Riccardo Nicolosi, Anne Hartmann (eds.)
Born to be Criminal

Lettre

Riccardo Nicolosi, Anne Hartmann (eds.)

Born to be Criminal

The Discourse on Criminality and the Practice of Punishment in Late Imperial Russia and Early Soviet Union. Interdisciplinary Approaches

[transcript]

Printed with financial support by the Ludwig-Maximilians-Universität Munich.

Bibliographic information published by the Deutsche Nationalbibliothek
The Deutsche Nationalbibliothek lists this publication in the Deutsche Nationalbibliografie; detailed bibliographic data are available in the Internet at http://dnb.d-nb.de

Cover layout: Maria Arndt, Bielefeld
Cover illustration: Tipi di criminali slavi e tedeschi
(Slavic and German Criminals). From: Cesare Lombroso, L'uomo criminale (Criminal Man). 5th Edition. Turin 1896. Atlante (Atlas), Tav. CI.
Typeset by Francisco Bragança, Bielefeld
Druck: Majuskel Medienproduktion GmbH, Wetzlar
Print-ISBN 978-3-8376-4159-2
PDF-ISBN 978-3-8394-4159-6

Content

II. On the Treatment of Social Deviance and Criminals in the Late 1920s-early 1930s

III. Political and 'Other' Prisoners – Literature of the Gulag

Acknowledgements

This volume grew out of the conference *The Born and the Common Criminal. The Discourse on Criminality and the Practice of Punishment in Late Imperial Russia and Early Soviet Union* that took place on 14-15 February 2015 at the Ludwig-Maximilians-Universität in Munich. The conference was conceived and organised by the editors in cooperation with Marc Junge of the Ruhr-Universität in Bochum. We would first of all like to thank all the authors who worked with such dedication on this volume together with us. We are grateful to the Ludwig-Maximilians-Universität in Munich, the Ruhr-Universität in Bochum and the Graduate School for East and Southeast European Studies for their financial and organisational support. A big 'thank you' is also due to Natalija Miller, Natalia Skradol, Frances Jackson and Rebecca Podlech for their much appreciated help in the course of the preparation of the volume.

Munich and Bochum, June 2017
Riccardo Nicolosi and Anne Hartmann

Introduction

Riccardo Nicolosi/Anne Hartmann

The title of the present volume – *Born To Be Criminal* – is intentionally ambiguous. On the one hand, it refers to Cesare Lombroso's theory of criminal anthropology and his idea of the "born criminal," and on the other it alludes to all those theories which connect criminality in a deterministic fashion to one's original environment or social class. These are the two focal points that unite the contributions in this collection. The authors' goal is to explore the continuities and disruptions in the perceptions of criminality, its causes and ways of fighting it that were dominant in late Imperial Russia and the early years of the Soviet Union. With this in mind, we collected here texts on both *the discourse on criminality*, that is, the conceptualisation of criminality in various disciplines and fields of research (criminology, criminal anthropology, psychiatry, journalism and literature) and *penal practice*, that is, different aspects of criminal law and of anti-crime policy. Thus, the volume is markedly interdisciplinary, with authors representing a variety of approaches in history and literary studies, from social history to discourse analysis, from the history of sciences and culture to text analysis.

In this volume, the concept of the "born criminal" covers theories of criminality which in the late 19th century postulated some kind of a biologically determined origin of criminal behaviour. It refers not only to Cesare Lombroso's controversial theory of the existence of individuals born with a tendency to commit crimes, but also to all those interpretations of criminal behaviour which, grounded in degeneration theory, included hereditary factors among the causes of criminality. However, this medicalisation of the criminal is analysed in our volume not only in the imperial context of the late tsarist era. Another question addressed here concerns the extent to which the figure of the born criminal, understood in a broad sense, played a role in the discourse of criminality and in the penal practices of the first Soviet years. Officially, anthropological explanatory models were decisively rejected in post-1917 Russia. The sociological school that replaced these models stressed the role of social factors as triggers of criminal behaviour, the assumption being that, as social conditions could be changed, the fertile ground for criminality would be eliminated. However, next to the prevailing discourse of resocialisation in the 1920s another approach set itself through, where the emphasis was on the importance of therapy and cure. According to this approach, which has not been sufficiently analysed until now, delinquents were to be seen as pathological cases and thus, their treatment was outside the realm of criminal law. However, the deterministic approaches to either social or biological factors do not exclude but rather complement each other (Beer 2008, 189-191).

It is much more difficult to conclude what image of the criminal determined the Soviet penal practice since the end of the 1920s, when diverse schools of legal theory had been silenced down and whatever was happening in this area was decided by functionaries and secret service officials. The consequences were tangible: offences against the law were politicised, and – according to a new definition of "normality" and "deviation" – whole groups were stigmatised. With the advent of the Great Terror in 1937 the public discussion concerning the causes of criminality and its treatment by penal bodies had been terminated. Information on life in camps was now channeled mostly through the so-called "Gulag literature" and thus documented only retrospectively and presented, once again, from a very particular angle. Its authors, all without exception former political prisoners, created an image of the criminal world that presented those imprisoned on criminal charges as fundamentally "different" and "alien." This, too, had far-reaching consequences for the categories applied, even if the references were usually to professional criminals and hard-core crooks who imposed a regime of terror in prisons. There was not much to be learnt from these sources about petty criminals and repeat offenders.

Our slim volume cannot by any means claim to provide a comprehensive coverage of the complex and broad topic. Rather, we have collected here case studies which aim to highlight rarely explored issues, and which will hopefully inspire further research in the area.

The *first part* of the volume, *Inborn Criminality and the Late Russian Empire*, continues a discussion which has become quite heated in the past years and which concerns the presence and function of biomedical discourses in late imperial Russia, and primarily Cesare Lombroso's criminal anthropology (Engelstein 1992; Sirotkina 2002; Goering 2003; Beer 2008; Morrissay 2010; Mogilner 2013). The lack of interest in the propagation of criminal anthropology and degeneration theory in Russian scientific discourse, which prevailed in scholarship for decades, had been justified by allusions to the "special paths" (*Sonderwege*) of Russian and Soviet culture when it came to biomedical theories and practices. A number of theoretical postulations were behind this trend. On the one hand, "social constructionism" was accorded a privileged position in Soviet medical historical research (see Iudin 1951 for a discussion specifically of psychiatry and criminal anthropology), and on the other hand, studies of Russia in Western Europe by and large rejected Foucauldian models. Researchers in the latter group claimed until very recently that tsarist Russia could not have been open to an understanding of society as a biological organism, which can potentially develop 'healthy' as well as 'pathological' states and which can, as a consequence, be 'cured' by scientific experts (physicians, psychiatrists, criminologists etc.). Adherents of this thesis argued that the populist-romantic, organic vision of society, which was prevalent in Russia until the beginning of the 20th century, would not have allowed biologically-based categories and stigmatisations to penetrate the social discourse. As evidence of this researchers would cite the preference for concepts such as *narodnost'* (folkness) instead of that of *race* (Knight 2000, 57-8; for a critical examination see Mogilner 2009).

Even Laura Engelstein, to whom scholars of Russia owe the long overdue re-discovery of biomedical visions of deviance in the last years of the tsarist rule, denies these discourses any significant role before 1905 (Engelstein 1992, 130). She attributes this to a special feature of the Russian culture in the late imperial era, which made it different from the West-European modernity and to which, as a consequence, Michel Foucault's theses on biopolitics cannot be applied (Engelstein 1993). According to Engelstein, in 19th century Russia there were no "dispositifs of power" in the sense in which Foucault uses the term to describe the bourgeois societies of Western Europe with their practices of discipline and control, where power is grounded not in laws, but in normalising mechanisms based on scientific knowledge. Engelstein questions the generalisability of Foucault's model of social development, according to which the police state of enlightened absolutism, where justice, law and punishment are in the foreground, is superseded by the "liberal" modern state, in which power and control are exercised through practices of self-regulation. The historian claims that in tsarist Russia one cannot observe a similar emergence of the modern state (Engelstein 1993, 343).

While Engelstein's critique of the applicability of Foucault's explanatory model of modernity for late imperial Russia is undoubtedly correct, the conclusions she draws concerning the limited circulation of biomedical concepts in Russia at the end of 19th century are questionable. While Engelstein deals exclusively with the discourse of sexual deviance, more recent studies have produced a more broad and varied picture of the emergence and development of biologistical discourses in Russia and thus convincingly refuted the claim of the Russian "special path." Of central importance here are the works of Daniel Beer (2008) and Marina Mogilner (2013). Coming from completely different theoretical and methodological perspectives, these scholars brought back forgotten biomedical discourses and practices of late imperial Russia and examined them as subjects of an archaeology of knowledge.

Daniel Beer, who performs a detailed analysis of biologistical models of crime as they were applied in criminology and criminal anthropology together with the degeneration discourse in psychiatry and the theory of psychic epidemics in mass psychology, explains the role of human sciences in the conceptualisation of the "liberal modernity" during the transition period from the tsarist rule to the early years of the Soviet Union. Beer criticises Laura Engelstein's thesis that in Russia the "modern liberalism" associated with human sciences failed. According to Beer, biomedical concepts were commonly used in late imperial Russia for discussions of the social body in categories of the normal and the pathological, as a driving force behind the "liberal and disciplining" project of the "healthification" (*ozdorovlenie*) of Russia (Beer 2008, 8). Beer also traces the survival of these pre-revolutionary discursive practices in the early bolshevik social experiment.

Emphasising overlaps between the political discourse and that of science, Beer explains how the biomedical discourse medicalised the earlier idealistic and postivistic paradigm of social organism and thus deprived it of its metaphoric character. He also talks about how this discourse became a diagnostic, therapeutic and repressive instrument in the struggle against expressions of social deviance by labelling them as pathologies, through the introduction of binary differentiations between the normal/healthy and the abnormal/sick. For Beer, what is special about the Russian discourse of degeneration is that it was seen ambivalently. Degeneration was understood simultaneously as an external and internal element of the Russian social organism, being both a manifestation of the 'atavistic' state of a backwards, uncivilised country, and a consequence of the 'harmful' modernisation processes associated with capitalism, urbanisation etc. Thus, Beer conceptualises a Russia-specific form of biopolitical modernity, in which – according to the Foucauldian model – the discursive authority of experts in human sciences (psychiatrists, criminologists, psychologists) played a central role, but which was different from the 'West European' modernity in that deviance was understood as omnipresent and normality was first of all to be created, before it could be protected.

A different interpretation of biomedical discourses in 19th century Russia is offered by Marina Mogilner in her work on the Russian tradition of "physical anthropology." Mogilner criticises Beer for giving an oversimplified picture of a heterogeneous Russian reality of the time, and for not differentiating between rather diverse scientific and ideological positions which are instead presented as equally important elements of a single, homogeneous biomedical discourse. Most importantly, she says, Beer fails to take into account the *imperial* factor, which she sees as fundamental for the biosocial imagination in Russia of the time (Mogilner 2010). Mogilner refers to more recent research on imperial cultures as cultures of difference and heterogeneity (Kappeler 1992; Burbank and Cooper 2010) to argue for a co-existence of contextually determined and variable understandings of 'norm' and 'deviance' in the Russian empire. The scholar reminds her readers that the Russian empire brought together multiple and sometimes incompatible with each other social and cultural realms, and that the definition of categories such as 'population' or 'ethnicity' was all but clear.

According to Mogilner, it is first of all the imperial flexibility in dealing with social and ethnic heterogeneity that provides the key to the special character of the Russian biomedical discourse, for which the "strategic relativism" of the empire (Gerasimov et al. 2009) represented an epistemological problem. This "strategic relativism" ran counter to the normalising practices of modern science with its clear distinction between the normal and the degenerative. Mogilner shows how the biomedical knowledge in Russia was adapting to the conditions of the empire with Lombroso's criminal anthropology being interpreted within the context of degeneration theory. While Lombroso understood the difference between the normal and the criminally pathological as anthropologically universal, Russian scientists tended to interpret "the born criminal" as a collective category in order to stigmatise social and ethnic groups and thus to control imperial diversity. For example, the psychiatrists who were also theoreticians of Russian nationalism, such as Ivan Sikorskii, Vladimir Chizh and Pavel Kovalevskii, diagnosed degenerative deviations from the norm among Tatars, members of religious sects, Jews and ethnic groups from the Caucasus and called for "an imperial monotony" by designating the borders of 'healthy' Russia. At the same time, when it came to conceptualising the figure of 'a born criminal,' the heterogeneous nature of the empire was reflected in a variety of theories defended by Russian criminal anthropologists of the time.

Marina Mogilner develops this interpretation of criminal anthropological discourses in the imperial context in her essay that opens the first part of the volume. According to Mogilner, the adaptation of Lombroso's criminal anthropology under the motto of the imperial "strategic relativism" gives rise to various new images of "the savage within" as an atavistic phenomenon, all them grounded in the "method of imperial comparison." Especially in the time before the Revolution of 1905 sociologists such as Maksim M. Kovalevskii, or even criminal anthropologists like Lombroso's follower Pras'kovia N. Tarnovskaia, tended to postulate different manifestations of atavism and degeneration for different ethnic groups. Mogilner points out that between the Revolution of 1905 and until the collapse of the empire in 1917 there occurred a shift in the biologistic discourse of criminality: physiognomic and anthropometric markers of a retarded criminal now played a secondary role with respect to "the hidden and therefore illusive and frightening signified" of the criminal.

Mogilner shows convincingly how even in this late imperial phase of the biologistic discourse of deviance in Russia what was thought of as primitive instincts, which Lombroso understood as atavistic in a universal sense of word, could be seen in completely different ways, depending on the context, – as healthy or degenerate, progressive or regressive. The aspiring Russian psychiatry post-1905 profited from this discursive shift, because it had at its disposal efficient scientific tools for diagnosing criminal deviance. At the same time, however, it had to always adapt its practices to the reality of the Russian 'imperial diversity,' where every attempt to medicalise the "atavistic savage" was doomed to have mixed, unstable and thus unsettling consequences, as Mogilner convincingly shows on the example of the first generation of Russian psychiatrists (Ivan Sikorskii, Pavel Kovalevskii, Vladimir Chizh). Even their colleagues who came after them (E.M. Budul, Ernest Erikson) and who tried to overcome the ambiguity of the Russian discourse of deviance by resorting to race theory, had to use the method of "imperial comparison" in order to construct "the savage within" (primarily the Jews). Mogilner concludes that only the early Soviet Union was able, thanks to its clear ideological orientation, to transcend the instability of the discourse of exclusion and to introduce the clear category of social "savagery."

The connection between criminal anthropology and Russian nationalism, the flip side of imperial diversity, is explored by **Louise McReynolds** in her text on Pavel I. Kovalevskii, one of the pioneers of Russian psychiatry. Kovalevskii, head of the department of psychiatry at the universities of Kharkov and Kazan and rector of the Warsaw University, founded in 1883 the first Russian psychiatric journal *The Archive of Psychiatry, Neurology, and Forensic Psychopathology* (*Arkhiv psikhiatrii, neirologii i sudebnoi psikhopatologii*). Its very title points to an affinity with Lombroso's journal *The Archive of Psychiatry, Criminal Anthropology, and Penal Sciences* (*Archivio di psichiatria, antropologia criminale e scienze penali*), and from the beginning of its existence the journal became an influential medium for propagating criminal anthropology in Russia (Salomoni 2009).

McReynolds shows how Kovalevskii's political conservatism influenced his work as a forensic psychiatrist when it came to a socio-political interpretation of biologistically determined criminal deviance. His nationalistic philosophy became even more apparent after 1905, and criminal anthropology for him became an instrument for modelling a healthy Russian nation. Both his internationally recognised professional publications and his popular writings for a broad audience with a consistently high print run, composed in the "alarmist" style reminiscent of Richard v. Krafft-Ebing, show clear evidence of the political implications of that particular version of forensic psychiatry, inspired by Lombroso and practiced by Kovalevskii.

Kovalevskii's forensic psychiatry is in the centre of **Riccardo Nicolosi**'s contribution, which focuses on the narrative dimension of Russian criminal anthropology where scientific and literary discourses come together. Kovalevskii's case studies are examined here as prime examples of the special style of writing in criminal anthropology. Until now researchers have almost completely ignored this side of the specialist texts, which emphasise the interconnection between atavism and degeneration – on the one hand, and narrativity – on the other. Nicolosi explores the mythopoetic foundation of Lombroso's idea of "inborn criminality" and its high potential of "tellability" by placing it in the context of psychiatric degeneration theory. In Kovalevskii's case studies the born criminal, characterised as an atavistic monster, is incorporated into a genealogical theory of degeneration, thus allowing the psychiatrist to come up with a comprehensive interpretation of the offender's bestiality which needs to be restrained.

Exploring atavistic phenomena and degeneration as narrative models allows Nicolosi to demonstrate a close interconnection between the poetics of science and the epistemology of literature in the field of criminal anthropology in late 19th century Russia. Seen from this perspective, the Russian literature of the time no longer appears to be "immune" to biologistic theories of crime, as researchers have been claiming. Instead, various narrative models of 'inborn criminality' become apparent, be it in the works of classical authors like Lev Tolstoi and Fedor Dostoevskii or in the writings of authors less popular today, such as Aleksei Svirskii und Vladimir Giliarovskii.

The *second part* of the volume, *On the Treatment of Social Deviance and Criminals in the Late 1920s-early 1930s* is dedicated to analyses of a period in which, as it would seem, the use of biologistical models for an explanation of criminal offenses completely died out. The October Revolution was perceived by its supporters as a breakthrough into a new era where, as many optimistically believed, a reconstruction of social relations would also lead to a gradual decrease of crime rates, with crime finally disappearing once the transition to communism has been achieved. In contrast to Lombroso scholars like Mikhail Gernet emphasised social reasons of criminality and its "changeability and dependence on place and time" (*ee izmenchivost' i zavisimost' ot uslovii mesta i vremeni*; Gernet 1974, 437). Evgenii Pashukanis, an influential legal scholar, even argued that the legal system as a whole would vanish as a remnant of the bourgeois society, just as the state itself would eventually die out (Pashukanis 1924). Whatever few delinquents might remain would be taken care of by welfare services. It is possible that there is a connection between this vision and the gradual suppression of concepts such as "crime" and "punishment" and their replacement through sociological categories such as "a socially dangerous act" and "a measure of social defense" (Berman and Hunt 1950, 640-641). The new legislation from the years of the New Economic Policy (NEP) was indisputably progressive. For example, *The Corrective Labour Code of the Russian Federation* (*Ispravitel'no-trudovoi kodeks RSFSR*) from 1924 contained a gradation of penalties and listed five types of detention institutions with regimes of varying strictness.

The project of humane punishment was aimed, programmatically and propagandistically, against the legal system of the West, which was supposed to be driven exclusively by a desire for revenge and humiliation of delinquents, and also against the tsarist *katorgas* and prisons with their chains and torture instruments. The Museum of Revolution in Moscow featured a special room with walls covered in black tapestries. This "Museum of Horror," as it was officially called, contained documents and objects from the earlier reign of terror. But as René Fülöp-Miller, who described the exhibition in his book *The Mind and Face of Bolshevism* (*Geist und Gesicht des Bolschewismus*) noted, for all its alleged condemnation of the tsarist practices, the Soviet government retained "the tried and tested" strategies of the previous regime, especially when dealing with political adversaries (Fülöp-Miller 1926, 430; see Leggett 1981, 175-176; Stettner 1996, 44-45).

Those who were seen as "socially close elements" could get away with a relatively mild sentence, usually just "correctional labour" (*ispravitel'nyi trud*). However, those who were regarded as oppositional to the system (high-profile tsarist officials and officers, clerics, business people, members of the Constitutional Democratic Party etc.) were treated as not eligible for correction and not suitable for integration into the society. Many of them were shot, others were sent away to concentration camps and forced labour sites (*prinuditel'nyi trud*). As early as on 5 September 1918 the decree "On Red Terror" was passed, which ordered that all necessary violence be applied to liberate the Soviet Republic from "class enemies" and "counterrevolutionaries."

Thus dangerously prescriptive and imprecise concepts were introduced, which postulated that it was one's origin and belonging to a social class, rather than a committed crime, that counted as the decisive criterion for the kind of measures that were to be taken by the state in a particular case. One of the consequences of the distinction between "socially close" elements and "socially distant" ones was the establishment of a double-track penal system, whose fatal results were not long in coming. Cheka was responsible for the first wave of terror. The "Extraordinary Commission" was not accountable either to courts of law or to any law-enforcing body. Even though Cheka and its special camps were dissolved in 1922 with the passing of the executive decision on the "reconstruction of socialist legality" (*vosstanovlenie sotsialisticheskoi zakonnosti*), its successors GPU and OGPU were awarded a similarly broad warrant to arrest, to interrogate and to punish. The "Northern camps of special purpose" (*Severnye lageria osobogo naznacheniia*, SLON), set up on the Solovetskii Islands as a special detention facility for political prisoners, were the seed from which the Gulag evolved.

In contrast, the detention centres of the People's Commissions for Justice and for Internal Affairs (the responsibilities of the rival authorities changed frequently) were primarily in charge of implementing regular court sentences, with "labour, health conditions, medical care and education" in prisons being controlled by external committees (Stettner 1996, 66). The guiding principle in the administration of punishment at that time, obvious also in the writings of most of those who were involved in these matters in practice, was the belief that delinquents could be re-socialised.

However, any examination of the *discourse* of the time on the subject of crime and its causes must take into account also a third group of institutions. As early as in 1922 the so-called "Cabinet for Criminal Anthropology and Forensic Medical Expertise" was opened in Saratov (*Kabinet kriminal'noi antropologii i sudebno-meditsinskoi ekspertizy*), whereupon similar institutions were organised in Moscow and other big cities. The State Institute for the Study of Crime and the Criminal under the auspices of the NKVD, opened in Moscow in 1925, was charged with coordinating the activities of the various cabinets, centres and institutes. The effort that went into the study of criminality in the hope of understanding and – hopefully – eliminating it altogether is remarkable. The great number of tested individuals, as well as numerous publications (partly in foreign languages) all testify to the dedicated engagement of those involved.

The markedly medical and psychiatric profile of most of the "cabinets" is also worth noting. For example, the "cabinet" in Saratov had a sociological department, but also departments researching the psychological, physical and nervous-psychiatric state of delinquents, as well as a section for hypnotherapy. The goal of the work was formulated as follows: "A study of the aetiology, pathology and pathogenesis of criminality as well as the personality of delinquents as carriers of the latter" (*izuchenie etiologii, patologii i patogenezisa prestupnosti, a takzhe i lichnosti prestupnika kak nositelia poslednei*; Ivanov 1925, 85). Significantly, the "Cabinet for the Study of the Criminal Personality and Crime" (*Kabinet po izucheniiu lichnosti prestupnika i prestupnosti*) in Moscow was subordinate to the Institute of Health in the capital (Moszdravotdel).

The delinquents were regarded as products, or rather – as victims of their circumstances, whereby social factors received much less attention than medical ones. A clinical diagnosis was supposed to establish psychological and physical anomalies, so that the criminal could then be classified as a sick person, who was first of all to be cured. The popularity of this approach came from a dogmatic interpretation of the belief in the "anti-criminal" character of socialism, in which there was no room for antagonistic social tensions. Hence, crime had to have a different cause, it had to come from the "nature" of the delinquent, even though Lombroso's thesis of the born criminal was allegedly rejected (for a critical discussion of this topic see Prozumentov and Shesler 2014, 52-53).

In the late 1920s the theories of the "criminal cabinets" came under attack as "bourgeois," their work and the academic publications of their staff were superseded by other developments in the Soviet society and ultimately suppressed. Professional publications as well as journalistic statements and generally available statistics on crime dynamics gradually disappeared from the public domain. A 1930 report on the state of crime, where the Head of the NKVD of the Russian Republic Vladimir Tolmachev listed various offences committed in the second half of the 1920s and grouped them based on factual information, rather than with reference to them as "counterrevolutionary activities," was the last document of this kind for decades to come (see the contribution by David Shearer in this volume). Now it was no longer legal scholars and experts in penal law who set the tone, but secret police. Head of the secret service Iagoda, his colleagues and successors had no knowledge of the penal code, and they most certainly did not have much interest in theoretical debates or empirical research (*ibid.*), which makes it difficult to reconstruct the motives behind their actions (on this, see the article by Marc Junge in this volume).

The change of direction occurred against the background of forced industrialisation and collectivisation as part of the First Five Year Plan, which brought about a massive increase in crime rates. At the same time it is hard to say to what extent there was an actual sudden explosion in the number of criminal acts, and to what extent the increase was due to a new taxonomy of crime as well as stricter and longer sentences. Such sentences were often imposed for a reason, namely, in order to transform OGPU camps into a "production giant" (Stettner 1996). In any case, it is obvious that the "traditional reading of crime" (Shearer 2009, 26) was now replaced with a politicisation of all acts criminal. This held true for all manifestations of social deviance including prostitution, hooliganism and alcoholism, which authorities in the 1920s still tried to handle by means of philanthropic measures. Now, an alcoholic could be accused of being an enemy of the people or "an accomplice of the *Trotskyite-Zinovievite gang*" (Lebina 1997). The transferral of responsibilities from the judiciary apparatus to secret police, as well as the substitution of a regulated legal process with speedy sentencing administered by extra-judicial committees (the *Police* and *Kulak Troikas*), accompanied this shift.

This "great turn" of the 1920s to the 1930s is the initial focus and point of departure of the contributions in the second part of this volume. The authors reconstruct the activities of bodies of state security and ask what became of the idea of "improvement" and why people who were once seen as "socially close" were now victims of mass repressions.

In January 1933 at a plenary session of the Central Committee of the VKP(b) in the presence of hundreds of delegates Stalin announced "the fundamental victory of socialism." This speech is the starting point of **David Shearer**'s chapter. Shearer shows that Stalin's declaration was accompanied by warnings as well as threats, whose spirit determined the future policy. According to Stalin, even if organised class resistance had been broken, it continued under the surface, as "quiet sabotage," "in the form of crime and lawlessness." Stalin saw theft and pilfering as particularly threatening, especially when it was socialist property that was being stolen or damaged. These acts were now regarded as counter-revolutionary activities, as they could destabilise the social order. In this vision, class enemies and criminals merged into one group. The counter-measures had to be correspondingly powerful, in order to protect the state whose integrity had top priority. These measures were implemented primarily by the secret police, thus significantly broadening its authority to exert power.

As Shearer shows, the consequences of thus policising or statising crime were far reaching. The so-called state crimes (*gosudarstvennye prestupleniia*) and crimes against administrative order were now considered to be as severe as political offenses to which Article 58 of the Penal Code referred: people with anti-social tendencies were mutating into anti-Soviet elements. Repeat offenders especially were seen as a fundamental danger for the Soviet order. They were, in Iagoda's view, incorrigible, being inherently hostile to the Soviet power. According to him, a tendency to commit repeated offenses was an atavistic trait, which he, however, interpreted not in biomedical but in social terms. The same mechanism drove the attribution of essentialist qualities to whole groups of the population that were branded as "hostile class aliens" or – somewhat later – as "ethnic aliens" and as such excluded from the society in the course of grand campaigns. Even if the Soviet officials emphatically rejected the thesis of a biological genesis of crime, they still believed, as Shearer says in his conclusion, "in a social and ethnic kind of atavism that produced recidivist criminals, incorrigibly harmful social elements, and enemy nations even within Soviet borders."

Here one can draw, even if with a slightly different emphasis, surprising parallels with the positions of some leading adherents of criminal anthropology in the 19th century. Could it be that in the 1930s the vacant position of the "born criminal" was taken over by the repeated offender, somebody who was accustomed to a life of crime, who had internalised it, so that it had grown into his flesh and blood? And was the ideology of "imperial monotony," fixated on the concept of "healthy Russia," now replaced by the project of Soviet homogeneity, so that the role of the "savage within" could again be played by somebody, namely by those groups that were socially or ethnically "different" from the "norm"?

Marc Junge, too, poses the question of possible political and historical roots of the state policy in the 1930s. His starting point is a puzzling fact: during the Great Terror it was precisely petty criminals, beggars, nomads, prostitutes etc. who were penalised systematically, collectively and with great severity, even though theoretically they were a "socially close element." Referring to his own earlier works, most of them co-authored with Rolf Binner, Junge asks himself and the readers whether the position commonly accepted in the Soviet Union in the 1920s, which demanded that criminality be regarded as a purely sociological phenomenon, was as broadly accepted as it was claimed, especially in light of the fact that the different institutions dedicated to the study of crime and criminals, as mentioned above, also had a pronounced biological and psychological profile. And did sociological approaches carry any weight at all later, in the 1930s? After all, it was becoming more and more difficult to characterise the Soviet Union as a society in transition, and thus to present criminals as victims of their social conditions. Junge suggests that addressing this question could also explain why the search for possible reasons of criminality was gradually abandoned, as were explanatory models that detected the roots of criminality in pre-revolutionary, capitalist conditions. According to the scholar, at that time an old principle from before the Revolution was revived, albeit in a different form, namely the classical theory of free will. Individuals had to decide whether they wanted to be integrated into the society, or else be excluded from it.

Like Shearer, Junge emphasises the determined position of the bodies of state security in the treatment of the repeat offenders classified as "incorrigible." This policy, implemented under Iagoda, continued also under his successor Ezhov. Repeat offenders were regarded as "the most dangerous criminal group" and received a prominent mention in the notorious NKVD Order 00447 from July 30, 1937. Junge poses the question of whether this extreme fixation on repeat offenders "indicates a connection between Lombroso's biological model and the penal policies instituted by the USSR." Even if his tentative answer is "yes," the historian refrains from a definite conclusion. He notes that more research is necessary, also in order to further investigate the thesis of the biological heredity of "class" postulated by Tracy McDonald and Lynne Viola.

For a significant number of camp inmates, even if by no means for all of them, there was hope that one day they would be released. According to Steven Barnes, on average about 20% of inmates were released every year (Barnes 2011, 10). At least until 1936 a reintegration of former prisoners into the Soviet society was propagated in both Soviet and foreign media as the official goal of the project. The word *perekovka* was used at the time to celebrate the successful "re-forging" of delinquents in the camps. However, there are few sources testifying to how the reintegration worked in practice. In her article **Anne Hartmann** shows how the concept of *perekovka* emerged at the point of intersection of penal policy and literature. The metaphor reflects the technological spirit of the First Five-Year Plan and is linked to the idea of writers being "engineers of the human soul." The Belomorkanal (White Sea Canal) project especially was a testing ground for the inmates as well as for the writers who were sent to the site in 1933 as members of a brigade of 120. Gor'kii and his fellow campaigners celebrated the Chekists as educators, and forced labour – as a source of inspiration for the writers. The impetus extended even further: as a "factory of human beings" and a "school of work" the camp was supposed to set an example for the whole country.

The Belomorkanal project was about the struggle against nature, also human nature. Except that, as Hartmann shows, there was no clear answer to the question of whether, and to what extent, the latter was to be transformed. While Iagoda, as we already mentioned above, did not believe that repeat offenders and class enemies could be "socially renewed," his wife Ida Averbach was more optimistic. In her opinion, just as the flow of the Volga river could be reversed, so, too, deeply ingrained behavioural patterns could be changed. Despite this, the discussions of *perekovka* clearly show that there was no agreement as to the relative importance of, on the one hand, biological and social determinism, and on the other – free will, and of people's potential for re-education versus the degree to which they could be deemed "incurable." The writers who reported on the project resorted to the category of "wonder" in their descriptions of how one could be re-born (*pererozhdenie*) overnight as a "new man."

The beginning of the Great Terror put an end to the literary and journalistic celebrations of the 'transformation' of camp inmates as a grand experiment in reforming people. Visitors were no longer allowed on sites and there was to be no reporting. As many of the protagonists of *perekovka* disappeared almost overnight, victims to a wave of arrests, so did the media reports on the victorious achievements and, more generally, the narrative of re-education and correction. From that moment on, insights into the camp life of the time could almost exclusively be gained retrospectively, from the descriptions of former inmates. These are the subject of the *third part* of the volume: *Political and 'Other' Prisoners – Literature of the Gulag*, where both contributions address specifically the question of how the criminal world is represented in camp memoir literature. We should be mindful of one particularity of Gulag literature and a related methodical problem, namely, that all the texts come from so-called "political prisoners," who during their imprisonment felt exposed on many levels to the shenanigans of professional criminals, sometimes in a life-threatening way. Their point of view and narrative position are largely determined by the victim perspective. On the other hand, we learn next to nothing about "accidental" prisoners and petty criminals. They were and remain a group deprived of its own voice, a group that did not particularly interest the political prisoners who wrote the accounts. If they are mentioned at all, it is only as those who were also oppressed by the gang bosses, the latter acting as their masters and demanding unconditional service, quickly corrupting the younger ones and turning them into career criminals in their own right.

In her chapter "Criminals in Gulag Accounts" **Renate Lachmann** first analyses the literature of the early 1930s, where Gulag was presented from an external point of view and where, in the spirit of the propaganda of the time, re-education was celebrated as a heroic endeavour or else criminals were romanticised and made to appear harmless, in the tradition of the gangster folklore of the 19th – early 20th century. Nikolai Pogodin's comedy *Aristocrats* (*Aristokraty*, 1935), which was also made into a feature film, is a representative example here. However, for those authors who had an immediate experience of life in the camps criminals represented hostile and threatening adversaries. Especially traumatic seem to have been encounters with serious or top rank criminals, who established their own terrifying regime and system of regulations in the camps. Remarkably, their reign usually receives more attention in the memoirs than the rule of guards and camp authorities.

Lachmann draws a distinction between an ethnographic and a moralistic view of the criminals, without, however, claiming that they are mutually exclusive. "Observers" such as Dmitrii Likhachev, Varlam Shalamov or Julius Margolin tried to learn the laws of this peculiar alternative society. They described its hierarchy and rank order, the code of honour and the punishments imposed internally. Of particular interest to them was the obscene language of the professional criminals (*urki, blatnye*), as well as the skin-language of prison tattoos and card games as the main leisure activity (whereby the professional criminals would normally try to dodge the labour duty). The moralistic perspective emphasises disgust and distancing, as the authors position themselves against what they experienced as a completely foreign, categorically different world. Lachmann quotes Aleksandr Solzhenitsyn and Evgeniia

Ginzburg: "they are not people," "the criminals are beyond the human." The scholar shows how this act of 'othering' turned the bandits into an "alien tribe" lacking human traits. Are we dealing here, yet again, with the figure of a "savage within"? In any case, the intellectual witnesses draw a clear border between themselves and the underworld of which they are not part. After all, they had the last word, and they could use the writing to compensate themselves for the loss of dignity they suffered: "In writing autobiographies, memoirs, diaries, stories, the victims recovered their intellectual and moral superiority."

In Lachmann's opinion *Sketches of the Criminal World* (*Ocherki prestupnogo mira*) by Varlam Shalamov offer a profound sociological analysis into the reality of the camps. This collection is also in the centre of **Leona Toker**'s contribution. For all the precision with which Shalamov depicted this counter-society and its corrupting influence on younger, still 'innocent' prisoners, he avoids two topics which apparently he saw as taboo zones of extreme horror: homosexuality and cannibalism. As Toker makes clear, the *Sketches* provide first-hand historical evidence, particularly on the "bitch war" (*such'ia voina*) which broke out when many criminals switched over to the service of the authorities. This phenomenon was especially widespread after the end of World War II. Such ex-gang members were seen by "criminals in law" (*vory v zakone*) as collaborators and thus enemies, but they enjoyed the support of camp bosses when it came to maintaining order and, if necessary, to settling bloody scores with those who were too unruly. On the other hand, the *Sketches* are "suffused with literary concerns." Like Solzhenitsyn, Shalamov, too, criticises the harmful effects of literary glorifications of thieves as romantic rebels and free agents. The writers' criticism reflects a particular understanding of literature, whereby literary texts are seen as exemplary models. However, both of them focus on the potential of literary texts to harm or to cause damage, while they apparently have little hope for the therapeutic power even of their own works.

We learn little about the causes of criminality from Shalamov's texts, even if he, according to Toker, had a clear opinion on the matter of biological versus social conditioning. For him the decisive factor was the environment, not heredity. The literary tales of criminals' heroic pursuits were part of the environment, as was the governmental policy that led to the spread of criminality. "The world of the *blatnye* must be destroyed," – such is Shalamov's conclusion, and it was not a plea for death penalty or longer sentences. His own position was wrought with internal contradictions. He wrote literary texts in order to enlighten readers and make them immune to the "corrosive attractiveness" of seductive, but deceptive narratives, but at the same time he himself did not quite believe in the power of his writings and did not seek to have them published.

References

Barnes, St. A. 2011. *Death and Redemption. The Gulag and the Shaping of Soviet Society*. Princeton and Oxford: Princeton University Press.

Beer, D. 2008. *Renovating Russia: The Human Sciences and the Fate of Liberal Modernity*. Ithaca and London: Cornell University Press.

Berman, H. J. and Hunt, D. H. 1950. "Criminal Law and Psychiatry: The Soviet Solution". *Stanford Law Review* 2, 635-663.

Burbank, J. and Cooper, F. 2010. *Empires and the World of History: Power and the Politics of Difference*. Princeton: Princeton University Press.

Engelstein, L. 1992. *The Keys to Happiness. Sex and the Search for Modernity in Fin-de-Siècle Russia*. Ithaca and London: Cornell University Press.

Engelstein, L. 1993. "Combined Underdevelopment: Discipline and the Law in Imperial and Soviet Russia." *American Historical Review* 98, no. 2, 338-353.

Fülöp-Miller, R. 1926. *Geist und Gesicht des Bolschewismus. Darstellung und Kritik des kulturellen Lebens in Sowjet-Russland*. Zürich et al.: Amalthea.

Gerasimov, I. et al. 2009. "New Imperial History and the Challenges of Empire." Gerasimov, I. et al. (eds.), *Empire Speaks Out. Languages of Rationalization and Self-Description in the Russian Empire*. Leiden and Boston: Brill, 3-32.

Gernet, M. 1974. "Predislovie k rabote 'Prestupnyj mir Moskvy'." Gernet, M., *Izbrannye proizvedeniia*. Moscow: Iuridicheskaia literatura, 401-437.

Goering, L. 2003. "Russian Nervousness: Neurasthenia and National Identity in Nineteenth-Century Russia." *Medical History* 47, 23-46.

Iudin, T.I. 1951. *Ocherki istorii otechestvennoi psikhiatrii*. Moscow: Medgiz.

Ivanov, G. 1925. "Iz praktiki Saratovskogo gubernskogo kabineta." *Sovetskoe pravo* 1, 84-95.

Kappeler, A. 1992. *Rußland als Vielvölkerreich. Entstehung, Geschichte, Zerfall*. Munich: C.H. Beck.

Knight, N. 2000. "Ethnicity, Nationalism and the Masses: *Narodnost'* and Modernity in Imperial Russia." Hoffman, D.L. and Katsonis, Y. (eds.), *Russian Modernity: Politics, Knowledge Practices.* Basingstoke et al.: Macmillan, 41-64.

Lebina, N. B. 1997. "Povsednevnost' 1920-1930-kh godov: 'bor'ba s perezhitkami proshlogo'." *Sovetskoe obshchestvo: voszniknovenie, razvitie, istoricheskii final.* Vol. 1. Moscow: RGGU, 244-290.

Mogilner, M. 2009. "Russian Physical Anthropology of the Nineteenth-Early Twentieth Centuries: Imperial Race, Colonial Other, and the Russian Racial Body." Gerasimov, I. et al. (eds.), *Empire Speaks Out. Languages of Rationalization and Self-Description in the Russian Empire.* Leiden and Boston: Brill, 155-189.

Mogilner, M. 2010. "Review: Daniel Beer, Renovating Russia: The Human Sciences and the Fate of Liberal Modernity, 1880-1930. Ithaca, NY: Cornell University Press, 2008." *Kritika: Explorations in Russian and Eurasian History* 11, no. 3, 661-672.

Mogilner, M. 2013. *Homo imperii. A History of Physical Anthropology in Russia.* Lincoln and London: University of Nebraska Press.

Morrissey, S. 2010. "The Economy of Nerves: Health, Commercial Culture, and the Self in Late Imperial Russia." *Slavic Review* 69, no. 3, 546-675.

Pashukanis, E. B. 1924. *Obshchaia teoriia prava i marksizm. Opyt kritiki osnovnykh iuridicheskikh poniatii.* Moscow: Kommunisticheskaia Akademiia.

Prozumentov, L.M. and Shesler, A.V. 2014. "Otechestvennye nauchnye kontseptsii prichin prestupnosti." *Criminology Journal of Baikal National University of Economics and Law,* no. 1, 49-58.

Salomoni, A. 2009. "La Russia." Montaldo, S. and Tappero, P. (eds.), *Cesare Lombroso cento anni dopo.* Turin: Utet, 249-261.

Shearer, D. 2009. *Policing Stalin's Socialism. Repression and Social Order in the Soviet Union, 1924-1953.* New Haven et al.: Yale University Press.

Sirotkina, I. 2002. *Diagnosing Literary Genius. A Cultural History of Psychiatry in Russia, 1880-1930.* Baltimore and London: The Johns Hopkins University Press.

Stettner, R. 1996. *"Archipel GULag": Stalins Zwangslager. Terrorinstrument und Wirtschaftsgigant. Entstehung, Organisation und Funktion des sowjetischen Lagersystems 1928-1956.* Paderborn et al.: Schöningh.

I. Inborn Criminality and the Late Russian Empire

The Empire-Born Criminal

Atavism, Survivals, Irrational Instincts, and the Fate of Russian Imperial Modernity[1]

Marina Mogilner

Criminality and the scholarly field of criminal anthropology that studied it as well as the public discourses of illegality and deviance that bred on them are used by scholars as indicators of Russia's partaking in global modernity. Intentionally or unintentionally, the historical discussion evolves around the "essence" of scholarly and popular discourses of deviance as a marker of Russia's normality, "combined underdevelopment," or essential difference vis-à-vis some normative version of modernity (Engelstein 1992; 1993; Beer 2008). My goal in the present article is to go beyond this well-established tradition and revisit the old debate from the vantage point of new imperial history and its primary concern with unintended and unexpected consequences of seemingly self-evident approaches and ideas. Empire, as a context-setting category, ascribes meaning to situations and relationships depending on specific circumstances, subcultures, and local knowledge (in the Geertzean sense). It invalidates the very project of comparing some universal and stable Russian deviance (and, by extension, Russian modernity) to some normative and equally self-evident Western model. Whether read through the Lombrosian or Foucauldian lenses, the discourses of norm and deviance as epitomes of modernity become conditioned by a specific imperial situation – the decisive factor

1 | The article was prepared within the framework of the Basic Research Program at the National Research University Higher School of Economics (HSE) and supported within the framework of a subsidy granted to the HSE by the Government of the Russian Federation for the implementation of the Global Competitiveness Program.

determining the configuration of power-knowledge relations (Gerasimov et al. 2009).

Empire embraces numerous, only partially congruent and mutually "translatable" sociocultural spaces and hierarchies and acts as a "switchman" between different contexts that change the meaning and mode of one's performance, ideas, and identity. Thus, ethnicity as a main marker of difference can coexist with and even substitute for social status. As we know, in the Russian Empire the legal estate of "aliens" (*inorodtsy*) was reserved for ethnic minorities, and being a Pole or a Jew implied a whole complex of social, economic, and legal characteristics defined by law. On the other hand, criminal behavior according to the imperial penal code might be interpreted as a "tradition" under particular circumstances. The empire's legal order or the "imperial rights regime" (Burbank 2006) implied a coexistence of multiple and often incongruent legal logics, institutions, and practices – beyond the scope of legal pluralism. Multidimensional imperial situations perpetuated hybridity: not necessarily in the sense famously defined by Homi Bhabha (as occurring exclusively within the colonial discourse) (Bhabha 2004), but more directly and indiscriminately producing hybrid – complex, hierarchical, relational, and situational – knowledge, identities, and discourses.

In this perspective, the main conflict regarding the take on deviance in late imperial Russia appears not to be between experts with their normative discourse of norm and the archaic state that did not embrace it. After all, there was nothing specifically Russian in these experts' alleged readiness to radically change their "social environment" (political revolution viewed as an option), in order to impose their clear-cut vision of norm and deviance over the entire society (Engelstein 1993; Beer 2008; Morrissey 2010). The main conflict seemed to be the essentially imperial dilemma: how to reconcile the "strategic relativism" of criteria and values produced by the fundamental factor of empire's heterogeneity and diversity with the systematizing and rationalizing impulse of modern scientific episteme and political culture (exemplified by the normative approach of experts) (Mogilner 2013). This tension inspired early reflections on the phenomenon of hybridity and relativizing critique of hegemonic discourses (Gerasimov et al. 2013). At the same time, it encouraged the strategy of "learned ignorance" about the empire as a way to make the unstable imperial situation more comprehensible.[2] The simultaneous proliferation of such antagonistic responses to the main conflict of Russian imperial modernity demonstrated the persistence of imperial strategic relativism as the impossibility of imposing a single "regime of truth" and interpretative strategy embracing the whole complexity of the Russian imperial condition.[3]

Strategic relativism at work can be vividly demonstrated in the applications of Lombrosian criminal anthropology in Russia. From the outset, Lombroso had been criticized for establishing the Eurocentric hegemonic discourse of norm and deviance as the universal and only scientific one. According to the first Russian anthropology professor and the leader of the Moscow school of liberal anthropology, Dmitrii Anuchin:

> The "anthropological" school should use real anthropological data and consider all known different human types. Anthropological data prove [...] that morphologically a normal man can belong to white or black races, have wooly hair – as a Negro or Hottentots do - or straight hair – as a Mongol or an American does; he can be tall

2 | "Learned ignorance" is Ann Stoler's term. She traces it to "deliberately educated ignorance" coined by W. E. B. Du Bois, "cultivated ignorance" by Foucault, and "sanctioned ignorance" by Gayatri Chakravorty Spivak, in which Stoler emphasizes the linguistic-aphasic rather than cognitive elements of occlusion of knowledge (Stoler 2009, 247). Such learned ignorance characterized, for example, the nineteenth century Russian populism that was blind to the diversity and interconnectedness of the social space of empire because it interiorized the perception of society as a holistic social order. For a more detailed discussion see Semyonov et al. 2013.

3 | "Strategic relativism" is based on and refers to Gayatri Chakravorty Spivak's concept of "strategic essentialism" (Spivak 1987, 205): "The opposite case constituting the distinguishing feature of the ideal type of empire [...] may be termed strategic relativism, which should be understood as the discourse and stance that relativizes the bounded and internally homogeneous nature of the constituent elements of the sociopolitical space and governance [...] and [...] produces the situation of uncertainty, incommensurability, and indistinction" (Gerasimov et al. 2009, 20).

as a Polynesian, a Patagonian, or a Kafr, or short as a Negritos, a Japanese, or a Lopar (Anuchin 1890, 337-338).[4]

Anuchin called generalizations based exclusively on European measurements arbitrary and unsubstantiated and compared this to a normative approach that assumed only "white [men] to be normal, while regarding Negroes, Mongols, and other types as abnormal, degenerative, and enfeebled representatives of the family Homo" (*ibid.*, 338).[5]

This implicitly anticolonial intellectual critique reflected the profound transformation of the Lombrosian concept of "inborn criminal" and explained why in Russia it became easily differentiated into an assortment of ethnically distinctive collective types, as in the following assertion: "In the development and general form of the skull, Lombroso has found a predominance of prognathic brachycephalism, that is, an approximation of the type of Tatars, Kalmyks, Otaitians, Arakurants [...]" (Mintslov 1881, 219).[6] The ethnicization of anthropometric characteristics of the "criminal type" logically led to a similar differentiation of the normative type into distinctive regional, racial, or social types. This was part of a typical imperial story of negotiating criteria and degrees of human difference (Mogilner 2013, 328-346). Not unlike other languages of imperial self-modernization, criminal anthropology became a means to systematically reorganize, rationalize, and possibly control imperial diversity. As I will show below, in the Russian Empire at the turn of the century, the program of imposing a single universal norm and marginalizing and criminalizing its variations as deviance had to be explicitly politically (indeed reactionary)

---

4 | "'Антропологическая' школа должна пользоваться данными действительной антропологии и включать в свой кругозор все известные разновидности человечества. Данные же антропологии доказывают, что [...] [в] морфологическом отношении нормальный человек может принадлежать к белой или к черной расе, иметь шерстистые волоса (так в оригинале – MM), как негр или готтентот, или прямые и гладкие, как монгол или американец; быть высокорослым, как полинезиец, патагонец, кафр, или малорослым, как негритос, японец, лопарь."

5 | "[...] как считать только белого человека нормальным, а в неграх, монголах и других видеть ненормальных, выродившихся и оскуделых представителей рода homo."

6 | "Ломброзо нашел в преступниках преобладание прогнатического брахицефализма, т.е. приближение к типу татар, калмыков, отаитян, арауканцев [...]."

motivated. But even in the latter cases, empire as a context-setting category relativized and mitigated the most radical attempts to impose and stabilize one universal normative discourse and the politics of deviance.

The methodological embrace of imperial diversity could lead to quite discriminatory political conclusions, including explicitly colonial ones. This was the case of professor Maksim Maksimovich Kovalevskii, sociologist and historian, a student of British political tradition and Caucasian customary law, a founder of the Party for Democratic Reforms, and a member of the Russian parliament (State Duma). A great part of Kovalevskii's charisma derived from his being a personal acquaintance of Karl Marx, for whom Kovalevskii served as a source of knowledge about the history of communal landownership, and who could encourage Kovalevskii to perceive deviants as historically formed social groups rather than individuals (Boronoev 1996; Semyonov et al. 2013, 64-68). "Let us imagine a Caucasian mountaineer who discusses some articles of the Criminal Code while being convinced that blood should be wiped away only by blood or compensated with cows and sheep," wrote Kovalevskii in 1905 in a leading Russian liberal newspaper. He continued, "When a circuit court sentences the murderer-Circassian to hard labor in Siberia, the closest relative of his victim follows him there to exercise the duty of revenge. Such facts are often mentioned in the courts' minutes and administrative correspondence" (Kovalevskii 1905, 2).[7] Kovalevskii grouped peoples of the Russian Caucasus with the Siberian natives – Chukchees, Kamchadals, and Yakuts – into one category of underdeveloped and uncivilized subjects of the empire whose "criminality" was not, strictly speaking, "inborn" in that it was a derivative of their primitive stage of development, but still structurally fundamentally incompatible with a modern society. Hence Kovalevskii recommended reservations based on the U.S. American Indian model and exclusion from the common civic space as a way of "punishment" of the primitives and a means to construct

7 | "Представьте себе кавказского горца, обсуждающего те или другие статьи уголовного кодекса и проникнутого убеждением, что кровь надо смывать кровью или взамен этого требовать коров и баранов. [...] Когда окружной суд приговаривает убийцу-черкеса к каторжным работам в Сибири, ближайший родственник жертвы спешит последовать за ссыльным, чтобы осуществить на нем долг мести. Такие факты не раз упоминаются судебными протоколами и административной перепиской."

a modern imperial society (*ibid.*). At the same time, "primitivism," "traditional society," "atavism," and "criminality" were not just general scientific concepts for Kovalevskii, and least of all connected exclusively to criminal anthropology. Their concrete meaning and practical implications depended on specific structures of empire (Kovalevskii 1886; 1890).

The alternative to this kind of liberal imperialism was a much more egalitarian and even populist vision of the coexistence of various local norms and local versions of degeneration – arranged into distinctive and horizontally differentiated national groups. This well-elaborated application of the principle of imperial relativism in criminal anthropology is most immediately associated with the best known Russian follower of Cesare Lombroso, the female physician Praskov'ia Nikolaevna Tarnovskaia, who studied Russian female murderers and prostitutes (Engelstein 1992, 138-143; Mogilner 2013, 339-340). She was literally obsessed with designating strict borders of her normative and deviant groups, constructing them as purely racially Russian. Carefully excluded from her sampling were

> all those cases, regardless of how interesting they are, where, after close scrutiny, one parent appears to be not indigenously [ethnic] Russian by birth. Thus I had to reject all convicts who had a parent originating from Finland, the Baltic provinces, western territories (*Zapadnyi krai*), as well as from the Caucasus, or descendants of Kazan and Crimean Tatars or other *inorodtsy*. We also excluded all women who had among their ancestors Jews and Armenians. We strictly excluded any admixture of extraneous blood that would produce racial mixture. In other regards, I did not select subjects for my analysis. I took all female murderers available to me from the mid-Russia provinces, Russian by origin (Tarnovskaia 1902, 2).[8]

8 | "[Исключались] как бы интересны они ни были, все те случаи, где, при ближайшем ознакомлении, один из родителей оказывался не коренным русским по рождению. Таким образом, приходилось откинуть всех осужденных, один из родителей которых был уроженцем Финляндии, Балтийских губерний, Западного Края, равно как и Кавказа, или происходил от казанских или крымских татар, или иных инородцев. Мы исключили также всех женщин, заведомо имевших в своем восходящем поколении евреев и армян, строго исключая из своих наблюдений примеси посторонней крови обусловливающие скрещения рас, – в остальном я не выделяла субъектов для своих наблюдений, а брала подряд всех представлявшихся мне женщин-убийц средних русских губерний, русских по происхождению."

Tarnovskaia's Russian female "criminal types" and "normal" peasant women were not in any way representatives of some universal anthropological norm and degeneration, and they did not simply stand for a politically deprived class and gender group upon which intellectuals projected their cultural and biological biases and utopias. Instead, they embodied the Russian ethnic/racial norm and Russian ethnic/racial atavism, and Tarnovskaia readily acknowledged the limitations of her results. She allowed that other pure racial groups in the empire exhibited their own specific forms of norm and degeneration, and thus implied the possibility of coexistence of multiple legal logics reflecting different sociobiological realities (Mogilner 2013, 339-340).

The main problem with this application of Lombrosian methodology was its political implications. The arrangement, under which each collective subject would have its own unique "born criminal" and thus would receive an individualized legal treatment, was possible only under the archaic particularistic imperial order. It was precisely the "old" imperial state that preferred local knowledge and individualized treatments of different imperial subjects (the proverbial "Jewish question" or "Finnish question" instead of a general nationalities policy) to universal expert paradigms. When consistently applied as a means to reconfigure the existing imperial order, the adaptations of Lombrosian agenda or conceptual repertoire *à la* Kovalevskii and Tarnovskaia yielded only two alternatives: a consistent modern colonialism on the example of Western overseas empires or some backward-looking (toward the old imperial particularistic order), even if rhetorically very modern and "progressive," social utopia. Neither alternative, when articulated explicitly in political terms, was able to completely satisfy the Russian intellectual public, including Kovalevskii and Tarnovskaia themselves. At the same time, in no way had this practical inadequacy diminished the significance of the very task of rationalizing and reorganizing the irregular and disorderly imperial diversity.

Rigorous intellectual work was being carried out in many academic and professional spheres outside of the proper domain of criminal anthropology. Categories such as "atavism," "survival," "irrational," and "primitive" could have been borrowed from ethnography, philosophy, sociology, or psychiatry, and used to structure broader interdisciplinary debates which actively splashed out into the public domain. Since the late nineteenth century, ethnographers, lawyers, physical anthropologists, general physicians, psychiatrists, pedagogues, officers of the Russian army, national and civic activists, and all kinds of politicians shared this rhetorical repertoire. This helped to keep the Lombrosian agenda on the radar without directly referencing the Italian criminal anthropologist or the "inborn criminal."

For example, evoking the concept of "survival" in the postreform courtrooms opened the door for an essentially Lombrosian social imagination (in its characteristic Russian imperial rendition) under the disguise of the respectful ethnographic genealogy going back to E. B. Tylor. In his *Primitive Culture* (1871), Tylor outlined the evolutionary vision of a uniform "prehistoric" society as a necessary stage in the development of all human collectives. He formulated the concept of survivals as "proofs and examples of an older condition of culture" that had no functional meaning in modernity (Tylor 1871, 15). When used outside its proper context and evolutionary chronotope, "survival" could easily have been read as "atavism" bearing an important message for modern experts. A paradigmatic example of such a substitution was the "Votiak trial" (1892-1896), when a group of Votiak men (today known as Udmurts) from the village of Old Multan in the taiga-covered triangle between the rivers Volga and Kama, was falsely accused in the ritual murder of a Russian (Geraci 2000). The two court convictions in this case were based mainly on the expert testimony of Imperial Kazan University professor, ethnographer Ivan Smirnov, who never claimed to be an admirer of Lombroso. A true Tylorian, he believed in the universal path of human progress toward civilized cultural and social forms and in the Russian imperial civilizing mission. As an expert, he blamed not the concrete Votiaks, but rather their archaic "survivals" that needed to be purged. As long as Votiaks as a group exhibited these "survivals," they were to occupy the niche of the "born criminal." At the same time, for those who still retained a belief in imperial civilizing power and in nonracial imperial Russianness, their condition remained theoretically curable (Mogilner 2016a).

In the last decades of the empire, this applied discourse underwent quite a dramatic evolution, made apparent by another paradigmatic trial – the infamous "Beilis case" (1911-1913) (Weinberg 2014). When the Jew Mendel Beilis was accused in the ritual murder of the Christian boy Andrei Iushchinskii, experts supporting this accusation blamed the crime not on certain atavistic "survivals," but on the savage nature of the whole Jewish race. This time, the whole group was conceptualized as a collective survival and hence firmly established as an "inborn criminal" with no chances for cure and social integration (Mogilner 2016a). The main expert for the prosecution, professor Ivan Alekseevich Sikorskii (1842-1919) of Kiev St. Vladimir University, believed that, to explain the motives of Mendel Beilis, "one has to confine himself to considerations of an historical and anthropological character" and treat the murderer as a "criminal anthropological type." "One must admit, with the anthropological criminologists," continued Sikorskii, "that the psychological basis of crimes of that type is sought in racial revenge" (Weinberg 2014, 99-100). To get rid of this "collective survival" of the primitive epoch, the modern society needed to isolate or purge completely the whole dangerous group motivated by the criminal impulse for revenge. In his court testimony, Sikorskii explicitly synthesized Lombrosian criminal anthropology with Tylorian ethnography, misrepresenting his concept of "survival" as a live phenomenon, not merely an empty shell of the practice that was supposed to have lost its cultural meaning and function long before. To this mix he added James Frazer, the author of the *The Golden Bough: A Study in Comparative Religion* (1890) – a groundbreaking exploration of animist rituals in primitive cultures. Frazer was needed to support Sikorskii's claim that the ritual killing of children of another ethnicity was a sign of living savagery (Mogilner 2016a).

As arbitrary as such syntheses might have seemed, they revealed the persisting importance of the Lombrosian agenda connecting atavistic and criminal/deviant (survival and modernity). This connection, however differently understood and expressed, remained theoretically and practically relevant for thinking about human diversity in the Russian Empire.

The savage within

As a semiotic system, this Lombrosian connection implied that external signs of atavism and degeneracy (signifiers) were indicators of an internal degenerate condition (signified). However the relationships between the signifier and the signified changed in the years that separated the Votiak case from the Beilis trial, with experts' attention shifting from the observable and measurable signifiers to the hidden and therefore illusive and frightening signified. This new shift became especially apparent during the interrevolutionary period of 1905-1917. "Savage hunters" from within the ranks of scholars and politicians sharing the modernist and nationalist perception of the society, rather unwillingly discovered the very same qualities they attributed to alien groups (primitivism, irrationality, reliance on instincts) in their own "constituency" – first of all, the Russian ethnocultural nation. From the Tylorian vantage point, there would have been nothing dramatic in such a discovery, but a more Lombrosian essentialized perception of human diversity (in categories of race or social class) could not rely on the idea of evolutionary transformation. If the "savage within" could not be purged without the destruction of the self, the only remaining option was to wholeheartedly embrace it as a positive kind of "savagery," with all its criminal connotations.

It is thus not accidental that in the 1950s and 1960s, an influential group of American historians of late imperial Russia, who showed almost no interest in its imperial nature, nevertheless posited as a key predicament of that period the conflict between social organization and elemental improvisation, consciousness and spontaneity, epitomized (for these historians) in the standoff between the Bolsheviks and the Mensheviks.

> For almost three decades, the members of the various factions of Social Democracy had been content to interpret the data of their life experience - and to define and phrase their varied and changing political stands - through the medium of the two conceptual and symbolic categories, "consciousness" and "spontaneity." It had been their common quest for consciousness, for a reasonable and responsible world view in the face of an alien and indifferent society, that had originally brought the members of the intelligentsia together. [...] The very intensity of their efforts to find a "conscious" identity had periodically given rise in many members of the intelligentsia to an opposite striving, to an urge to break out of their isolation and to give free, "spontaneous," expression to their feelings - by "fusing" with an outside popular force. [...] The concepts of consciousness and spontaneity reflected the conflict between these two modes of orientation. They reflected the split that many members of the intelligentsia were making between reason and feelings (Haimson 1955, 209-210).

The author of this passage, the historian Leopold Haimson, presented the Mensheviks as resenting the savage face of their class base – a substantial part of the Russian proletariat that was presumably "completely unadapted to their new factory environment, 'driven by instincts and feelings rather than consciousness and calculation,' who gave the mass movement 'its disorganized, primitive, elemental character'" (Haimson 1964, 634). The Bolsheviks took over the Mensheviks because they more successfully resolved the dilemma of the "savage within."

Indeed, a comprehensive analysis of Vladimir Lenin's exhaustively documented writings reveals the suggestive dynamics of his usage of the notion of "class instinct" ("revolutionary instinct"), as contrasted to rational forms of organization or theoretical thinking. For more than ten years, from 1893 to 1903, he referred to the role of "instinct" only negatively. These were his political opponents, populists, who "believed in the communist instincts of the 'communal' peasant" and "the socialist instincts of the people" (Lenin [1894], 275; Lenin [1901], 281, 299; Lenin [1902a], 388). They were "demagogues" provoking "base instincts in the masses." In response, Lenin demanded that "all revolutionary instincts and strivings" be subordinate to "a centralized, militant organization that consistently carries out a Social Democratic policy" (Lenin [1902a], 463, 477; Lenin [1902b], 202; Lenin [1902c], 269). Lenin believed that only "the backward worker[s] from the lower or middle strata of the masses" could be "guided by their instincts" (Lenin [1899], 291-292); that "because of the extremely low cultural level of the Caucasian workers, their struggle against the employers has naturally been of a more or less instinctive, spontaneous nature" (Lenin [1902d], 324-325). The turning point in his perception of irrational and instinctive social action as having a pedagogic and creative value (Lenin [1904], 273) came in November 1903, when Lenin suddenly admitted that the workers' "proletarian instinct may teach us 'leaders' something too" (Lenin [1903], 116). After January 1905, references to the newly understood "instinct" literally flooded his writings, appearing in dozens of articles over the year. There was no longer anything savage in "sober proletarian instinct" (Lenin [1905a], 57), so "comrades [...] will have to be guided [...] by their revolutionary instinct" (Lenin [1905b], 69; Lenin [1905c], 300). By April 1905 Lenin had already begun directly juxtaposing the "revolutionary instinct of the working class" to "fallacious theories" (Lenin [1905d], 207, 208), and by May had completely reversed the hierarchy of values, declaring the priority of instinct over rational thinking and organization.[9]

9 | "Workers have the class instinct, and, given some political experience, they pretty soon become staunch Social-Democrats. I should be strongly in favor of

Somewhat lagging behind the Bolsheviks, Russian liberals and nationalists also sought reconciliation with the formerly estranged and repressed "savage" within their target audiences. In March 1909, Peter Struve published a programmatic article, *Intelligentsia and the National Face* (*Intelligentsiia i natsional'noe litso*), in which he demanded that the Russian intelligentsia become self-consciously "nationally Russian." The period 1908-1909 was one of the radical political reorientation of Struve, who had been perceived as one of the leading liberal ideologists and politicians in Russia (just as in the 1890s he was a recognized leader of the Social Democrats). What was striking about this article was not so much its ideological message (the turn from liberalism toward statism and nationalism) as its very different mental mapping of social reality:

> Once they thought that nationality meant race, that is, the skin color, the width of nose ("nasal index"), and so on. But nationality is something much more apparent and at the same time delicate. It is spiritual attractions and repulsions. To become aware of them, one does not have to use anthropological instruments or genealogical studies. They live and tremble in our soul (Struve 1909, 3).[10]

A renowned intellectual and rationalist, Struve rejected any objective and institutionalized (rational) forms of social differentiation. Declaring that the future of the state depends on the success of national cohesion and mobilization, he entrusted these important tasks to "spiritual attractions" that "tremble in our soul" – that is, the most irrational instincts lying at the very core of the trope of primitivism.

The same instincts appeared to be located in the Self and the Other, to be healthy and degenerate, criminal and perfectly legal, progressive and retrograde or atavistic. Their meaning was far from stable and universal; it was defined by a particular configuration of the imperial situation, a certain political agenda, a vision of the imperial or post-imperial future.

---

having eight workers to every two intellectuals on our committees" (Lenin [1905e], 408).

10 | "Когда-то думали, что национальность есть раса, т.е. цвет кожи, ширина носа ('носовой указатель') и т.п. Но национальность есть нечто гораздо более несомненное и в то же время тонкое. Это духовные притяжения и отталкивания, и для того, чтобы осознать их, не нужно прибегать ни к антропологическим приборам, ни к генеалогическим изысканиям. Они живут и трепещут в душе."

Evidently, the shift from the signifier to the signified did not produce any stability regarding the notions of norm and deviance. Likewise, it did not result in a less groupist and more individualized treatment of "inborn criminality," of organic deviance and difference. It nevertheless cleared the way for psychiatrists as the main experts on irrational instincts, attractions, and repulsions. They now became the most vocal and authoritative diagnosticians of different social conditions, the most qualified users of the established conceptual repertoire of deviance, from "criminal type" to "survival," "savage," and so on. No wonder the story of Russian psychiatry as a profession and, most important, as a powerful social and political discourse chronologically coincides with the timing of the semiotic shift, which, in turn, coincides with the epoch of rising mass politics and its nationalization in the empire (Brown 1981; 1987; Etkind 1993; Menzhulin 2004; Beer 2008). This story is yet to be written as an imperial history from the perspective of the discovery of internal savagery in the dynamic late imperial situation.[11] Russian psychiatrists inherited the tradition of ethnicization of deviance and faced the new challenge of reordering and rationalizing hidden internal irrational instincts alongside "external" imperial diversity.

Imperial comparison of deviance

Professor Ivan Sikorskii, a Kiev psychiatrist and neurologist, the infamous expert on Jewish racial savagery at the Beilis trial, was a typical representative of those Russian psychiatrists who most consciously embraced the ideology of modern – in fact post-imperial in terms of its political makeup and horizon – Russian nationalism (Mogilner 2013, 185-200). Professor Pavel Ivanovich Kovalevskii, another prominent Russian psychiatrist and a leading Russian nationalist, represented the same cohort.[12] In 1883, only three years after Cesare Lombroso founded a special journal for the Italian school of criminal anthropology, *Archivio di psichiatria, antropologia criminale e scienze penali*, Kovalevskii began editing the Russian *Archive of Psychiatry, Neurology, and Forensic Psychopathology* (*Arkhiv psikhiatrii, neirologii i sudebnoi psikhopatologii*). The *Archive*, just as

11 | I attempt to suggest such a history in Mogilner 2016b.

12 | On P. I. Kovalevskii see also Louise McReynolds' and Riccardo Nicolosi's contributions to this volume.

individual academic and popular publications by Sikorskii, Kovalevskii, or another highly positioned member of the group, professor Vladimir Fiodorovich Chizh, exhibited a trademark blend of Lombrosian rigidity of "types," their groupist and ethnicized interpretation and a strong fixation on irrational instincts. Kovalevskii claimed approvingly that Russians felt "instinctual, biological nationalism" (Kovalevskii 1910, 76), which for him was a healthy instinct, for he understood nationalism as a synthesis of the rational "act of thinking" with "national feeling," an "animal, gregarious, organic and inborn phenomenon" (Kovalevskii 1915, 3).[13] However, in the cases of Tatars or especially Jews the same "animal, gregarious, organic" signaled dangerous, criminal, and "predatory" (Kovalevskii 1900, 103).

Sikorskii went even further, exposing the dangerous and overtly criminal nature of irrational instincts of the Russian religious sectarians who contaminated the Russian national body from within. In other contexts, however, he presented these same instincts as revealing sectarians' true religiosity and existential Russianness (Mogilner 2013, 167-200). To differentiate between the two interpretations, Sikorskii needed a third element, which he found in collective Jews whose irrational nature lacked any ambiguity and as such presented an absolute threat to the emerging post-imperial Russian national modernity. The resulting construct of the "savage within" was a hybrid product of superimposition of atavistic Jewish and primitive Russian; social environment and determinism of race; uplifting religious emotions and primitive ecstasy; complex (Russian sectarian) hallucinations and ugly (Jewish) hiccup and vomiting; individual etymologies of male degenerate psychoses (individual medical cases in Sikorskii's analysis of sectarian movements were exclusively restricted to male sectarians), and generic sexualized descriptions of female hysteria (exemplified by a hiccupping and vomiting young Jewess from one of his medical reports – on the one hand, and female leaders of the common worships of one of the Russian sects that he studied – on the other). Regardless of how scientific Sikorskii's mode of discussing the atavistic and criminal was, his "savage" remained hybrid, elusive, unstable, and hence even more frightening (Mogilner 2016b).

It became the task of the younger generation of psychiatrists, more extreme in terms of their readiness to part ways with the old imperial

---

13 | "[…] нацональное чувство" – "явление животное, стадное, органическое и прирожденное."

complexity, to eliminate ambiguity from the unstable constructs of their mentors. A graduate student of Vladimir Fiodorovich Chizh, E. M. Budul (later known in his native Latvia as Hermanis Buduls, 1882-1954),[14] attempted to do this in his dissertation, *On Comparative Racial Psychiatry* (*K sravnitel'noi rasovoi psikhiatrii*, 1914). He racialized psychiatric statistics collected at Iur'ev (Tartu) University Clinic for nervous disorders and elaborated a comparative method of measuring degrees of inborn versus socially acquired psychological and mental deviance. One of his main focuses was hysteria – the same hysteria that Sikorskii famously diagnosed among the racially degenerate Jews and Russian sectarians alike. The disciplinary mainstream of the time understood hysteria as a culturally determined disorder receding with the advancement of societal progress. In modern history it was believed to affect predominantly subalterns: women, peasants, and Jews (Gilman 1991) – all three main elements of Sikorskii's elusive concept of internal savagery. Budul attempted to disengage the elements of this triad (especially Jews from the Russian peasants) by composing a complex hierarchy of racial versus cultural forms of primitivism observable within the imperial borders. He diagnosed hysteria – a malady of the savage and feminine groups – among the animist Yakuts, Ostiaks, Tunguzs, and Kalmyks, whose culture he associated with "hysterical" rituals and self-mutilations, and who otherwise could hardly be linked to Jews as a people of culture, monotheist religion, and "capitalist" economic behavior. In Budul's dissertation, inborn – that is, racial – predisposition toward hysteria and self-mutilation became the two basic features of primitivism that made cultural differences between Yakuts and Jews irrelevant.

To them Budul opposed the Russian nation. He admitted its relative cultural backwardness, which, however, was expected to disappear with time ("psychic epidemics of this type are comparatively frequent in Russia because it still lags behind Western Europe" [Budul 1914, 182]).[15] Simultaneously, Budul dismissed any organic foundations of sectarian hysteria. In Budul's interpretation, sectarians, not unlike Votiaks of the

14 | He is regarded as "the founding father of Latvian psychiatry" (Kuznecovs 2013, 149).

15 | "В России психические эпидемии названного рода наблюдаются сравнительно часто только потому, что культура в России еще не пошла так далеко вперед, как в Западной Европе."

Multan case, exhibited "survivals" that were theoretically curable. As in Sikorskii's works, in Budul's dissertation, Russian hysteria revealed itself in "the most beautiful hallucinations with religious and terrible fantasies,"[16] while Jewish hysteria was exemplified by the hiccupping and vomiting peasant Jewish girl. Budul stabilized these two extreme poles on the scale of relative imperial savagery, which enabled him to evaluate biological and social danger represented by each particular non-Russian group between Russians/Slavs and the Jews. For example, he described Bashkirs as suffering simultaneously from cultural and biological causes of degeneration and hence as destined to remain half-modern/half-savage. Unlike them, sectarians, together with other backward groups of Slavs, were on their way toward the top position on the comparative imperial scale – the position designated for the Russian race-nation in its ideal state. If the fate of the Jews had been "scientifically" predetermined, the fate of other primitives (such as Yakuts or Ostiaks) described in the dissertation as being quite close to the degenerate Jews, remained unspecified and seemed to depend on political rather than scholarly judgment.[17]

Medical practice as social-political technique

Since the late nineteenth century, Russian physicians and especially military physicians who partook in the postreform vanguard military discourse of population politics, tended to connect ethnicity, atavism, and deviance. While zemstvo and private doctors still exhibited more diverse professional attitudes, annual reports of the physicians of Russian military hospitals routinely classified patients by nationality (a category officially absent from state statistics). Physicians of neurological and psychiatric divisions of these hospitals especially readily combined the ethnicity of their patients with race and almost always provided descriptions of "signs of anthropological degeneration" that ranged from anomalies in skull and facial features à la Lombroso to hysteria or other "organic" psychiatric disorders.[18]

16 | "[…] самыми красивыми галлюцинациями с религиозными и страшными фантазиями".

17 | See a more detailed analysis in Mogilner 2016b.

18 | As a typical example, see Kiselev (1889). In a special section, Kiselev treats "signs of anthropological degeneration" among eleven melancholic patients of his

Dr. Ernest Vilgel'movich Erikson was such a typical military physician. He received his medical doctorate in 1900 for dissertation, *On the Influence of the Cerebral Cortex and Subcortical Node on the Reduction of the Spleen*, defended at St. Petersburg Military-Medical Academy under the supervision of Professor Bekhterev (Erikson 1900). However as a clinical psychiatrist and neurologist he made the Lombrosian connection between atavism and criminality his major field of scholarly interest. The results of his medical and anthropological observations appeared in professional journals, including *Bulletin of Psychology, Criminal Anthropology and Hypnotism* (*Vestnik psikhologii, kriminal'noi antropologii i gipnotizma*), edited by Vladimir Bekhterev, *Natural Science and Geography* (*Estestvoznanie i Geografiia*), *Neurology Bulletin* (*Nevrologicheskii Vestnik*), and others (Erikson 1899; 1901; 1902; 1905). Erikson's most productive period was in the early twentieth century, just before the first Russian Revolution, when he served as a military physician in the Caucasus. There he developed a research agenda for each "psychiatrist and psychologist" interested in the connection between atavistic (inborn, racially determined) and criminal: "do inborn features of the psyche of some tribes and races of this region play any role in the etiology of murders and brigandage in the Caucasus, and do psychiatric and nervous diseases also play a role in these crimes (and if so – to what degree)?" (Erikson 1906, 48).[19] Registering signs of physical degeneration and collecting anthropometric statistics were seen by Dr. Erikson as absolutely necessary elements of medical practice in the Caucasus (Erikson 1909a, 1).

Surely, the colonial distances were more apparent there than anywhere else in the empire, and "criminality" of the local population was a well-

hospital psychiatric division. He found these signs in the form of their skulls and in the form and size of their ears: "[...] one patient's right ear was bigger than the left one, along with the better developed right side of the skull; another patient's right ear was smaller than the left ear, and the skull exhibited asymmetry." "[...] у одного больного правое ухо было больше левого совместно с большим развитием правой стороны черепа; у другого правое ухо было меньше левого при асимметрии черепа" (Kiselev 1889, 129).

19 | "[...] не имеют ли значение в этиологии убийств и разбоев на Кавказе врождённые особенности психики отдельных племён и рас, населяющих край, и не играют ли в этого рода преступлениях также некоторой роли, а если играют, то в какой степени – психические и нервные болезни людей?"

established trope in academic, professional, and political debates. For Erikson, however, the Caucasus and the medical treatment of deviance there represented nothing specifically colonial or particularly unique. In all other places where he worked in the military hospitals, from Siberia and the Far East to the Warsaw district military hospital (*Varshavskii uiazdovskii voennyi gospital'*), he developed the same approach, the same research agenda and the same understanding of the connection between atavism, deviance, and criminality. An acute feeling of professional and social responsibility as an expert on irrational instincts, who possessed the real power of interpretation of the hidden signified, penetrated his routine medical reports and scholarly writings regardless of the geographical location in the empire where he observed his patients. When cultural and racial differences between the patients he treated seemed to be less apparent than in the Caucasus, Erikson resorted to the method of imperial comparison. He arrived at this method independently, out of practical considerations and well before Budul had elaborated it in his dissertation.

As a psychiatrist at the Warsaw district military hospital, Erikson evaluated and treated a highly diverse soldier population reflecting not only the demography of the Privislenskii krai, but the demography of the Russian Empire in general (including a small minority of conscripts from the Caucasus). Under these circumstances, Erikson calibrated his scale of normalcy in such a way that his Jewish patients came to embody the benchmark of the lowest and hopeless organic deviance (racial degeneracy, atavisms, organic psychosis, criminal inclinations, social danger). His Russian patients represented the opposite pole of culturally determined and curable deviance. All other national cases could be safely located between the two extremes.

It makes sense to compare the impact of an unpleasant letter from home on a Russian and a Jew: a healthy and strong Russian man, at least as he is perceived in his unit, often faints away or experiences a wild hysterical or neurasthenic attack, or can sometimes go and hang or shoot himself. Under the same circumstance, a Jew most often exhibits an unusually strong anger and a desire for revenge. He wants to escape home and take the law into his own hands, however he is not likely to attempt suicide and in any case is not going to take to drinking "in pain", which is so customary among the Russian soldiers (Erikson 1907a, 12).[20]

From the onset, Erikson's typical Russian was a "healthy and strong" man whose neurotic reaction was caused by the difficult circumstances of military service in the western borderlands of the empire, which were alien to him, far away from home and family. At the same time, in his assessment of the Jewish psychopathological reaction, Erikson had anticipated Sikorskii's infamous claim during the Beilis trial that Mendel Beilis acted out of "racial revenge." Erikson characterized his very real individual Russian patient-soldiers as "dreamers and mystics" (*ibid.*), just as seven years later Budul would insist that the aggregated Russian hysteria revealed itself in "the most beautiful hallucinations with religious and terrible fantasies."

In a routine medical-statistical report compiled for the psychiatric division of the Warsaw hospital in 1906, Erikson introduced its Jewish patients as representatives of a "tribe producing the greatest numbers of hysterics, neurasthenics, and different kinds of degenerates."[21] In the context of the report, such an introduction justified Erikson's and his fellow physicians' diagnoses and choices of treatment, including harsh measures of isolation, painful medical procedures applied for experimental purposes, and complete disregard for information supplied by the patients themselves (Erikson 1907b, 138; Erikson 1908). Patients' aggressive criminal instincts and the tribal "desire for revenge" released physicians of any moral and professional constraints.

20 | "Стоит сравнить действие неприятного письма, полученного из дому, на русского и на еврея: русский подчас совершенно здоровый и крепкий мужчина, по крайней мере считавшийся таковым на службе, сплошь да рядом падает в обморок или обнаруживает бурный приступ истерического возбуждения, а случается – пойдет и повесится или застрелится; у еврея при тех же условиях вспыхивает разве только гнев необычайной силы, появляется жажда мести, стремление убежать со службы домой и расправиться самолично, но он вряд ли сделает покушение на свою жизнь и во всяком случае не запьет "с горя", что так обычно у русских солдат."

21 | "[...] нет другого племени, среди которого было бы столько истериков, неврастеников и разного рода дегенератов [...]."

In 1910, if not earlier, Erikson suggested that military-medical examiners had to consider the nature of racially specific neuroses and psychosis when making decisions about the military fitness of conscripts (Erikson 1909b; Erikson 1910b, 159). The semiotic shift from the signifier to the signified manifested itself in this suggestion, especially when Erikson criticized the traditional Lombrosian approach based on the analysis of external signs of atavism. As a practical physician working with patients whom he perceived as individual representatives of their race, Erikson knew that anthropometric indicators were good for constructing a generic "criminal type" but not sufficient for differentiating between ethnically and racially marked specific "criminal types." In addition, external signifiers did not allow for a convincing presentation of Jewish conscripts as an absolute degenerate type. In most cases, the average length and width of skulls of Erikson's Jewish patients were normal. Erikson's expectations of finding mostly dolichocephalic skulls among his Jewish patients also failed miserably. As he reasoned, the Jewish race evolved from ancient dolichocephaly to modern brachicephaly, and if "one sees mental illness as a phenomenon of degeneration and atavism, then our material has to yield many dolychocephals" (Erikson 1909a, 5).[22] He was disappointed to discover that this was not the case, and that in general no meaningful correlation existed between the "height of skull and forms of mental disorder." (*ibid.*, 6).[23] Nor did he find Lombrosian hyperdeveloped jaws of "born criminals" among his Jewish patients. The only "degenerative" anatomic sign presumably signaling atavism was, in his view, the Jewish ear: "Very often Jews have ears protruding on both sides, with more or less outspread helix and comparatively prominent Darwin's tubercle. This feature is so characteristic of the Jewish people that often ears alone are enough to disclose who you are dealing with" (Erikson 1909a, 17).[24] Left with nothing but ears, Erikson concluded that instincts and neuroses

22 | "Если смотреть на душевные болезни как на явление вырождения и атавизма, то следовало бы в нашем материале найти много долихоцефалов."

23 | "Отыскивать какую либо связь между высотою черепа и формами душевного расстройства не представляется возможным."

24 | "Уши, торчащие в обе стороны, с большим или меньшим развернутым helix'ом и сравнительно сильно выступающим Дарвиновым бугорком очень часто встречаются у евреев. Это признак настолько характерный для данной народности, что часто по ушам можно сказать, с кем имеешь дело."

and psychoses were more effective indicators of the "savage within" and that the task of practical psychiatrists and neurologists was not only to collect anthropometric statistics and diagnose and cure illnesses but also to explain the meaning, nature, and danger, when applicable, of impulses, instincts, and abnormal behavior. In his formulation of the task of practical psychiatry, the distinction between medical practice and social policing was disappearing. The signified as the main object of diagnostics provided much broader opportunities for almost unrestricted ideological creativity (as long as formal conventions of scientific narrative were observed).

Physicians of the Warsaw hospital could discuss specific instincts and irrational impulses from a formally psychiatric point of view, as during their meeting on February 26, 1910, when Dr. E. Nilson presented on "soldiers' morbid impulses toward escape."[25] However the medical-social discourse of deviance that these psychiatrists shared necessitated generalizations about racial impulses and the application of imperial comparison for differentiating between the degrees of social danger presented by these impulses to society. During the discussion of Dr. Nilson's presentation, his colleagues predictably assumed that the predisposition toward vagrancy was an atavistic and a racially determined quality. They could have heard about "drapetomania" – the psychiatric diagnosis attributed by the American nineteenth century psychiatrists to blacks and described as an uncontrollable urge to run away from their 'master' and change places (Cartwright 1851; Beynton 2001), or they just reasoned about "lower" races in a similar logic. They immediately ran into the problem of how to differentiate between the atavisms of nomadic peoples of the empire, of Roma and Jews, on the one hand, and the "Vagrant Rus'" (Russian colonizers, pilgrims or seasonal workers), on the other. This diversion from the psychiatric aspect of the problem, summarized by Erikson as "where are the borders of the inherited instinct and the expressions of psychopathology?" (Erikson 1910, 153-154),[26] to a social-political formulation of the same problem was inevitable and in fact quite conscious.

The same blurred border between medical and social-political aspects characterized the psychiatric construction of the phenomenon of self-

25 | "О болезненных побуждениях к побегу у солдат."

26 | "[...] где границы унаследованного инстинкта и где проявление психопатологии?"

mutilation (*chlenovreditel'stvo*) as a problem of practical relevance for the medical community and for the modernizing imperial society in general. Since the late nineteenth century, hundreds of unpublished reports and published articles penned by physicians serving in different military hospitals in the Russian empire detailed characteristically Jewish self-mutilations, which, as one medical doctor from the Warsaw military hospital noted, were "well-known to any old military physician" (Nil'son 1909, 98).[27] The proliferation of this literature was obviously connected with the attempts to limit Jewish presence in the Russian army by stressing their cunning schemes to avoid conscription and their physical (and moral) unfitness (Holquist 2001; Petrovsky-Shtern 2008; Mogilner 2013, 269-296). However by the 1910s, this practical and obviously anti-Semitic discourse was being more and more contaminated by the racialized understanding of Jewish self-mutilation as an expression of Jewish racial atavism. While Budul in his dissertation creatively presented self-mutilation as a key atavistic indicator of a primitive condition connecting Jews and peoples of shamanistic cults, clinicians such as Erikson generalized a few cases from their practice using the already established multidisciplinary (ethnographic, psychiatric, historical, sociological) framework of savagery to their advantage. Not only did they systematize individual and very diverse medical cases as variations of one typical criminal case of conscious self-mutilation with the aim of avoiding military conscription, but they conceptualized these cases as atavisms by randomly connecting them to specific "savage" Jewish rituals and cults. Erikson was ready to see in any Jewish medical complaint an instance of self-mutilation connected to some live atavistic Jewish ritual. Thus he diagnosed a specific Jewish paralysis of the upper left hand produced by the tradition of wearing tefillin (Erikson 1911). Jewish religion, Jewish rituals, Jewish instincts, Jewish neuroses and psychoses, and Jewish physicality formed one powerful image of the ultimate and dangerous (aggressive, violent, perverted) savage persisting in modern times.

Of course, there were politicians and professionals who rejected this interpretation of Jewish savagery and this application of imperial comparison, and who understood the real danger of their ideological and, most important, practical implications for the Jews and the imperial

27 | "Всякому старому военному врачу хорошо известны обычно практикуемые способы членовредительства."

society. Thus, Solomon Vermel', psychiatrist of the Kazan circuit mental hospital (*Kazanskaia Okruzhnaia lechebnitsa dlia dushevno-bol'nykh*), felt compelled to devote quite a few pages in his own study of Jewish mental patients of Kazan hospital to exposing Erikson's medical inaccuracy, ideological bias, and poor knowledge of Jewish culture: "I dedicated so much time to this issue because at present, when all and everyone everywhere find simulation and self-mutilation, Dr. Erikson's 'discovery' may affect not just [the legal] condition of many people, but, quite possibly, their very lives" (Vermel' 1917, 36).[28]

However even in this case of open professional confrontation with Erikson, the collective nature of the "patient" (as representing race, nationality, or class, or even an ideological community), and the perception of each individual deviance as an expression of a group defect or atavism (even if culturally constructed), as well as the promise to offer the only true and scientifically informed interpretation of irrational instincts remained embedded in the discourse. Yes, Vermel' was a Jew and a Jewish activist, whereas Erikson, regardless of the Swedish origin of his family name, perceived himself as a Russian and was a Russian nationalist and defender of radical colonialism (just as Sikorskii, with his obviously Polish-sounding family name, or Budul who was a Latvian and imperial Russian nationalist). Yes, the opponents of Vermel' used their psychiatric expertise to scientifically homogenize Jews and Russians/Slavs in order to stabilize the fluid and unordered imperial situation according to their ideological preferences. But Vermel' equally tended to homogenize at least the Jews according to his own sociopolitical idea. His Jewish deviance was constructed as less "inborn" and more "common," that is, socially and culturally determined, yet it remained a collective stigma and a collective promise, as well as the indicator of a civilizational status of the whole group. Vermel' normalized Jews by applying to them Lamarckian and sociologically sensitive interpretations of heredity, and at the same time accepted that the more developed a national culture was, the more "complex and intricate," "beautiful and bright" was the pattern of mental illness that it produced. Vermel' also needed an imperial comparative

28 | "Я так долго остановился на этом вопросе потому, что в наше время, когда нередко всем и каждому везде видится симуляция и членовредительство, 'открытие' д-ра Эриксона может оказать влияние не только на положение, но, может быть, и на жизнь многих людей."

scale to rehabilitate the Jewish deviance as a phenomenon of developed modernity and sophisticated national culture.

Not surprisingly, both clinicians, Vermel' and Erikson, referred in their medical publications to Lombroso, who continued to influence their professional language and ideological outlooks. Whereas Erikson encouraged a semiotic shift toward the signified within what had been considered the classic version of criminal anthropology, Vermel' appealed to the authority of Lombroso as a critic of scientific foundations of anti-Semitism, which the Italian criminal anthropologist tellingly called "atavism." The Russian translation of Lombroso's *Anti-Semitism and Modern Science* (1894) came out in 1906 with an introduction by the well-known lawyer and member of the Russian parliament, Osip Iakovlevich Pergament (Lombroso 1906). This, however, turned out to be a double-edged weapon in the hands of Jewish activists, because Lombroso's discussion of anti-Semitism as an essentially atavistic manifestation of human intolerance included a radical denunciation of "barbaric" Jewish rituals quite in line with Erikson or Budul. As the most outrageous example, Lombroso mentioned the "barbaric tradition of circumcision, which, as Spenser has proved, is only a symbolic survival of human sacrifice." Lombroso presented it as a ritual case of self-mutilation. The most orthodox Jews, claimed Lombroso, "used their teeth or sharpened stones for this cruel ritual, the same way this had been done by our ancestors who lived in caves" (Lombroso 1906, 14, 15).[29]

The Soviet reinvention of savagery: Epilogue

Whatever the ideological position or the vision of the post-imperial society, the Lombroso-inspired conversation about atavism and criminality, savagery, and modernity structured hegemonic idioms of the politics of exclusion. All candidates for the exclusion – the born criminal, the savage, the hidden enemy, the degenerate race, or most often some combination of the above – were collective actors. Their normalization and integration was hardly possible as an individual choice. These idioms are easily

29 | "[…] варварский обычай обрезания, являющийся, как это доказал Спенсер, лишь символическим пережитком человеческих жертвоприношений […]"; "Они доходят до того, что пользуются для жестокого обряда обрезания зубами или заостренными камнями, как наши предки, жившие в пещерах."

distinguishable in the early Soviet context of ideological and professional debates. Without doubt, they persisted after 1917, but they changed their meanings in the structurally new situation. First, in the Soviet society, the entire old-regime modernized elite, regardless of political loyalty, came to embody archaism. Second, constructivism and developmental utopianism dominated nationalities policies, posing a powerful alternative to organicist concepts of race. Third, the Jew ceased to personify a savage within – now the Lombrosian reading of anti-Semitism as an atavism defined the official ideology. Interviewed by the Jewish Telegraphic Agency in January 1931, Stalin remarkably branded anti-Semitism as a survival, articulating it in perfectly Lombrosian terms:

> National and racial chauvinism is *a relic of man-hating customs, characteristic of the era of cannibalism*. Antisemitism is an extreme expression of racial chauvinism, and as such *is the most dangerous survival of cannibalism*. Antisemitism is useful to the exploiter, for it serves as a lightning conductor enabling capitalism to evade the blows of the toiling masses. Antisemitism is a danger to the working people, inasmuch as it is *a false path leading them into the jungle* away from the right road. Communists, therefore, as consistent internationalists cannot but be irreconcilable and avowed enemies of antisemitism (Antisemitism 1931, 1; emphasis added).

The operationalization of these idioms by the Soviet regime that had built them into its aggressive social engineering and legal system (consider the social category of the "formers" – *byvshie*) changed the wording and, eventually, the symbolism of the language of exclusion. Adapting to the cultural background and education level of the new political elite, the old metaphor that had originated in the most advanced human sciences was replaced by a literally more down-to-earth (but still scholarly) notion of "vermin." In her study of the evolution of the political etymology of the term "vermin" (*vreditel'*) in the early Soviet public discourse, Galina Orlova shows that what had begun as a purely agricultural term became incorporated into a critical social discourse about local village landowners in 1924, and two–three years later evolved into the discourse about enemies-savages within the Soviet project (Orlova 2003). These vermin were "born criminals" because they belonged to particular social classes, and even the most loyal of them could yield to the temptation of unleashing their inherent survivals at any moment. However their anthropological traits did not matter, and their internal instincts were not seen as irrational and illusive. The Lombrosian connection between atavism and criminality became purely sociological. Social origin distinguished "vermin" from "common criminals" born into "progressive classes": even though the latter had committed a crime, they did this under the influence of cultural "survivals" that were not organic, and hence could be corrected. "Vermin" of the late 1920s was the opposite of the common criminal who was not structurally predetermined to sin against the Soviet society.

The Soviet state institutionalized the principle of group subjecthood on the basis of class political philosophy and national evolutionism, not biological races and their civilizational hierarchy, thus preferring one specific interpretation of savagery and exclusion. It could do this because the Soviet regime was an ideological regime. The old empire had not had time or opportunity to reach this stage – it had collapsed at the moment when a number of different notions of subjecthood and versions of the politics of exclusion were debated in the political and professional fields. As I have attempted to show, even the most uncompromising proponents of the radical strategy of elimination of racialized savages had to embrace the method of imperial comparison in order to construct their ultimate "savage within" – a method that remained relevant and meaningful only as long as the imperial situation of underrationalized and unstable diversity persisted.

The Soviet regime modified the language of exclusion, the connection between atavism/inborn nature and criminality/danger for a particular project of modernity, and the relevance of the semiotics of the external anthropological signifiers and the internal signified. But most important, it redefined the old imperial situation that had informed the meaning of this language of exclusion and the archetypal Lombrosian semiotic construct behind it.

References

Antisemitism 1931. "Antisemitism Danger to Working People [Interview with Josef Stalin]." *Daily News Bulletin* (Jewish Telegraphic Agency) 12, no. 14, 1.

Anuchin, D. 1890. "Izuchenie psikhofizicheskikh tipov. D. A. Dril': 'Psikhofizicheskie tipy v ikh sootnoshenii s prestupnost'iu i ee raznovidnostiami,' M. 1890." *Vestnik Evropy* 3, no. 5, 337-341.

Baynton, D. C. 2001. "Disability and the Justification of Inequality in American History". Longmore, P. K. and Umansky, L. (eds.), *The New Disability History: American Perspectives.* New York: New York University Press, 33-57.

Beer, D. 2008. *Renovating Russia: The Human Sciences and the Fate of Liberal Modernity, 1880–1930.* Ithaca and London: Cornell University Press.

Bhabha, H. 2004. "Of Mimicry and Man: The Ambivalence of Colonial Discourse." Stoller, A. L. and Cooper, F. (eds.), *Tensions of Empire: Colonial Cultures in a Bourgeois World.* Berkeley: University of California Press, 152-162.

Boronoev, A. O. (ed.) 1996. *M. M. Kovalevskii v istorii rossiiskoi sotsiologii i obshchestvennoi mysli: sbornik statei k 145-letiiu rozhdeniia M. M. Kovalevskogo.* St. Petersburg: Izdatel'stvo St. Peterburgskogo Gosudarstvennogo Universiteta.

Brown, J. 1981. *The Professionalization of Russian Psychiatry, 1857–1911.* Ph.D Diss., University of Pennsylvania.

Brown, J. 1987. "Revolution and Psychosis: The Mixing of Science and Politics in Russian Psychiatric Medicine, 1905–13." *Russian Review* 46, no. 3, 283-302.

Budul, E. M. 1914. *K sravnitel'noi rasovoi psikhiatrii: Dissertatsiia na stepen' doktora meditsyny.* Iur'ev: Tipo-litografiia Ed. Bergmana.

Burbank, J. 2006. "An Imperial Rights Regime: Law and Citizenship in the Russian Empire." *Kritika: Explorations in Russian and Eurasian History* 7, no. 3, 397-431.

Cartwright, S. A. 1851. "Report on the Diseases and Peculiarities of the Negro Race." *New Orleans Medical and Surgical Journal.* May 7, 331-336.

Engelstein, L. 1992. *The Keys to Happiness: Sex and the Search for Modernity in Fin-de-Siècle Russia.* Ithaca and London: Cornell University Press.

Engelstein, L. 1993. "Combined Underdevelopment: Discipline and the Law in Imperial and Soviet Russia." *American Historical Review* 98, no. 2, 338-353.

Erikson, E. V. 1899. "Iz vospominanii o Batume i ego okrestnostiakh." *Estestvoznanie i geografiia* 6, 1-27.

Erikson, E. V. 1900. *O vliianii mozgovoi kory i podkorkovykh uzlov na sokrashchenie selezenki. Dissertatsia na stepen' doktora meditsiny E. V. Eriksona. Iz fiziologicheskoi laboratorii pri klinike dushevnykh i nervnykh boleznei prof. V. M. Bekhtereva*. St. Petersburg: Tipografiia kn. V. G. Meshcherskogo.

Erikson, E. V. 1901. "Dushevnye i nervnye bolezni na Dal'nem Vostoke." *Nevrologicheskii vestnik* 9, no. 4, 172-229.

Erikson, E. V. 1902. "Dushevno i nervno bol'nye v Abastumane v sezon 1902 g." *Protokoly zasedaniia Imperatorskogo Kavkazskogo meditsinskogo obshchestva (Tiflis)* 7, 170-192.

Erikson, E. V. 1905. "Alkogolizm na Kavkaze." *Obozreniie Psikhiatrii, Nevrologii i Eksperimental'noi psikhologii* 2, 98-122; 3, 198-214.

Erikson, E. V. 1906. "Ob ubiistvakh i razboiakh na Kavkaze." *Vestnik psikhologii, kriminal'noi antropologii i gipnotizma* 3, no. 1, 21-53.

Erikson, E. V. 1907a. "Materialy k voprosu o pokushenii na samoubiistvo sredi nizhnikh chinov v voiskakh Priviskenskogo kraia (Po nabliudeniam v psikhiatricheskom otdelenii pri Varshavskom Uiazdosvskom voennom gospitale za 1906 god)." *Meditsinskii sbornik Varshavskago uiazdovskago voennogo gospitalia* XIX, no. I-III, 11-15.

Erikson. E. V. 1907b. "Psikhiatricheskoe otdelenie pri Varshavskom Uiazdovskom voennom gospitale i kolichestvo, sostav i dvizhenie v nem bol'nykh za 1906 god." *Meditsinskii sbornik Varshavskago uiazdovskago voennogo gospitalia* XIX, no. I-III, 114-140.

Erikson, E. V. 1908. "Psikhiatricheskoe otdelenie pri Varshavskom Uiazdovskom voennom gospitale za 1907 god." *Meditsinskii sbornik Varshavskago uiazdovskago voennogo gospitalia* XX, no. I-III, 5-40.

Erikson, E. V. 1909a. "Antropologicheskie issledovaniia evreev na material psikhiatricheskogo otdeleniia pri Varshavskom Uiazdovskom voennom gospitale." *Meditsinskii sbornik Varshavskago uiazdovskago voennogo gospitalia* XXI, no. I-III, 1-121.

Erikson, E. V. 1909b. "Zametka o prizyvnykh, proshedshikh cherez psikhiatricheskoe otdelenie pri Varshavskom Uiazdosvskom voennom gospitale v techenie 1908 goda." *Meditsinskii sbornik Varshavskago uiazdovskago voennogo gospitalia* XXI, no. I-III, 79-85.

[Erikson, E. V.] 1910a. "Zasedanie 26 fevralia 1910 goda." *Meditsinskii sbornik Varshavskago uiazdovskago voennogo gospitalia* XXII, no. I-III, 153-156.

[Erikson, E. V.] 1910b. "Zasedanie 10 marta 1910 goda." *Meditsinskii sbornik Varshavskago uiazdovskago voennogo gospitalia* XXII, no. I-III, 156-159.

Erikson, E. V. 1911. "Znachenie tefillina v razvitii paralicha ruki u evreev." *Voenno-meditsinskii zhurnal* 132, 498-508.

Etkind, A. 1993. *Eros Nevozmozhnogo: Istoriia psikhoanaliza v Rossii*. St. Petersburg: Meduza.

Geraci, R. 2000. "Ethnic Minorities, Anthropology, and Russian National Identity on Trial: The Multan Case, 1892-96." *Russian Review* 52, no. 4, 530-554.

Gerasimov, I. et. al. 2009. "New Imperial History and the Challenges of Empire." Gerasimov, I. et al. (eds.), *Empire Speaks Out: Languages of Rationalization and Self-Description in the Russian Empire*. Leiden: Brill, 3-32.

Gerasimov, I. et al. 2013. "The Postimperial Meets the Postcolonial: Russian Historical Experience and the Postcolonial Moment." *Ab Imperio* 14, no. 2, 97-135.

Gilman, S. 1991. *The Jew's Body*. New York: Routledge.

Haimson, L. 1955. *The Russian Marxists and the Origins of Bolshevism*. Cambridge, MA: Harvard University Press.

Haimson, L. 1964. "The Problem of Social Stability in Urban Russia, 1905-1917 (Part One)." *Slavic Review* 23, no. 4, 619-642.

Holquist, P. 2001. "To Count, to Extract and to Exterminate: Population Statistics and Population Politics in Late Imperial and Soviet Russia." Suny, R.G. and Martin, T. (eds.), *A State of Nations: Empire and Nation-Making in the Age of Lenin and Stalin*. Oxford: Oxford University Press, 110-143.

Kiselev, V. G. 1889. "Otchet po otdeleniiu dushevno-bol'nykh Tiflisskogo voennogo gospitalia za 1888 god." *Meditsinskii sbornik, izdavaemyi Imperatorskim Kavkazskim Meditsinskim Obshchestvom* 26, no. 50, 107-134.

Kovalevskii, P. I. 1900. *Psikhologiia prestupnika po russkoi literature o katorge*. St. Petersburg: Russkii meditsinskii vestnik.

Kovalevskii, P. I. 1910. *Natsional'noe vospitanie i obrazovanie v Rossii*. St. Petersburg: Akinfiev.

Kovalevskii, P. I. 1915. *Psikhologiia Russkoi Natsii*. St. Petersburg: Otechestvennaia tipografiia.

Kovalevskii, M. M. 1886. *Sovremennyi obychai i drevnii zakon (Obychnoe pravo u osetin v istoriko-sravnitel'nom osveshchenii)*, 2 vols. Moscow: Tipografiia V. Gatsuk.

Kovalevskii, M. M. 1890. *Zakon i obychai na Kavkaze*, 2 vols. Moscow: Tipografiia A. I. Mamonova i Ko.

Kovalevskii, M. M. 1905. "Otnoshenie Rossii k okrainam." *Russkie vedomosti* October 9, 2.

Kuznecovs, V. 2013. "Latvian Psychiatry and Medical Legislation of the 1930s and the German Sterilization Law." Felder, B. F. and Weindling, P. J. (eds.), *Baltic Eugenics: Bio-Politics, Race and Nation in Interwar Estonia, Latvia and Lithuania, 1918–1940*. Amsterdam and New York: Rodopi, 147-168.

Lenin, V. I. [1894] 1977. "What the 'Friends of the People' Are and How They Fight the Social-Democrats." *Lenin Collected Works*, 4th printing. Vol. 1. Moscow: Foreign Languages Publishing House, 129-332.

Lenin, V. I. [1899] 1977. "Apropos of the Profession De Foi." *Lenin Collected Works*, 4th printing. Vol. 4. Moscow: Foreign Languages Publishing House, 286-296.

Lenin, V. I. [1901] 1977. "Review of Home Affairs." *Lenin Collected Works*, 4th printing. Vol. 5. Moscow: Foreign Languages Publishing House, 251-301.

Lenin, V. I. [1902a] 1977. "What Is to Be Done?" *Lenin Collected Works*, 4th printing. Vol. 5. Moscow: Foreign Languages Publishing House, 347-568.

Lenin, V. I. [1902b] 1977. "Revolutionary Adventurism." *Lenin Collected Works*, 4th printing. Vol. 6. Moscow: Foreign Languages Publishing House, 184-205.

Lenin, V. I. [1902c] 1977. "On the Tasks of the Social-Democratic Movement." *Lenin Collected Works*, 4th printing. Vol. 6. Moscow: Foreign Languages Publishing House, 269-270.

Lenin V. I. [1902d] 1977. "On the Manifesto of the League of the Armenian Social-Democrats." *Lenin Collected Works*, 4th printing. Vol. 6. Moscow: Foreign Languages Publishing House, 324-327.

Lenin, V. I. [1903] 1977. "Letter to Iskra." *Lenin Collected Works*, 4th printing. Vol. 7. Moscow: Foreign Languages Publishing House, 114-117.

Lenin, V. I. [1904] 1977. "One Step Forward, Two Steps Back (The Crisis in Our Party)." *Lenin Collected Works*, 4th printing. Vol. 7. Moscow: Foreign Languages Publishing House, 201-423.

Lenin, V. I. [1905a] 1977. "Fine Words Butter No Parsnips." *Lenin Collected Works*, 4th printing. Vol. 8. Moscow: Foreign Languages Publishing House, 56-62.

Lenin V. I. [1905b] 1977. "A Letter to Y. D. Stasova and to the Other Comrades in Prison in Moscow." *Lenin Collected Works*, 4th printing. Vol. 8. Moscow: Foreign Languages Publishing House, 66-70.

Lenin V. I. [1905c] 1977. "The Revolutionary-Democratic Dictatorship of the Proletariat and the Peasantry." *Lenin Collected Works*, 4th printing. Vol. 8. Moscow: Foreign Languages Publishing House, 293-303.

Lenin V. I. [1905d]) 1977. "Plan of a Lecture on the Commune." *Lenin Collected Works*, 4th printing. Vol. 8. Moscow: Foreign Languages Publishing House, 206-210.

Lenin V. I. [1905e] 1977. "Speech on the Question of the Relations between Workers and Intellectuals within the Social-Democratic Organisations." *Lenin Collected Works*, 4th printing. Vol. 8. Moscow: Foreign Languages Publishing House, 407-408.

Lombroso, Ch. 1906. *Evrei i nenavist' k nim*. Trans. G. Z., Introd. ("Evreiskii vopros i Narodnaia svoboda") by O. Ia. Pergament. Odessa: Tribuna.

Menzhulin, V. 2004. *Drugoi Sikorskii: Neudobnye stranitsy istorii psikhiatrii*. Kiev: Sfera.

Mintslov, R. 1881. "Osobennosti klassa prestupnikov." *Iuridicheskii vestnik* 10, 216-246.

Mogilner, M. 2013. *Homo Imperii: A History of Physical Anthropology in Russia*. Lincoln and London: University of Nebraska Press.

Mogilner, M. 2016a. "Human Sacrifice in the Name of a Nation: The Religion of Common Blood." Avrutin, E. et al. (eds.), *The Worlds of Ritual Murder: Culture, Politics, and Belief in Eastern Europe and Beyond*. Bloomington: Indiana University Press (forthcoming).

Mogilner, M. 2016b. "The Discovery of the Irrational: National Psychiatry and the Russian Imperial Dilemma of the 'Savage Within'." *East Central Europe* 43, 99-133.

Morrissey, S. 2010. "The Economy of Nerves: Health, Commercial Culture, and the Self in Late Imperial Russia." *Slavic Review* 69, no. 3, 546-675.

Nil'son, E. 1909. "Po povodu nabora prizyvnykh v P-m uezde Varshavskoi gubernii v 1908 g." *Meditsinskii sbornik Varshavskogo uiazdovskogo voennogo gospitalia* XXI, no. I-III, 87-99.

Orlova, G. 2003. "Rozhdenie vreditelia: otritsatel'naia politicheskaia sakralizatsiia v strane sovetov (1920-e)." *Wiener Slawistischer Almanach* 49, 309-346.

Petrovsky-Shtern, Y. 2008. *Jews in the Russian Army 1827–1917: Drafted into Modernity*. Cambridge: Cambridge University Press.

Semyonov, A. et al. 2013. "Russian Sociology in Imperial Context." Steinmetz, G. (ed.), *Sociology and Empire. The Imperial Entanglement of a Discipline.* Durham, NC: Duke University Press, 53-82.

Spivak, G. Ch. 1987. *In Other Worlds: Essays in Cultural Politics.* New York and *London*: Routledge.

Stoler, A. 2009. *Along the Archival Grain: Epistemic Anxieties and Colonial Common Sense.* Princeton, NJ: Princeton University Press.

Struve, P. 1909. "Intelligentsiia i natsional'noe litso." *Slovo,* March 10, 3.

Tarnovskaia, P. N. 1902. *Zhenshchiny-ubiitsy: Anthropologicheskoe issledovanie s 163 risunkami i 8 antropometricheskimi tablitsami.* St. Petersburg: Tovarishchestvo khudozhestvennoi pechati.

Tylor, E. 1871. *Primitive Culture: Researches into the Development of Mythology, Philosophy, Religion, Art and Custom.* Vol. 1. London: John Murray.

Vermel', S. S. 1917. *Dushevnye bolezni u evreev (iz Kazanskoi Okruzhnoi Lechebnitsy).* Kazan: Tipo-litografiia universiteta.

Weinberg, R. 2014. *Blood Libel in Late Imperial Russia: The Ritual Murder Trial of Mendel Beilis.* Bloomington and Indianapolis: Indiana University Press.

P. I. Kovalevskii

Criminal Anthropology and Great Russian Nationalism

Louise McReynolds

Pavel Ivanovich Kovalevskii would be surprised to find himself a *desaparecido* in postrevolutionary histories of prerevolutionary Russia. He appears in an occasional cameo role in studies that address criminality, specifically noted for his connections to Cesare Lombroso and the late-nineteenth-century fascination with degeneration, in particular at that point where criminal anthropology intersected with forensic psychiatry. Despite the subsequent repudiation of his theory that criminals are born atavistic creatures identifiable by their physiognomy, Lombroso remains a familiar historical figure. Kovalevskii, on the other hand, finds his name mentioned only sporadically and primarily in relation to the medicalization of reactionary politics at the *fin-de-siècle* (McReynolds 2013; Goering 2003; Brown 1987; Beer 2008; Miller 1998).

The son of a priest from rural Ukraine, or "Little Russia" as he understood his *rodina*,[1] Kovalevskii was in fact a highly respected and pioneering psychiatrist. He enjoyed an international reputation; a number of his books were translated into French and German, just as he and his wife translated contemporary western psychiatric works into Russian. Although it is not clear what original analyses he contributed to psychiatric research in general, his work on epilepsy was translated, as were some of his psychiatric analyses of historical figures. He always cited Western scholars in his work because he considered himself an equal in the profession. Kovalevskii was Russia's Philippe Pinel, removing the chains from the inmates of Kharkov's infamous asylum, the Saburov Dacha; he was its Jean-Martin Charcot, with his emphasis

1 | He identified himself as a *maloross* (Kovalevskii 1912, 184).

on the neurological origins of mental illness; and, he was its Lombroso, with his argument that jurisprudence must turn its focus from the crime to the criminal. Kovalevskii's curriculum vitae is impressive: editor and publisher from 1883 of the first Russian-language psychiatric journal, *The Archive of Psychiatry, Neurology, and Forensic Psychopathology* (*Arkhiv psikhiatrii, neirologii i sudebnoi psikhopatologii*);[2] author of another first, a Russian textbook on psychiatry, to which he later added a supplement for jurists (Kovalevskii 1880 and 1905); chair of the psychiatric department at Kharkov University; then rector at Warsaw University; later chair of psychiatry at Kazan University; and finally director of psychiatric branch of the Medical Surgical Academy in St. Petersburg. Notably, before his final stint in Petersburg, he worked in areas of the Russian empire that had substantial non-ethnic Russian populations. In sum, he influenced a generation or more of psychiatrists all around the empire, many of whom would practice in the nascent USSR.

Furthermore, his influence extended well beyond academics. Kovalevskii turned himself into a prominent public intellectual, one who popularized psychiatry when he psychoanalyzed in print a number of historical figures, including tsars Ivan the Terrible, Peter I, Paul, plus Napoleon and, incongruously, Nebuchadnezzar (Kovalevskii 1994).[3] By the 1890s he was giving public lectures and publishing books oriented toward lay readers, explaining his psychiatric theories in easily accessible language and images, outstanding for his graphic and alarmist vocabulary.[4] He also began writing popular guides to the health spas in Borjomi in 1892 and Kislovodsk in 1894. This figures into a curious gap

2 | However, *Archive of forensic medicine and public hygiene, published by the medical department of the Ministry of the Interior* (*Arkhiv sudebnoi meditsiny i obshchestvennoi gigieny, izdavaemoi meditsinskim departamentom MVD*), which began publication in 1865 and continued from 1871 as *Herald of public hygiene, forensic and practical medicine, published by the Chief Medical Inspectorate of the Ministry of the Interior* (*Vestnik obshchei gigeny, sudebnoi i prakticheskoi meditsiny, izdavaemoi pri upravlenii Glavnogo Vrachebnogo Inspektora Ministerstva Vnutrennykh Del*) and continued until 1917, was the first to offer articles about forensic psychopathology. Psychiatric luminaries Dmitrii A. Dril' and Vladimir M. Bekhterev sat on its editorial board.

3 | Some of these were translated into German.

4 | Most prominently: Kovalevskii 1894.

in his biography, when "a serious (but undisclosed) illness" sidelined him from professional activities, 1897-1903; it may be presumed he was taking in the waters for his health, about which he later wrote with authority (Petriuk 1996, 57-61). Especially after the 1905 revolution, he turned his writing to nationalism. In 1908, he joined the All-Russian National Union (*Vserossiiskii natsional'nyi soiuz*), a political party committed to maintaining the autocracy and the territorial integrity of the empire, but within an ill-defined structure of modernity that favored scientific progress, as long as it had no ripple effects on society or monarchist politics (Kotsiubinskii 2001). His popular biography of Tsar Alexander III, written in 1912 (Kovalevskii 2005), praised the autocrat's devotion to Russia without subjecting him to the psychoanalysis that he had the others. Kovalevskii's lonely death in a Belgian town in 1931 belies his status and influence.[5]

Lombroso can be summoned to recover Kovalevskii's eminence, although not by reducing the latter to a disciple of the former. As Nicole Rafter and Mary Gibson observed in their translation of *The Criminal Woman, the Prostitute, and the Normal Woman*, Lombroso remains "recognized as one of the most fertile, if uncritical, thinkers in nineteenth-century Europe, and a man whose work marked a turning point in conceiving of the body as a sign of human worth" (Rafter and Gibson [eds.] 2004, 4). Daniel Pick, in an article fundamental to any assessment of Lombroso, locates the Italian criminologist squarely within the context of post-*Risorgimento* Italy; by the same token, Kovalevskii has much to tell us about Russia, one generation into the Great Reforms, and then in the aftermath of 1905. As Pick pointed out, "the designation of the criminal is bound up in complex ways with the opposing but reciprocal process of defining a good citizen, or the good subject, in specific societies, in particular periods" (Pick 1986, 61). This smacks of Michel Foucault's philosophies of the social construction of the political body. Laura Engelstein (1993) and Daniel Beer (2008) have, among others, cited the French mandarin to illustrate some of the problems inherent in Russian liberalism, but here I move in the other direction, to Russian conservatism, as it can be understood through Kovalevskii's ideas about psychopathology.

5 | Sources usually give his dates as "1849-1923," but in fact he emigrated in 1924, and his correspondence with other émigrés suggests that "the reports of his death have been greatly exaggerated" (Petriuk 2009, 77-87).

Like Lombroso, Kovalevskii's analyses had political implications with regards to citizenship, or more precisely, subjecthood in the Russian empire. Foucault brings attention to the criminal's loss of civil liberties under liberal republicanism, in that this political system legislated that the appropriate punishment for those who violated the social contract was to be excluded from political participation in that society (Foucault 1995). Kovalevskii's politics are considerably less concerned about individual law-breakers; he concentrates on the pathology of the degenerate body in such a way as to shift attention away from the diseased individual, to the social and other external causes of those illnesses that were associated with the brain. In his conclusions, he consistently looks for ameliorative measures that would conserve the social collective. "Only the society (*obshchestvo*) or commune (*obshchina*) can save the individual," he wrote (Kovalevskii, 1903, 231).[6]

Kovalevskii began his medical career in the 1870s by studying the physiology of the nervous system, which for him laid the basis for psychiatry in that it literally connected body to mind. He wrote his dissertation on the sensory organs, and diagnoses of physical changes in them were always central to his research.[7] For him, the function of psychiatry was to identify and treat mental illness, and because he looked for somatic causes for insanity, he was naturally drawn to the fascination with degeneracy at the *fin de siècle* that had inspired Max Nordau to dedicate his best-selling book on the subject to Lombroso. In the opening editorial of *Arkhiv* Kovalevskii announced that "our journal is a refuge for articles on pathology, criminology, and forensic psychopathology." Specifically, the journal would focus on *nervnaia zhizn'*, by which he meant the nervous system, that aspect of human biology that affected human behavior. Moreover, insisting on his foundation as a naturalist, Kovalevskii connected humans to other animals, setting people apart because of the greater complexity in their physiological systems. Asserting that "there is no place for philosophical discussions" in his journal, he

6 | "Только общество или община может спасти единицу."

7 | For example, he opens *Forensic Psychopathology* (*Sudebnaia obshchaia psikhopatologiia*): "*Разстройства органов чувств.* Душевныя болезни выражаются разстройством в области органов чувств, мышления, поступков или произвольных движений, а нередко и в органах растительной жизни, – поэтому мы считаем необходимым коротко наметить эти разстройства, дабы быть понятыми при изложении отдельных душевных болезней" (Kovalevskii 1896, 1).

made the point that "every thinking person cannot but agree with the argument that each individual is the product of the sphere in which he grew: he is a product of his parents, the nature surrounding him, other people, and environmental conditions" (Arkhiv 1883, Vol. 1, 2-3).[8]

The inaugural issue also featured an article by Kovalevskii's mentor, A. U. Freze, historicizing the relationship between body and soul, establishing the modern physiological connection that dated back to Adam and Aristotle (Freze 1883). *Arkhiv* thereafter became the platform for other doctors to report the findings from their various studies of criminal and mentally ill populations. In these pages, Kovalevskii fixed the Russian link between "madness and badness" and the near impossibility of separating the two. As I have argued elsewhere, Russian criminologists did not try to coordinate religious faith with scientific knowledge in the spirit of Thomas Aquinas (McReynolds 2013, 56-59). This can be seen clearly in their use of *dusha*, which translates most literally as the "soul," but can also refer to metaphorical concepts associated with the soul, such as mind and spirit, or even the person him/herself. The adjectival form *dushevnaia* applied to *bolezn'* meant "mental illness" in the psychiatric sense, and this also imputed a social and medical significance to insanity. Comfortable that faith and knowledge derived from different sources, the heart and the mind, respectively, Kovalevskii remained a devout Orthodox whose religiosity could be recognized in his sympathy for those stricken with *dushevnye bolezni*, regardless of their criminal actions. The present penal code was "unchristian" in its use of punishment to exact retribution (Kovalevskii 1903, 272). He shared the same sentiments as the esteemed neurologist Professor Ivan Sechenov:

> Society cannot regard the vices of its members as anything other than the product of heredity, ignorance, crudeness of morals, inadequate upbringing, confusion, poverty, idleness, etc. Therefore society does not have the right to treat its

8 | "Общество не может видеть в проступках своих членов что-либо иное, нежели продукт наследственности, невежества, грубости нравов, ущербности воспитания, замешательства, бедности, лености и т.д. Каждый мыслящий человек не может не согласиться с тем, что три фактора влияют на образование физической и психической организации человека: наследственности, воспитания, условия, среди которых он развивался."

immoral members badly, or to punish them as a means of exacting vengeance for their actions (Kovalevskii 1881, 25).[9]

For all his insistence on the biological, physiological materiality of psychiatry as a science, the ways in which he applied forensic psychiatry to criminology made his diagnoses ultimately political. Kovalevskii determined that most criminal behavior could be attributed to deteriorating social conditions – conditions that he also maintained had a material basis – and could be improved through state intercession in jurisprudence by way of medicine rather than law enforcement. Kovalevskii wanted clinics for the mentally ill built in every province, at local and government expense (Kovalevskii 1905, 293). A recurring theme that echoed in his works, including the journal that he edited, was the lack of proper identification of and treatment for the mentally ill, who were too often put in jails rather than clinics for their actions, especially when they turned violent and homicidal.[10]

Kovalevskii began writing in the 1880s, after Lombroso had begun focusing less on atavism and more on the notion that criminals are "born," and identifiable by their degenerated physiognomy and behavior. Conceding that people could be born with inclinations toward criminality, Kovalevskii nonetheless considered the habitual criminal a minor character in the larger social drama. His brief section on "the criminal" in a book devoted to degeneration and the battle with criminality was written in the vocabulary of Lombroso, but without citing the Italian (Kovalevskii 1903, 231-254).[11] Bad skin, bad teeth, bad attitudes: any jailor

9 | "Общество не может смотреть на пороки своих членов иначе, как на продукт наследственного расположения, невежества, грубости нравов, дурного воспитания, недоумения, бедности, праздности, лени и пр. Поэтому оно не имеет право относиться с злобою к своим порочным членам и тем менее наказывать их в виде возмездия за дурные дела."

10 | He insisted that "everyone who commits a crime should be placed in a psychiatric facility and the research should be in the hands of psychiatrists." "Всякий, кто совершает преступление, должен быть помещен в психиатрическую лечебницу, и что расследование должно быть в руках психиатров" (Kovalevskii 1909, 25).

11 | "The criminal" is covered 23 of 370 pages, although admittedly some sections of the book had been published elsewhere, separately.

or anthropologist could spot a criminal (Kovalevskii 1881, 19). Kovalevskii noted that the non-criminal population also contained a number of nature's throwbacks,[12] and he sometimes wrote of indicators of atavism associated with Lombroso, such as wisdom teeth (which he connected to sadism) (Arkhiv 1898, Vol. 32/1, 10).

These individuals, however, were of secondary interest to Kovalevskii. His *Arkhiv* stands out for the laudatory attention it fostered on the Italian school of criminology, but what the Russians seemed most engrossed with was what Rafter and Gibson identified as the recognition of "body as a sign of human worth." The Italian phrase that Lombroso used, *uomo delinquente,* translates as "criminal man," and the Russian in Kovalevskii's work, *prirozhdennyi prestupnik,* as "born criminal," were also translated into their different national and cultural contexts. In any case, Kovalevskii could not be reduced simply to being a disciple of Lombroso because not only were the criminal codes not identical in Russia and Italy, nor were social ideas about what constituted criminal behavior. Kovalevskii could seemingly always detect a somatic explanation for lawless behavior, and in the larger theoretical disagreement over whether criminals were "born" or "culturally constructed," he drew the middle ground that combined the two in diathesis: degenerate traits created by social circumstances could be inherited, potentially condemning the victim to a life of crime (Kovalevskii 1903, 282-291). Like a number of other forensic psychiatrists, Kovalevskii collected a sizeable amount of data from prisons, because he considered many of the incarcerated to be mentally ill rather than criminal. He was most interested in the kinship (*rodstvo*) between the criminal and the insane, and his observation "such people die out, not leaving descendants" (Kovalevskii 1881, 12-14)[13] suggests that he feared the individuals less than the causes of their conditions.

12 | See his article on Prof. D. N. Zernov's statistics on non-criminals in Arkhiv 1896, Vol. 27/3, 124-125. Psychiatrists Dmitrii Dril' and Vladimir Chizh, both of whom enjoyed close ties to Kovalevskii, expressed the deepest sympathy for Lombroso's theories. But by the time of the Italian's death in 1909, Dril' has soured on the notion of the "born criminal" (*Russkoe slovo*, 9, 24 October 1909, nos. 231, 244). Also, Chizh noted in 1893 that he appreciated that Lombroso was giving less stress to atavism (Arkhiv 1893, Vol. 22/3, 105-118).

13 | "Такие особы умирают, не оставляя после себя потомство."

Because the line between badness and madness was so blurred in his vision, whether at court or in the clinic, he always looked for the potential for treatment. He believed that "the goals of criminal justice can only be satisfied by medical-psychiatric research" (Kovalevskii 1909, 23).[14] In his two-volume textbook for "medical personnel (*mediki*) and jurists," he used a number of court cases at which he had testified and observations from his clinical practice to assert the relationship between criminality and insanity, the central motif in his medico-political worldview (Kovalevskii 1881). Two fundamentals that the two groups – insane and criminal – shared in common were that in both instances some can be treated, and that the causes for both can be inherited. Society's objective with each is to isolate them for treatment to help them; the corollary of protecting the general population, then so important to American jurisprudence, for example, assumed a secondary status in Kovalevskii's estimation.[15] In his specific recommendations for treating the various layers of the criminal class, he included possibilities for re-entry for all except the insignificant few who showed no possibilities for reform, and even they belonged in colonies rather than prisons (Kovalevskii 1903, 363-370). Characterizing the Petersburg population as potentially "an army of psychopaths," he argued that possibly 90 percent of the insane were going untreated (Kovalevskii 1903, 39; see also Kovalevskii 1887). The "battle with criminality" for him was simply one in the larger war against a degeneracy that affected everyone, given that "half the people we know show some signs of degeneration" (Kovalevskii 1903, 39).[16] Theft could be interpreted as a symptom of mental illness (*ibid.*, 322). "Jails," he hammered repeatedly, "have outlived their time" (*ibid.*, 22).[17]

14 | "[...] цели уголовного правосудия могут быть достигнуты посредством медицинских психиатрических исследований."

15 | Frederick W. Griffin (1910, 17) wrote that "the sole object of punishment being the safety of society [...] society is never safe with the insane murderer at large."

16 | "Добрая половина наших знакомых демонстрирует те или иные признаки вырождения." The "battle with criminality" (*bor'ba s prestupnost'iu*; Kovalevskii 1909, 257-370), concentrates on the inadequacies of contemporary jurisprudence because of the rising criminal statistics. But answer lies in treating criminals as we do the mentally ill, not punishment.

17 | "Тюрьмы пережили свое время."

Contemporary society was both perpetrator and victim. Kovalevskii drew the link between modernity and mental health, with civilization the source of the degeneration that began with the body and then moved up through the veins and cells into the brain. The combination of heredity and deteriorating social conditions posed a long term threat that had to be addressed immediately (Kovalevskii 1886). He had been instrumental in organizing the first congress of psychiatrists in 1887, and in his opening speech he highlighted the social and political ramifications of ignoring mental illness. One part of his plan entailed a campaign for moral improvement, a theme he echoed in 1898 when he began his turn toward the general public with a guide he published about need for clean living in order to combat nervous disorders (Morrissey 2010, 659). Most people who broke the law did so as a reflexive action under stress, not because they were congenitally inclined to do so.

In many ways, Kovalevskii's ideas are commensurate with political attitudes about to engulf Russia in revolution because of the combined success of the Great Reforms to chart a path toward modernity, and the subsequent failure of modernity to satisfy most of the anticipations that it heightened. Balancing the weight of influence between heredity and environmental social conditions, he argued that upbringing (*vospitanie*) levied greater influence than birth on personal behavior (Kovalevskii 1894, 39). Kovalevskii focused his attention on the two illnesses that could be most closely tied to the degeneration of both the individual body and the social whole: alcoholism and syphilis. Horrifically, these two degenerative diseases were especially vicious because some of their nasty effects could be inherited, in the ways that forced children to continue paying for the sins of their fathers. The damaged genes could be "archived" and passed along, even skipping generations (Kovalevskii 1903, 76).

In *Nervous Diseases of Our Society* (*Nervnye bolezni nashego obshchestva*, 1894), Kovalevskii directed the attention of his concerned audience to his theme that mental illness was a social rather than personal concern. The three determining influences were: heredity, upbringing, and "conditions of life" (*zhiznennye usloviia*) (Kovalevskii 1894, 7). However, these could collectively be simplified as the consequences of an abnormal nervous system, usually infected by either syphilis or alcoholism, and then potentially passed along to offspring. Both well-grounded in history, these diseases originated in destructive social behaviors that had become even more pronounced with the stresses exacerbated by modern civilization (*ibid.*, 20). Repeating the graphic details of the destruction they wrought, Kovalevskii gave measured advice about child-rearing and healthy life styles: avoid alcohol, tobacco, and morphine; mothers should nurse their own babies, even though this was a perceptible hardship; the village was incomparably healthier than the city; and parents should avoid the "English system" of feeding rare meat and wine to their children (Kovalevskii 1903, 28). In remarkable contrast to Western social theorists of the era, he did not ascend a soapbox to preach about abstinence or temperance. In his popular self-help books Kovalevskii expounded for frank discussion of syphilis, particularly because so many young women were being infected by spouses and then passing it on through pregnancy (*ibid.*, 30). The disease must be considered "terrible, but not shameful" (*ibid.*, 50). Significantly unlike Lombroso, he considered sexual desire in women a normal phenomenon (*ibid.*, 63).[18]

Kovalevskii fleshed out his diagnoses describing the lives of one family of his patients. Beginning with the husband's graduate studies in Paris, where he contracted syphilis, Kovalevskii details the spiral downward through their five children, even to the grandchildren (Kovalevskii 1894, 57-119). The only child who was spared was the son who moved to the village and lived a clean life, breathing fresh air; unfortunately, this man's son inherited a damaged nervous system. His *Degeneration and Rebirth* (*Vyrozhdenie i vozrozhdenie*, 1903) was reminiscent methodologically of American Richard Dugdale's 1877 sociological study of *The Jukes: A Study in Crime, Pauperism, Disease and Heredity*. Where Dugdale's analysis essentially criminalized the lower classes, Kovalevskii's family history differs substantively in that he looks at the educated and wealthy rather than illiterate and impoverished (Dugdale 1910).[19] But the Russian psychiatrist did not segregate his patients according to class, sex, or ethnicity; he diagnosed a peasant woman with the same professionalism and consideration that he did a Georgian officer. Perhaps because they were dealing with such disparate control groups, Kovalevskii's study did not inspire eugenics, as Dugdale's did, but I would argue instead

18 | Lombroso thought it an indicator of "born" prostitutes.

19 | Numerous sociologists cited this as a justification for eugenics.

that cultural differences had more influence on the difference between American and Russian attitudes toward the poor (discussed below).[20]

The most damning heritable pathology that could be handed down as a result of both alcohol and syphilis was epilepsy, a somatic disease visited upon the innocent that played an important role in his larger ambition of educating Russians to prevent the slide into degeneracy. Kovalevskii found the vital pathological connection between body and mind in epilepsy, the equivalent of original sin visited upon children by incautious parents.[21] Always grounding illnesses in history to establish the precedent that intensified with civilization, Kovalevskii normalized this *bolezn'*; he dated it back to ancient Greece, and spread it across time and space, connecting it with cultural understandings of mental illness. This was a subject that he popularized, and many of his readers would have been aware that literary favorite Fedor Dostoevskii suffered the falling sickness. Kovalevskii described a number of familiar characters, men who if not epileptic themselves, were associated with seizures: David, Goliath's slayer, when fleeing King Saul's melancholic wrath; strongman Hercules was also given to seizures; and so was Martin Luther. Several of the historical figures whom he psychoanalyzed, including Mohammed and Joan of Arc, he characterized as epileptics, although the medical research cannot confirm that either was. In other words, this implied that all readers had had some sort of unknowing contact with an epileptic and therefore should not feel threatened by them.

The socio-medical importance of epilepsy lay in its resistance to precise diagnosis and treatment, and especially in the unpredictability of the type and length of seizures. Epileptics suffered differently, which made it a particularly engrossing illness for nineteenth-century medicine, especially neurobiologists and psychiatrists such as Kovalevskii who insisted upon the neurological basis to mental illness. He was a member of the international consortium of doctors, including supernovas Charcot and Richard v. Krafft-Ebing, studying epilepsy (Friedlander 2001). What matters for our purposes is that because he was a participant in the larger conversation, the points that he emphasized about epilepsy

20 | Kovalevskii did note a class basis to certain kind of mental illness, but ascribed these to "historical development" (Kovalevskii 1905, 207).

21 | He wrote on this often, finally pulling his ideas together in a textbook (Kovalevskii 1898a).

can be contrasted with those coming from other cultural contexts. All psychiatrists and neurologists included epilepsy within the framework of criminal anthropology because of the numbers of epileptics accused of committing crimes in the throes of a seizure. Additionally, epilepsy found itself integrated into degeneration theory, in addition to other scientific models for studying social and environmental impacts on behavior.

Kovalevskii's 350-page textbook on epilepsy included a section on its "forensic-psychiatric meaning." As he introduced this chapter, "The reality of our new legal institutions persuades us that the majority of law-breaking actions, especially criminal, are committed under the influence of an epileptic fit" (Kovalevskii 1898a, 324).[22] Then he divided the disease itself in two: "somatic" and "psychotic." In the first instance, both body and mind were seized, and in the second, the mind only. Somatic epilepsy could be associated with, for example, sexual desire, cocaine use, diabetes, or more prosaically, the brain's cortex (*ibid.*, 93-104, 109). Psychotic epilepsy was characterized by "mental derangement" (*dushevnoe rasstroistvo*), which could be the result of "pathological-anatomical changes that condition both epilepsy and psychosis." Furthermore, this epilepsy could appear "together with or independent of other psychoses" (*ibid.*, 134).[23] Primarily, Kovalevskii understood psychotic epilepsy as a pathological condition that could explain erratic behavior of seemingly any sort.

Furthermore, epilepsy was often hereditary and chronic, but could be particularly difficult to diagnose because seizures could be of short duration or with extended lengths of time – sometimes years – in between. Therefore, when a crime had been committed, the criminologists were dependent upon the observations of witnesses about the physical appearance and actions of the accused. Throughout his career Kovalevskii remained insistent upon the need for professional care for those accused of crimes committed while possibly in the throes of an epileptic fit, and the length of time needed to observe suspects under clinical conditions justified his argument for special facilities. What is most telling here is Kovalevskii's underlying assumption that the tsarist government should,

22 | "Деятельность наших новых судебных учреждений достаточно убеждает нас в том, что масса преступлений, особенно уголовных, совершается под влиянием приступов эпилепсии."

23 | "Эпилепсия может проявляться вместе или независимо от других душевных расстройств."

and could, foot what would have been the extraordinarily high medical costs for such a venture. This is best understood as an aspect of Russian conservatism, which held the autocracy responsible for social policy without the perceived need to take finances into consideration when designing it; ironically, that this attitude characterized the subsequent Soviet socialist government reminds of the continuation of a number of political expectations about the role of government vs. the individual that crossed the 1917 divide. Even when he granted that private clinics could be built for "the wealthy, spoiled by the comforts of life," he added the caveat that these required strict medical supervision because of the potential for abuse by the indolent rich (Kovalevskii 1905, 293).

Another major issue for nineteenth-century forensic psychiatry was pathological *affekt*, which posed a number of the same problems for diagnosis as an epileptic fit because it depended upon witnesses to the physiological changes that the accused had undergone. Kovalevskii methodically described the three stages of "pathological *affekt*," an emotional outburst that signaled complete loss of memory, which would relieve the accused of legal culpability (Kovalevskii 1896, 21-25, *et passim*).[24] The primary difference between the two seems to lie in the idea that epilepsy could be inherited, and *affekt* could have resulted from physiological damage to the brain, such as a blow to the head.[25] Each was characterized by the sufferer taking a reflexive action, but pathological *affekt* was the result of a burst of passion that overwhelmed the subject's ability to reason.[26] However, Kovalevskii was specifically careful to distinguish *affekt*, a diseased condition, from emotional passion: "passion can provide the soil from which *affekt* develops, but the converse is not

24 | A court case at which he testified about this, *The Trial of Lt. Schmidt* (*Delo podporuchika Shmidta*), reprinted in Vladimirov 1892, 60-93.

25 | In one particularly interesting case, of Georgian Prince Mikeladze who had struck a superior officer, Kovalevskii detailed the case to distinguish that the prince had suffered "pathological *affekt*" (emotional outburst that signaled complete loss of memory) rather than an epileptic fit. The physiological basis of his misbehavior lay in a head injury suffered years earlier (Kovalevskii 1881, 170-183).

26 | "Free will does not exist". "Свободы воли не бывает" (Kovalevskii 1896, 23).

possible" (*ibid.*, 92).[27] A person could be born (*prirozhdennyi*) with an inclination for *affekt* (*ibid.*, 94).

In both instances, the sufferer lost control of his or her free will, understood in physiological rather than religious terms. Both epilepsy and pathological *affekt* could explain a loss of the kind of moral reasoning that would permit a god-fearing person to commit murder. However, western jurisprudence differs from that for which the Russian psychiatrists argued, because it asks jurors to evaluate whether or not the accused could distinguish right from wrong when not in the throes of a seizure. To return to Pick's point about the reciprocal relationship between a society's criminals and its "good subjects," in the specificity of turn-of-the-century Russia, the two could not be neatly separated at all. The unfortunate epileptic sitting behind bars because the inadequately trained prison doctor could not diagnose him properly would still be a "good Russian." One tirade of which Kovalevskii never tired was the need for professional forensic psychiatrists, on the government payroll, at court in order to protect these thoroughly decent Russians.[28]

Indeed, Russians took a more humane attitude toward epileptics than, for example, Americans in this era, evident from contrasting court cases in which epilepsy was used as a defense. In the American example, if the defense argued successfully that the epileptic had committed murder during a seizure, the sentence could be reduced from the death penalty to life in prison (Friedlander 2001, chapter 9). Kovalevskii's testimonies reveal considerably more compassion, and Russian juries considerably more sympathy through their acquittals (McReynolds 2013, chapter 2).[29] In addition, as the eugenics crusade gained momentum in the United States, its adherents included epileptics among the social groups that should not be permitted to procreate; by 1914 thirteen states had legislated against the right epileptics to marry (Friedlander 2001, 263).[30] Although Kovalevskii

27 | "Страсть может обеспечить почву для развития аффекта, а вот обратное исключено."

28 | He wanted them attached officially and salaried rather than serving haphazardly as expert witnesses. He lays out his case in Kovalevskii 1881, 377-406.

29 | Kovalevskii publishes his reports to the courts throughout his journal as well as his monographs.

30 | Teddy Roosevelt also supported eugenics for a time.

worried in print about the dangers to society of the generations passing down increasingly damaging diseases, I have not found a word of support for eugenics. The closest I have found to his use of marriage as a method of social control is to support for early nuptials in order to evade syphilis.[31] Even so reactionary a psychiatrist as Vladimir Chizh, after analyzing a connection between epilepsy and *coitus interruptus*, would not deny epileptics the right to copulate, which in his consideration could only happen within the bonds of matrimony (quotes in: Kovalevskii 1898a, 215). And as Kovalevskii pragmatically pointed out, it would be impossible in any case to prevent people who wanted to marry from doing so (Kovalevskii 1903, 81).

The more he involved himself with social issues, the greater role he assumed as a public intellectual. This became pronounced in his turn toward nationalism, articulated first in his 1898 handbook on the Black Sea resort at Ialta. Was he influenced by his own illness and subsequent recovery at the health spas in Crimea? Continuing to write for a general audience, introduced a new theme: that of the progressive nature of Russian imperialism. Critiques of local hygiene and entertainments at the spas appear alongside historical synopses of the "tens of thousands of women and children" tortured and taken prisoner by Crimean Tatars until the Russian annexation in 1774. Under Russian suzerainty, such "brigandage has been replaced with pears and grapes" (Kovalevskii 1898b, 22).[32] These themes would be repeated in his later books on the pearl of the empire: the Caucasus, whose piedmont by 1914 had become Russia's primordial homeland (*prarodina*).[33]

Kovalevskii's newfound attention toward nationalism resonates in the vocabulary of his forensic psychopathology. Two points in particular matter for our purposes about the Kovalevskii connection between criminal anthropology and Great Russian nationalism. First, his position as a public intellectual gives his opinions a sort of "populist gravitas." Second, Kovalevskii expressed his nationalism in much of the same theoretical imagery about the influence of both the socio-political

31 | Despite a lifetime concern with the hereditariness of pathologies from sexually transmitted diseases, Kovalevskii did not favor social intervention to prevent marriage, not even when the betrothed were consanguineous, and therefore their children doomed from the outset (Kovalevskii 1903, 56-57).

32 | "Разбой был заменен грушами и виноградом."

33 | Kovalevskii 2005, 38. See also Kovalevskii 1914 and Kovalevskii 1916a.

and the physical environments that he used when discussing criminal anthropology. Heredity remained paramount, as tribes passed on their physical and psychological attributes to their descendants, many of which had developed as a result of environmental factors.

Although he noted that "nation" (*natsiia*) was not a Russian word, and he rarely deployed the term "race," Kovalevskii had a very specific understanding of nation that depended upon the unity of language, territory, religious belief, and historical customs that permitted him to describe a nation as he would an individual. People were born (*prirozhdennyi*) with specific national identities that he considered both physical and spiritual (Kovalevskii 2005, 45).[34] But now, in place of degenerative psychoses, Russians were inheriting an "instinctual, biological nationalism" (Kovalevskii 1912, 76). Although he recognized minor differences among "Great," "Little," and "White" Russians, he treated them as a collective. Substituting them for modern society's pathological victims, Kovalevskii adopted a much brighter tone for the Russian future.[35]

For Kovalevskii the empire established by Peter was indivisible, and this provided the cornerstone of his political identity. If the empire was *rossiiskii*, that is, multi-ethnic, its creator (*sozdatel'*), the House of Romanovs, was *russkii* (Kovalevskii, 1914, 6).[36] The German-born Catherine the Great could be a genuine (*chisto iskonno*) Romanov by virtue of her having devoted herself to the Russian empire, language, and culture. Kovalevskii was in fact a great admirer of one contemporaneous American president, Teddy Roosevelt, for the brand of nationalism that celebrated a healthy, invigorated populace. In 1912 he had pointed out that "the president of the free republic, Roosevelt, declared directly and openly:

---

34 | He specifically avoided using the word *narod* because of its cultural association with the peasantry in Russia.

35 | He noted that Great Russians had Mongol blood, Little Russians were influenced by the steppe tribes, and White Russians by Poland and Latvia; nonetheless, they constituted together the Russian nation (Kovalevskii 2005, 40-41).

36 | He was also quick to write: "The Russian people is the creator of the Imperial Russian Power." "Русский народ есть создатель Российской Державы."

the American citizen is only he who devotes his whole soul to America. Why should Russia think otherwise?" (Kovalevskii 1912, 8).[37]

This seeming open-mindedness, however, depended upon all such nations within the territory of empire to reject their own and adopt Russian culture and customs. In 1910 Kovalevskii published the first of at least three editions of *Nationalist Upbringing and Education in Russia* (*Natsional'noe vospitanie i obrazovanie v Rossii*), which was essentially a popularized history of Russia that centered on the evolution of national consciousness (Kovalevskii 1910). Kovalevskii used the same theme that he had in describing the ways to combat the generational threat of degeneration: *vospitanie*, "upbringing." The educational system that had broken the initiative of so many young students in the 1880s was now taken to task for its failure to pay adequate attention to Russia's language and history. The reactionary ministers of education Ivan Delianov and Dmitrii Tolstoi, once applauded for returning the focus to the classical languages that acquainted Russian students with the civic virtues found Western antiquity, found themselves chastised for this as a disservice because it came at the expense of Russian language and culture (Kovalevskii 1903, 103-108). The outbreak of the Great War spawned an even more aggressive strain of nationalism, once again drawing from his background in psychiatry. *The Psychology of the Russian Nation* (*Psikhologiia russkoi natsii*, 1915) (Kovalevskii 2005, 37-100), a relatively short and highly propagandistic treatise, attempted to explain not only why the Russians were better positioned psychologically to triumph, but also why the German barbarians were nationalistically determined to be defeated.[38]

Jews, though, posed the most perceptible threat to Russia because, despite their being a distinguishable nation themselves, the fact that they lacked their own homeland mandated that they lived in those of other people's; those living in the Russian empire had refused to

37 | "Президент свободной республики Рузвельт заявил прямо и открыто: американский гражданин только тот, кто всей душой предан Америке. Почему в России должны думать иначе?"

38 | Of the multitude of virtues that essentialized the Russian nation, my particular favorite is "the superfluity of common sense" (Kovalevskii 2005, 76).

assimilate into his idea of the Russian nation.[39] Even though "some of his best friends were Jews," like most other Russian nationalists Kovalevskii wrote a particularly insidious strain of anti-Semitism into his theories.[40] Psychiatrist Ivan Sikorskii has always managed to grab top billing in this narrative, having gained special notoriety for testifying to the Jewish practice of "blood libel" at the trial of Mendel Beilis in 1911 (Weinberg 2013, 152-154).[41] In part Kovalevskii's anti-Semitism drew from the familiar images of the boy Jesus driving the money changers from the temple, which in late imperial Russia was associated with the capitalism that threatened a misplaced nostalgia for a uniquely "Russian way of life" (Kovalevskii 1915, 7). Kovalevskii tested the patience of even the disgracefully anti-Semitic Orthodox Church for arguing in *The Bible and Morality* (*Bibliia i nravstvennost'*) that Christians should drop the Old Testament from their Bible, because Jehovah and Jesus were not the same God, and therefore the two testaments of divine revelation shared nothing in common. Once released from its arrest by censors in 1906, the booklet went through at least fourteen editions (Kovalevskii 1916b). He also wrote *Jesus, the Galilean* (*Iisus Galeleianin*) in 1907, a tract positing that Jesus was not a Jew, but rather a Galilean (Kovalevskii 1907).[42] Evidence of his disdain for the liberal intelligentsia, Kovalevskii liked to compare them to Jews because he saw both groups as self-loathing because they denied their national selves (Kovalevskii 1912, 7).[43]

---

39 | According to Kovalevskii, impudence (*derzost'*) was their mainstay, as they refused to adopt the religion and languages of the countries in which they lived; to have done so would have been to join the Russian nation (*ibid.*, 44).

40 | He recognized Jews as a distinct nationality, one without a homeland, which they lacked because they preferred to live as parasites on other peoples' lands; in Little Russia and White Russia, they turned the natives into "white Negros" (Kovalevskii 1912, 184-208). In the various editions and reprints, *Russkii* does not always appear, although the book is specifically about Russian nationalism.

41 | It helped, too, that Sikorskii's son Ivan invented the helicopter.

42 | French Orientalist Ernest Renan, later associated with scientific racism, also wrote about Jesus being able to shed his "Jewish" characteristics because he was a Galilean.

43 | Earlier, however, he had found it laudatory that Jews were not afraid to voice their patriotism, unlike some Russians. See also Kovalevskii 1903, 108.

* * * *

Although it is unlikely that Kovalevskii will be given pride of place in the new textbook of Russian History proposed by President Vladimir Putin in 2013 and being written by a collective at the Institute of History at the Russian Academy of Sciences, he is nonetheless currently enjoying a comeback.[44] His psychobiographies have been republished in several editions since 1991, and his *Nationalism and National Upbringing in Russia* reappeared in 1996. In 2005 Evgenii Troitskii edited a reprint edition as a trilogy of *Psychology of the Russian Nation; Upbringing of Youth;* and *Alexander III: Nationalist Tsar* (Kovalevskii 2005). Troitskii begins with an essay on the importance of acquainting contemporary readers with Kovalevskii's thought on nationalism, especially in the wake of the disastrous collapse of the Soviet Union and horrors of Chechen violent nationalism; this marks a return to the Caucasus that were so crucial to Kovalevskii's sense of empire. Moreover, Troitskii quotes American conservative Samuel Huntington's *Who Are We? The Challenges to America's National Identity* as a means to invoke the notion that other societies facing the threat of radical Islam feel a comparable threat to their sense of national self (Kovalevskii 2005, 101).[45]

Although it is Kovalevskii's popular works rather than his work on criminal anthropology that are being recirculated, he himself derived his nationalism from his ideas about madness and badness. His emphasis on upbringing and environmental factors in creating a personality within the context of a national identity resonates just as easily today. The rehabilitation of Kovalevskii the nationalist provides insight into contemporary Russian conservatism, particularly that aspect with renewed roots in the institution of the Orthodox Church. Although the contemporary Russian legal system still has more in common with its Soviet predecessor than the tsarist system of jury trials in which Kovalevskii worked (Solomon 2015, 59-78), his notion that when the criminal is perceived as the victim,

44 | As are other influential prerevolutionary academic conservatives, such as D. Ia. Samokvasov, archeologist, archivist, and public intellectual (Shchavelev 1998). Shchavelov also edited and annotated Samokvasov's correspondence, published by the same firm in 2007.

45 | Notably, both Russia and the United States are predominantly Christian and Caucasian.

"society does not have the right to [...] punish them as a means of exacting vengeance for their actions" has implications for rule of law in post-Soviet Russia. Because every society will decide for itself, even when its political leaders exercise a decisive influence, when the actions and behavior of an individual must be considered "criminal" and how he or she should be punished.

References

Arkhiv 1883-1894. *Arkhiv psikhiatrii, neirologii i sudebnoi psikhopatologii.* Ed. by P. I. Kovalevskii. Khar'kov: Tip. M. Zil'berberga.

Beer, D. 2008. *Renovating Russia. The Human Sciences and the Fate of Liberal Modernity, 1880-1930.* Ithaca: Cornell University Press.

Brown, J. 1987. "Revolution and Psychosis: The Mixing of Science and Politics in Russian Psychiatric Medicine, 1905-13." *Russian Review* 46, 283-302.

Dugdale, R. 1910. *The Jukes: A Study in Crime, Pauperism, Disease, and Heredity.* New York: G. P. Putnam's Sons.

Engelstein, L. 1993. "Combined Underdevelopment: Discipline and the Law in Imperial and Soviet Russia." *The American Historical Review* 98, no. 2, 338-353.

Foucault, M. 1995. *Discipline and Punish: the Birth of the Prison.* Translated from the French by Alan Sheridan. New York: Vintage Books.

Freze, A. U. 1883. "Istoricheskii ocherk o dushe." *Arkhiv psikhiatrii, neirologii i sudebnoi psikhopatologii* 1, no. 1, 1-19.

Friedlander, W. 2001. *The History of Modern Epilepsy: the Beginning, 1865-1914.* Westport, Conn.: Greenwood Press.

Goering, L. 2003. "'Russian Nervousness': Neurasthenia and National Identity in Nineteenth-Century Russia." *Medical History* 47, no. 1, 23-46.

Griffin, F. E. 1910. "Insanity as a Defense to Crime." *Journal of the American Institute of Law and Criminology* 1, no. 2, 13-28.

Kotsiubinskii, D. A. 2001. *Russkii natsionalizm v nachale XX stoletiia: rozhdenie i gibel' ideologii Vserossiiskogo natsional'nogo soiuza.* Moscow: Rosspen.

Kovalevskii, P. I. 1880. *Rukovodstvo k pravil'nomu ukhodu za dushevnymi bol'nymi.* 2nd ed. Khar'kov: Tip. M. Zil'berberga.

Kovalevskii, P. I. 1881. *Sudebno-psikhiatricheskie analizy*. 2nd ed. Khar'kov: Tip. M. Zil'berberga.

Kovalevskii, P. I. 1886. *Obshchaia psikhopatologiia*. Khar'kov: Tip. M. Zil'berberga.

Kovalevskii, P. I. 1887. "Vstupitel'naia rech' P. I. Kovalevskogo." *Trudy pervogo s"ezda otechestvennykh psikhiatrov*. St. Petersburg: Stasiulevich.

Kovalevskii, P. I. 1894. *Nervnye bolezni nashego obshchestva*. Khar'kov: Tip. M. Zil'berberga.

Kovalevskii, P. I. 1896. *Sudebnaia obshchaia psikhopatologiia*. Warsaw: Tip. VUK.

Kovalevskii, P. I. 1898a. *Epilepsiia, eia lechenie i sudebno-psikhiatricheskoe znachenie*. St. Petersburg: Tip. M. Akinfieva i I. Leont'eva.

Kovalevskii, P. I. 1898b. *Ialta*. St. Petersburg: Arkhiv.

Kovalevskii, P. I. 1903. *Vyrozhdenie i vozrozhdenie. Prestupnik i bor'ba s prestupnost'iu*. 2nd ed. St. Petersburg: Tip. M. Akinfieva i I. Leont'eva.

Kovalevskii, P. I. 1905. *Dushevnye bolezni: Kurs psikhiatrii dlia vrachei i iuristov*. 5th ed. St. Petersburg: Tip. M. Akinfieva i I. Leont'eva.

Kovalevskii, P. I. 1907. *Iisus Galeleianin*. St. Petersburg: N.p.

Kovalevskii, P. I. 1909. *Bor'ba s prestupnost'iu putem vospitaniia*. St. Petersburg: Vol'f.

Kovalevskii, P. I. 1910. *Natsional'noe vospitanie i obrazovanie v Rossii*. St. Petersburg: Akinfiev.

Kovalevskii, P. I. 1912. *Russkii natsionalizm i natsional'noe vospitanie v Rossii*. 3rd ed., supplemented, 2 vols. St. Petersburg: Tip. M. Akinfieva i I. Leont'eva.

Kovalevskii, P. I. 1914. *Kavkaz*. St. Petersburg: Tip. M. Akinfieva i I. Leont'eva.

Kovalevskii, P. I. 1915. *Psikhologiia russkoi natsii*. Petrograd: Otechestvennaia tipografiia.

Kovalevskii, P. I. 1916a. *Zavoevanie Kavkaza Rossiei: istoricheskie ocherki: s kartami i risunkami*. St. Petersburg: Tip. M. Akinfieva i I. Leont'eva.

Kovalevskii, P. I. 1916b. *Bibliia i nravstvennost'*. St. Petersburg: Tip. M. Akinfieva i I.Leont'eva.

Kovalevskii, P. I. 1994. *Odarennye bezumiem. Psikhiatricheskie eskizy iz istorii*. Kiev: Vyd. Ukraina.

Kovalevskii, P. I. 2005. *Psikhologiia russkoi natsii. Vospitanie molodezhi. Aleksandr III – tsar'-natsionalist*. Moscow: Granitsa.

McReynolds, L. 2013. *Murder Most Russian: True Crime and Punishment in Late Imperial Russia.* Ithaca: Cornell University Press.

Miller, M. 1998. *Freud and the Bolsheviks.* New Haven: Yale University Press.

Morrissey, S. 2010. "The Economy of Nerves: Health, Commercial Culture, and the Self in Late Imperial Russia." *Slavic Review* 69, 645-675.

Petriuk, P. T. 1996. "Pavel Ivanovich Kovalevskii." Kut'ko, I. I. and Petriuk, P. T. (eds.), *Istoriia Saburovi dachi.* Kharkov, 57-61.

Petriuk, P. T. 2009. "Professor Pavel Ivanovich Kovalevskii – vydaiushchiisia otechestvennyi uchenii, psikhiatr, psikholog, publitsist i byvshii saburianin." *Psikhichne zdorov'ja* 3, 77-87.

Pick, D. 1986. "The Faces of Anarchy: Lombroso and the Politics of Criminal Science in Post-Unification Italy." *History Workshop Journal* 20, 60-86.

Rafter, N. and Gibson, M. (eds.) 2004. *The Female Criminal.* Durham: Duke University Press.

Shchavelev, S. P. 1998. *Istorik russkoi zemli.* Kursk: Roszdrava.

Solomon, P. H. 2015. "Post-Soviet Criminal Justice: The Persistence of Distorted Neo-Inquisitorialism". *Theoretical Criminology* 19, no. 2, 159-178.

Vladimirov, L. E. 1892. *Zashchititel'nyia rechi i publichnyia lektsii.* Moscow: A. A. Levenson.

Weinberg, P. 2013. *Blood Libel in Late Imperial Russia: The Ritual Murder Trial of Mendel Beilis.* Bloomington: Indiana University Press.

Criminality, Deviance, and Anthropological Diversity

Narratives of Inborn Criminality and Atavism in Late Imperial Russia (1880-1900)

Riccardo Nicolosi

"Lombroso was here. He is a naive and limited old man." (Tolstoi 1953, 150).[1] With this ironic sentence Lev Tolstoi marked Cesare Lombroso's visit to Iasnaia Poliana in August 1897 in his diary. Lombroso, the founder of the Italian positivist school of criminology, also known as "criminal anthropology," had come to Moscow in order to attend the International Medical Congress (Mazzarello 1998; Sirotkina 2002, 75-79). He spontaneously decided to visit Tolstoi in order to verify his theory of a correlation between genius and degeneration on the "living object." From the very beginning, Lev Tolstoi had a central role in his study *The Man of Genius* (*Genio e follia* or rather *L'uomo di genio* as it was later retitled):[2] it is no coincidence that Tolstoi's portrait was on the cover of the sixth Italian edition of *L'uomo di genio* (1894) and on the cover of the collection of essays edited by Hans Kurella *Degeneration and Genius* (*Entartung und Genie*, 1894). Thus, Tolstoi embodied the paradoxical connection between these "two seemingly irreconcilable terms" (Lombroso 1894, 4).

During the visit, Lombroso and Tolstoi maintained their diametrically opposed positions concerning the nature of crime and the legitimacy of punishment. Lombroso explained the biological deviance of the criminal, his diminished responsibility due to heredity and the influence of the milieu, and the right of civilised society to defend itself against the born criminal. But Tolstoi remained deaf to all of these arguments, "he

1 | "Был Ломброзо, ограниченный наивный старичок."

2 | Six editions between 1864 and 1894.

knit his terrible eyebrows and hurled menacing flashes of his deep-set and penetrating eyes [at Lombroso]; finally he erupted, exclaiming 'This is all nonsense! All punishment is criminal!'"[3]

The encounter between Tolstoi and Lombroso and their talking at crossed purposes could be seen as a symbol for an apparently widespread "immunity" of late 19th-century Russian literature to biologistic theories of crime, something which distinguishes it from other European literatures of that era. In Russia, there seems to be a lack of literary texts which turned criminal anthropological concepts such as "atavism" or "inborn criminality" into structure-forming elements of fiction, as happened in Émile Zola's *The Beast Within* (*La bête humaine*, 1890) or in Bram Stoker's *Dracula* (1897).

At first glance, there is a gulf in late-imperial Russian culture between scientific and literary discourse as far as concepts of inborn criminality are concerned. Lombroso's theories were widely adopted within scientific discourse, especially in the area of forensic psychiatry and, just as in France or Germany, they were integrated into degeneration theory, a then dominant concept throughout Europe (Engelstein 1992, 128-164; Beer 2008, 97-130; Mogil'ner 2008, 358-396; McReynolds 2013, 47-78; Salomoni 2009).[4] Psychiatrists like Pavel I. Kovalevskii and Vladimir F. Chizh or criminologists like Dmitrii A. Dril' medicalised the criminal,

3 | "Aber Tolstoj [...] runzelte nur seine schrecklichen Brauen und schoss aus seinen tief in den Höhlen liegenden Augen drohende Blitze, bis er schließlich erwiderte: 'Nichts als Träume! Jede Strafe ist ein Verbrechen!'" (Lombroso 1902, 396). Lombroso may not have been able to convince Tolstoi of the truth of his criminal anthropological ideas, but he was at least able to confirm his earlier diagnosis of Tolstoi's degenerate genius. Even though the Russian novelist "astonishingly" showed no signs of mental degeneration, his "excessive impulsiveness" and the nervous disorder of his son Lev L'vovich were clear symptoms of a rampant familial degeneration that could be traced all the way back to "psychopathological" ancestors (Mazzarello 1998, 75; Mariani 1901).

4 | In an article from 1884 in the journal *Archive of Psychiatry, Criminal Anthropology, and Penal Sciences (Archivio di psichiatria, antropologia criminale e scienze penali)*, of which Lombroso was editor, Raffaele Garofalo describes the emergence of a positivist school of criminology in Russia, as inspired by Italian criminal anthropology. In it, he makes particular reference to the works of Rudol'f R. Mintslov and Dmitrii A. Dril' (Garofalo 1884).

interpreting his social deviance as the result of a degenerative aberration (see above).[5] This interweaving of medical and social diagnostics provides scope for the institutional legitimation of psychiatry: it positions itself as the leading discipline in the fight against social pathologies in turn-of-the-century Russia (Brown 1981; Becker 2003, 221-266).

Russian literature at that time, however, conceptualises the perpetrator more as a morally "fallen person" than a biologically "hampered" one.[6] *Neschastnyi* ("unfortunate," "unlucky") is a common term here: a good example of this trend is Fedor Dostoevskii, who underlined in his essay *The Environment* (*Sreda*, 1873) that the Russian people call a delinquent *neschastnyi* because they recognise in him their own flawed human nature and feel compassion for him (Dostoevskii 1980, 16). Dostoevskii uses this Christian concept in many of his novels, for example in *Crime and Punishment* (*Prestuplenie i nakazanie*, 1866), where "Raskolnikov personifies the quintessential *neschastnyi*" (McReynolds 2013, 117).

We also find no unambiguous conceptualisation of the anthropological otherness, or indeed monstrousness of criminals in factual literature about Siberian penal camps. In Nikolai M. Iadrintsev's *The Russian Community in Prison and Exile* (*Russkaia obshchina v tiur'me i ssylke*, 1872), the penal camp turns into an utopian sphere, where inmates form a community oriented towards the common good, an *obshchina* in the sense of the Russian Populists (*narodniki*): a kind of social avant-garde, which becomes a model for a Russian society, untouched by Western civilisation. Even in Chekhov's *The Island of Sakhalin* (*Ostrov Sakhalin*, 1890), where he describes the society of prisoners not as a "community", but as a "gang" (*shaika*; Chekhov 1978, 92), and stylises the penal camp as a chaotic "non-place of Russian culture" (Frank 2001, 44), felons are considered "quite normal people with docile, somewhat stupid faces" (*obyknovennye liudi s dobrodushnymi i glupovatymi fizionomiiami*), whose stories are characterised by "drabness and sparseness of content" (*beztsvetnost['] i bednost['] soderzhaniia*; Chekhov 1978, 131). According to Chekhov, the criminal is a thoroughly "common" criminal due to his "normal" banality.

5 | See, inter alia: Mechnikov 1878-1880; Kovalevskii 1881; 1896; 1903; Chizh 1894; 1895; Dril' 1884; 1895; Mintslov 1881. On Kovalevskii see Louise McReynolds' article in this book.

6 | Concerning the epistemic differentiation between a "fallen" and a "hampered" person in the criminological discourse of the 19th century see Becker 2002.

However, this gulf between criminal anthropology and literature in Russia can only be noted if you consider literature and science two separate areas that differ essentially in terms of logic, referentiality and modes of representation. As far as the 19th century is concerned, though, this differentiation is anything but true: especially in the life sciences, narrative and rhetoric methods were a decisive factor. Charles Darwin's theory of evolution serves as a prime example, where narration – Gillian Beer (1983) calls it "Darwin's plots" – and rhetoric – especially analogy and metaphors (Depew 2009; Campbell 1997) – constitute indispensable elements of argumentation. In the field of 19th-century criminal anthropology and degeneration discourse, overlapping and reciprocal phenomena between scientific and literary discourse are even more striking (Nicolosi 2017). Thus, the search for *narratives* of atavism and inborn criminality has to start within scientific discourse. This is because narrativity is the "epistemic bridge" that allows us to interrelate scientific and literary discourse productively – beyond the (illusionary) opposition between fact and fiction. Firstly, I shall explain which narrative potential can be found in Lombroso's theory of atavism and inborn criminality – above all by means of its integration into the theory of degeneration. The analysis of a forensic psychiatry case study by leading Russian psychiatrist Pavel Kovalevskii will then show how this potential is implemented in narration. In a last step, I shall demonstrate how this way of looking at "narrated science" allows us to discover narratives of atavism and inborn criminality in late 19th-century Russian literature. According to my definition, Russian literature of this period works with *non*-criminal anthropological, *anti*-criminal anthropological and *crypto*-criminal anthropological narratives.

The Narrative Potential of Criminal Anthropology

Criminal anthropology is closely linked to the name of Cesare Lombroso, the founder of the "positivist school" of Italian criminology, which, during the final third of the 19th century, advocated new approaches to the study of criminality. These approaches were adopted throughout Europe and subject to heated debate (Montaldo and Tappero 2009, 193-287; Pick 1989, 109-152; Nye 1984, 97-133; Wetzell 2000, 39-71). Setting itself up in opposition to the classical school of criminology, the positivist school did not wish to focus on the crime as a juridical "abstraction," but rather on the criminal and his quantifiable psychophysical predisposition (Lombroso

1910; Ferri 1926). In his magnum opus *Criminal Man* (*L'uomo delinquente*), Lombroso puts forward the idea of the anthropological otherness of certain types of criminals, which he understood in terms of atavistic regression. Lombroso's concept of the "born criminal" (*criminale nato*), the centre-piece of his theory of atavism, signifies a radical biologisation of criminality: it is no longer a purely social phenomenon of deviance, but a medical problem (Gibson 2002).

The success of criminal anthropological theories across Europe towards the end of the 19th century was, however, not so much rooted in their scientific nature, which in fact had been disputed from the outset, as above all in their mythopoeic dimension. As has already been pointed out, Lombroso moulds the born criminal into a mythological figure, who "[maintains] symbolic relations with all of the elements in the realm of confusion, of chaos, of evil, of the night" (Strasser 1984, 89). The born criminal's abnormal monstrousness stems directly from the gothic novel: Lombroso's retrospective description of his "discovery" of atavism in the introduction that he wrote for the British edition of his daughter Gina Lombroso Ferrero's book *Criminal Man According to the Classification of Cesare Lombroso* (1911) serves as an example of this. During the autopsy of a famous robber from Calabria, Vilella, Lombroso discovers an anatomic anomaly on the skull, the median occipital fossa, which, prior to this, has been found only "in inferior animals, especially rodents":

> This was not merely an idea, but a revelation. At the sight of that skull, I seemed to see all of a sudden, lighted up as a vast plain under a flaming sky, the problem of the nature of the criminal – an atavistic being who reproduces in his person the ferocious instincts of primitive humanity and the inferior animals. Thus were explained anatomically the enormous jaws, high cheek-bones, prominent superciliary arches, solitary lines in the palms, extreme size of the orbits, handle-shaped or sessile ears found in criminals, savages, and apes, insensibility to pain, extremely acute sight, tattooing, excessive idleness, love of orgies, and the irresistible craving for evil for its own sake, the desire not only to extinguish life in the victim, but to mutilate the corpse, tear its flesh, and drink its blood (Lombroso 1911, XIV-XV).[7]

---

7 | For an analysis of this mythopoeic nativity scene of a new academic discipline, see Villa 1985, 148-150; Frigessi 2000, 345-348.

If the born criminal is no different from a vampire, it is not surprising that Count Dracula in Bram Stoker's novel is characterised as a born criminal (Andriopoulos 1996, 48; Schönert 1991).

Even better possibilities of "narrating" the born criminal emerge from the already-mentioned integration of the theory of atavism into degeneration theory, which can also be observed in Lombroso's work. Originally, Lombroso conceived atavism based on a purely *analogical* model: The existence of a special anthropological variety, the *homo delinquens*, is "proven" by an enormous number of morphological, psychological and sociocultural signs that reveal significant analogies between criminals, "primitive peoples," primordial human beings and certain species of monkeys. The delinquent therefore turns out to be a throwback from an earlier phase of human development, or the remnant of a primitivism that was believed to have been overcome (Frigessi 2000, 346-47).

Even for that period, this analogical method was anything but scientific. From the third edition of his book onwards, Lombroso adds a pathological element in order to consider atavism in *causal* relations (Villa 1985, 163-205): He speaks about hampered development as a degenerative sign, primarily caused by heredity. According to Lombroso, degeneration becomes regression, revealing the original, primitive nature of humankind: being "hampered cultural men," criminals cannot overcome an early phylogenetic phase in their development, where crime is a natural phenomenon (Velo Dalbrenta 2004, 67).

The integration of atavism and degeneration gave rise to the possibility of narrating criminality, something which Russian criminal anthropological discourse made use of from the very beginning (see above). Starting with Bénédict Augustin Morel, the "inventor" of degeneration theory in French psychiatry, narrativity took a central position in degeneration, which itself became unthinkable beyond this narrative model. Morel defines mental and nervous diseases within a causal-temporal scheme, which interprets cause and development of these diseases based on the theory of heredity (Morel 1857).[8] The transmission

8 | Morel's theory is based on the pre-experimental concept of heredity of the 19th century (see Prosper Lucas' *Traité philosophique et physiologique de l'hérédité naturelle*, 1847-50), which sees metaphysical speculation take centre stage ahead of empirical provability.

of acquired pathological changes to subsequent generations does not mean that a specific disease is directly inherited, but rather that a general weakening of the nervous system is passed on, a so-called "nervous diathesis." By way of permanent transformation and accumulation, this diathesis develops progressively and metamorphotically, taking on all kinds of psycho-physical and moral disorders in ascending order according to their severity. Eventually, the family concerned becomes extinct over the course of just a few generations. This rapid degeneration is facilitated by a devastating interaction of endogenous and exogenous factors: harmful environmental influences inscribe themselves into the genetic make-up of a particular family and weaken the nervous system to such an extent that it can no longer defend itself against further exogenous "attacks" – or indeed against metamorphotic changes within the pathologies (Huertas 1992; Dowbiggin 1985).

Degeneration theory gains its scientific evidence exclusively from its narrative structure: only genealogical narration can produce a context of meaning between phenomena for which there would not otherwise be any evidence (Föcking 2002, 301). Morel's genealogical line of degeneration is nothing but a finite story with a beginning – the "crack" (*fêlure*) in the family's genotype –, a progressive, irreversible set course and an inevitable ending. This "crack" is a kind of "proto-event" within the narrative, the crossing of the border between the normal and the pathological. It constitutes the closed cosmos of degeneration, the prohibition boundary of which can no longer be crossed.

Following the theory of degeneration that developed after Morel, as found in the works of Valentin Magnan, Richard v. Krafft-Ebing, Paul J. Möbius, and others,[9] all phenomena of deviance are included in the narrative – that is, not only mental illnesses but also abnormal social behavior such as criminality or prostitution: there is no sign of deviance that cannot become a symptom of degeneration (Nye 1984; Chamberlin and Gilman [eds.] 1985; Roelcke 1999). The narrative therein acts as a dynamic construct that enables a maximum semiotic openness as well as a hypertrophic narrative coherence. This guarantees the narrative's high level of flexibility in describing disparate conditions of deviance and compensates for a lack of empirical provability: ultimately, the theory has

9 | See, inter alia Legrain and Magnan 1895; Krafft-Ebing 1898; Möbius 1900.

never got beyond the status of a speculative hypothesis (Weingart et al. 1988, 77-80).

Degeneration as a narrative is a basic schematic pattern, a *master narrative*,[10] which can be told in endless variations. In this context, case studies become indispensable elements of the explanation of the theory because they tell the *master narrative* again and again and thereby "confirm" it (Düwell and Pethes [eds.] 2014). Shaping degeneration into a finite story calls for a psychiatrist narrator, who selects particular elements from the amorphous continuum of happenings, from the vitalistic notion of boundless "life" (Foucault 2002, 287-304), – the "crack" in the family's genetic make-up, specific events and pathological conditions in the life of the patient and his ancestors – and puts them together in a story. That is, he sets a "line of meaning" to run through the happenings and, in doing so, puts the selected elements into a particular perspective. The protagonists of the individual case histories are born into the already-existing narrative world of degeneration, from which there is no escape. Their metamorphoses as a result of the various pathologies that afflict them do not represent the renewed crossing of a border, but rather the confirmation of a – medically and semiotically unchangeable – state (*état*) (Foucault 2003, 291-321). Valentin Magnan's psychiatric case studies exemplify how phenomena of criminality can become a feature of degeneration narratives when criminal behaviour is understood as one of the possible manifestations of degenerate state (Magnan 1892, 115-123).

At the same time, however, the integration of criminality into the degeneration narrative often results in authors distancing themselves from Lombroso's theory of atavism, as many do not regard degeneration and atavism as compatible phenomena. Valentin Magnan, in particular, points out that degeneration may represent a retrograde movement to a more imperfect evolutionary state, but not in the sense of an atavistic regression: atavism signifies to the "return to a state that is regarded as normal" (Legrain and Magnan 1895, 76), whereas degeneration constitutes a *new* pathological form in Magnan's eyes.

Although these attempts to distance oneself were made not least for strategic reasons and conceptual overlaps between the two theories certainly did exist (Galassi 2004, 139-190), the European reception of Lombroso's criminal anthropology is characterised by the fact that it

10 | On "master narratives" see Abbott 2002, 47.

highlights precisely this difference between atavism and degeneration in order to deny the existence of the born criminal as an anthropological species and to view the biologically determined criminal as one of many manifestations of degeneration. Degeneration theory makes it possible to be equally mindful of endogenous and social factors in the aetiology of crime, whereas Lombroso had not conceptualised the pathological side of the born criminal as being primarily dependent upon the social milieu.[11]

In the case of the Russian reception of Lombroso's criminal anthropology, scholars have detected a similar privileging of degeneration as an explanatory model for criminality, the specifics of which are located in the emphasis placed on social factors as opposed to biologistic moments (Beer 2008, 103-110; Salomoni 2009). For our context, it is nevertheless important to stress that some Russian authors assume a complementarity of atavism and degeneration, which leads to an increase in the tellability of criminality in the case studies. This position was particularly championed by the Khar'kov school of Russian psychiatry centred around Pavel Kovalevskii, which from 1883 onwards published the first Russian journal of psychiatry *The Archive of Psychiatry, Neurology, and Forensic Psychopathology* (*Arkhiv psikhiatrii, neirologii i sudebnoi psikhopatologii*) and adopted both the theory of degeneration and criminal anthropology: Kovalevskii, for example, maintains a biological relationship between "madmen and born criminals" (*pomeshannye i prestupniki ot rozhdeniia*) because both allegedly were forms of a "degeneration of humankind" (*vyrozhdenie chelovecheskogo roda*; Kovalevskii 1881, 12, 14).[12] In Kovalevskii's forensic psychiatry case studies, this mix of atavism and degeneration manifests itself in the development of narrative models of criminality, in which the epistemic power of the degeneration narrative is enhanced by the mythopoeic shaping of the born criminal into the embodiment of evil.

11 | The theory of degeneration was championed in France - contrasting polemically with Lombroso's theory of atavism - by, amongst others, Charles Féré (*Dégénérescence et criminalité*, 1888) and - together with Valentin Magnan - Paul Legrain (*La médicine légale du dégénéré*, 1894). In French criminology, it was Gabriel Tarde (*La criminalité comparée*, 1886) who became the most influential critic of Lombroso.

12 | See also from *Arkhiv*: Beliakov 1882; Troitskii 1885. On atavism as a subcategory of degeneration, see also Sikorskii 1904 and Orshanskii 1910.

Pavel Kovalevskii's forensic psychiatry case studies

Among Russian psychiatrists, Pavel Kovalevskii is the one who makes best use of the narrative potential of degeneration theory: he is a true master of the degeneration story.[13] His *Forensic Psychiatry Case Studies* (*Sudebno-psikhiatricheskie analizy*, 1881) show how the born criminal as a degenerate becomes the protagonist of stories that display his fascinating and at the same time horrifying anthropological otherness, in order that this then be tamed by the analytical view of the psychiatrist narrator. Astonishment functions as the basic narrative principle of the case studies: the monstrous cruelty of the perpetrators is astonishing – it is most likely no coincidence that one of them is named "S. Vovk" (Kovalevskii 1881, 30), meaning "wolf" in Ukrainian – as is the unexpected suddenness of the crimes; however, the semiotic performance of the psychiatrist is equally astonishing, as he first presents his readers with apparently unreadable forensic signs only to interpret them – just a scientific Sherlock Holmes – as "clear" signs of degeneration.

The story of P. M. Pogorelov, who cruelly murdered his wife in 1879 is a typical example (*ibid.*, 79-128). Kovalevskii was an expert in the murder trial of 1880 and thus became himself a second protagonist in the story he told. At the beginning, Kovalevskii presents the case in the form of a "neutral" description of the facts: he briefly depicts the unobtrusive life of the land surveyor Pogorelov, his love marriage to a general's daughter, and their altogether peaceful life despite the difference in social status. Then he describes the first signs of Pogorelov's abnormal behaviour during the days prior to the murder, which concerns those around him due to his logically unmotivated speech and actions. The objectivity of the report is suddenly shattered by the portrayal of the "horrible picture" (*uzhasnaia kartina*) of the murder scene, as seen by eye witnesses:

> Pogorelov is sitting by the door on the bedroom floor astride the chest of his wife, who is dressed in only a shirt, the right side of her face and an eye horribly disfigured, a pool blood around her head, and pulling accusingly at her tongue: "Here's your 'muzhik', now that's the last you'll ever say." [...] It was a struggle

13 | See my analysis of Kovalevskii's degeneration case study in *Nervous Diseases of Our Society* (*Nervnye bolezni nashego obshchestva*; Kovalevskii 1894, 57-119): Nicolosi 2007, 148-152.

to get the rope around Pogorelov and tie him up. He was swearing, shouting that he would kill them all, then he fell silent and lay motionless with his eyes closed (Kovalevskii 1881, 84-85).[14]

The psychiatrist's analytical work begins after this first carefully constructed climax. Kovalevskii initially gives a seemingly conclusive explanation of the murder as a contrived act of a non-pathological individual merely feigning his insanity in order to receive a milder sentence. Prefaced by a rhetorical question ("is this indeed the case?" [*no deistvitel'no li eto tak?*]; *ibid.*, 97), then follows the "correct" interpretation of the murder as the action of a degenerated person with a defective constitution, who killed during an epileptic seizure – an astonishing explanation for the layman. Kovalevskii inscribes Pogorelov into the narrative scheme of degeneration, underlining the pathological heredity within his family and interpreting epilepsy as one of numerous syndromes in which the degeneration could have manifested itself. Pogorelov's congenital defect is determined by way of a horrific, but for its time typical pseudo-deduction:

P.'s parents showed signs of nervous disorders: his father had a series of strokes which led to his death; his mother suffered from headaches. It follows that Mr. Pogorelov did not inherit a healthy brain, but that of an invalid, and which was, depending on the environment, susceptible to all manner of deviations from the healthy state (*ibid.*, 93).[15]

This narrative setting puts Pogorelov in the closed world of degeneration, from which he can no longer escape. Pogorelov's pathological otherness

14 | "Погорелов, у дверей на полу спальни, сидит на груди своей жены, распростертой в одной рубахе, с страшно изуродованной правой стороной лица и глазом, лужей крови около головы, и тянет жену за язык, приговаривая: 'вот тебе и мужик, теперь не будешь больше говорить.' [...] Погорелова едва стащили веревкой и связали. Он бранился, кричал, чтобы всех резали, потом замолчал и лежал неподвижно с закрытыми глазами."

15 | "Родители П. обнаруживали нервное расстройство: отец страдал ударами, от которых и умер, – мать головными болями. Следовательно, г. Погорелов унаследовал не здоровый мозг, а инвалидный, расположенный ко всевозможного рода уклонениям от известного здорового состояния, в зависимости от жизненных условий."

becomes an *anthropological* otherness in an *atavistic* sense when Kovalevskii describes the epileptic murderer in Lombroso's categories. In later editions of his work, Lombroso explains epilepsy as a new mainstay in the concept of the born criminal: "inborn criminality and moral insanity [are] nothing but variations of epilepsy" (Kurella 1910, 59). Furthermore, Kovalevskii lists numerous stigmata that according to Lombroso are characteristic for a delinquent; amongst them reduced skin sensitivity. Here however, it is the cruelty and monstrosity of the crime that are especially emblematic:

> Epileptics commit the most terrible, savage and disturbing crimes. [...] And the witnesses of these crimes really cannot help but be astonished, to the point of numbness, by the brutality displayed by the epileptic criminal. Usually, when they commit murder, epileptics do not content themselves with a single blow; on the contrary they seem to get drunk on their atrocity, finishing off the deed on the already dead victim with a kind of gusto. These crimes are made all the more terrible by the fact that they turn out to have been *committed without any reason, without any motive*, or for such a *paltry reason* that even at first glance, the whole folly and senselessness of the act becomes apparent, as does the criminal's ailing state of mind (Kovalevskii, 1881, 106).[16]

Kovalevskii masterfully incorporates the fascination for mythological evil, characteristic of Lombroso's idea of the born criminal, into a narrative. At the same time however, Kovalevskii seems to be the one who, by virtue of his knowledge, is able to tame the pre-civilised instincts: the phenomena portrayed lose their concerning unreadability because he interprets them as symptoms of hereditary degeneration. The accuracy of Kovalevskii's medico-semiotic work is confirmed performatively in the final court scene,

16 | "[Э]пилептики совершают самые страшные, зверские и поражающие преступления. [...] И действительно, свидетели этих преступлений невольно поражаются, до оцепенения, проявлением зверства преступника-эпилептика. Обыкновенно, совершая убийство, эпилептики не ограничиваются одним ударом, напротив, они как-бы упиваются своим зверством и с каким-то увлечением довершают его уже над мертвой жертвой. Еще более ужасными представляются эти преступления потому, что они являются или совершенно без всякого повода, мотива, или-же при таком *ничтожном поводе*, что уже с первого взгляда выясняются вся нелепость и бессмысленность его, а также и болезненное состояние умственных способностей преступника."

where Kovalevskii himself serves as an expert. His expertise stretches beyond the usual limits and appears again like a narrative *coup de théâtre*, leading to a new climax of suspense. Instead of repeating the already mentioned diagnosis of epilepsy in court, Kovalevskii predicts that the defendant will have another seizure in the very near future. And, indeed:

> Suddenly, a frenzied cry rang out in the court. The raving began. Four men could scarcely contain Pogorelov. [...] His face is a picture of horror. The sick man hallucinates intensely. "Butchery, they're butchering people! Oh! Guards! Help, help! Guards!" [...] The fit of raving, under the influence of which the crime had been committed, was repeated in that very courtroom in front of witnesses and served as the best confirmation of the experts' opinion and to convince the judges (*ibid.*, 123-124).[17]

The semiotic power of the forensic psychiatrist Kovalevksii not only reaches into the past, but also into the future.

Narrative models of inborn criminality in late 19th-century Russian literature

Based on these observations of the possibility of narrating atavism and inborn criminality, we can discern three narrative models in Russian literature at the end of the 19th century: *non*-criminal anthropological, *anti*-criminal anthropological and *crypto*-criminal anthropological models. The first model constitutes the concept of the criminal as *neschastnyi* as mentioned above: this concept is older than criminal anthropology and does not seem to interact with it. The following analysis will therefore focus on the other two narrative models.

17 | "[В]друг в суде раздался неистовый крик. Буйство началось. Четыре человека едва удерживали Погорелова. [...] [Л]ицо выражает ужас. Больной сильно галлюцинирует. 'Режут, людей режут! Ай! Караул! Спасите, спасите! Караул!' [...] Припадок буйства, под влиянием которого совершено было преступление, повторился в том самом суде при освидетельствовании и послужил самым лучшим подтверждением мнения экспертов и убеждения судей."

Anti-criminal anthropological narrative models: A. I. Svirskii and L. N. Tolstoi

Anti-criminal anthropological narrative models were developed by writers like Lev Tolstoi in his last novel *The Awakening* (*Voskresenie*, 1899) or the less well-known Aleksei I. Svirskii in his sketches (*ocherki*) about the criminal world of the 1890s (Svirskii 2002). On the one hand, the prefix *anti-* means that Tolstoi and Svirskii explicitly refer to criminal anthropology in order to disprove its hypotheses. Svirskii, for instance, disputes the comparability of prison inmates' tattoos with primitive peoples' tattoos, which, for Lombroso, is a sign of the atavism of born criminals (*ibid.*, 97-106; Lombroso 2000).

Tolstoi in turn, not only rejects criminal anthropology in *The Awakening* in an argumentative manner, but also discredits it in a performative way. This is typified by the court proceedings scene, in which a narcissistic prosecutor characterises the defendants using terminology taken from criminal anthropology to prove their guilt in his closing speech: "He spoke of heredity, of innate criminality, of Lombroso, of Tarde, of evolution, of the struggle for existence, of hypnotism, of hypnotic suggestion, of Charcot, and of decadence" (Tolstoy 2005, 68).[18] In doing so, he concludes that it is necessary to sentence the defendants in order to protect society from the risk of infection coming from the criminal as a pathological phenomenon:

> "Gentlemen of the jury!" the prosecutor continued meanwhile, gracefully swaying his slim body. "The fate of these people is in your hands, as is to some extent the fate of society, which is influenced by your verdict. You must fathom the significance of this crime, the danger to society that lurks in such pathological, as it were, individuals as Maslova. You must guard it against infection; it is your duty to guard the innocent, healthy elements of society against contagion, if not destruction" (*ibid.*, 69).[19]

18 | "Тут была и наследственность, и прирожденная преступность, и Ломброзо, и Тард, и эволюция, и борьба за существование, и гипнотизм, и внушение, и Шарко, и декадентство" (Tolstoi 1936, 72).

19 | "Господа присяжные заседатели, – продолжал между тем, грациозно извиваясь тонкой талией, товарищ прокурора, – в вашей власти судьба этих лиц, но в вашей же власти отчасти и судьба общества, на которое вы влияете своим приговором. Вы вникните в значение этого преступления, в опасность,

However, it is not the ironic characterisation of the prosecutor and his fashionable "scientific" rhetoric alone that serves as a method of banalisation of criminal anthropology. The underlying argumentation is debunked as a false conclusion, too: the claim of the prosecutor that one of the defendants was a "victim of heredity" (*zhertva nasledstvennosti*) is refuted by the counsel for the defence, who stresses that the parents of his client are unknown:

In conclusion, this lawyer made a thrust at the prosecuting attorney by remarking that, although the splendid reasonings of the prosecutor on heredity explain the scientific questions of heredity, they hardly hold good in the case of Bochkova, since her parentage was unknown (*ibid.*, 70).[20]

The prosecutor replies that with the theory of heredity it would not only be possible to deduce the crime from heredity but also heredity from the crime:

After this lawyer had finished, the prosecutor rose again and defended his position on the question of heredity against the first lawyer, stating that the fact that Bochkova's parentage was unknown did not invalidate the truth of the theory of heredity; that the law of heredity is so well established by science that not only can one deduce the crime from heredity, but heredity from the crime (*ibid.*, 71).[21]

представляемую обществу от таких патологических, так сказать, индивидуумов, какова Маслова, и оградите его от заражения, оградите невинные, крепкие элементы этого общества от заражения и часто погибели.' И как бы сам подавленный важностью предстоящего решения, товарищ прокурора, очевидно до последней степени восхищенный своею речью, опустился на свой стул" (*ibid.*, 73).

20 | "В заключение адвокат в пику товарищу прокурора заметил, что блестящие рассуждения господина товарища прокурора о наследственности, хотя и разъясняют научные вопросы наследственности, неуместны в этом случае, так как Бочкова – дочь неизвестных родителей" (*ibid.*, 74).

21 | "После этого защитника опять встал товарищ прокурора и, защитив свое положение о наследственности против первого защитника тем, что если Бочкова и дочь неизвестных родителей, то истинность учения наследственности этим нисколько не инвалидируется, так как закон наследственности настолько

On the other hand, Svirskii and Tolstoi achieve the rebuttal of criminal anthropology in this *anti*-narrative model by way of setting individual destinies of criminals against Lombroso's anthropological diversity. These testify to a human "normality" of the criminal as an individual and not as a "species." Prince Nekhliudov, protagonist in *The Awakening*, acting as the author's *porte-parole*, for instance argues:

These so-called depraved types, deviating from the normal, were, according to Nekhludoff, none other than those very people who have sinned less against society than society has sinned against them [...] (*ibid.*, 249).[22]

Svirskii's sentimental stories about delinquents often serve to re-individualise and re-humanise an at first seemingly monstrous criminal. In *The Beast* (*Zver'*), a story about the inmate and executioner "Kandyba", his metamorphosis is told from the perspective of a first-person narrator, who is one of Kandyba's fellow prisoners. Upon his arrival in the prison, the first-person narrator hears the rumours about Kandyba's monstrous brutality, which circulate in the prisons and prison camps:

Kandyba was a strong, courageous and cruel man. Monstrous legends were told about him in the prisons. It was said that Kandyba had whipped many people to death. [...] It was also said that once, when he was on the run and lost in the taiga, he killed his comrade and lived off the body of his murdered companion for seven days. Such was the repute of Kandyba, the famous executioner of Sakhalin (Svirskii 2002, 225-226).[23]

установлен наукой, что мы не только можем выводить преступление из наследственности, но и наследственность из преступления" (*ibid.*, 74-75).

22 | "Эти так называемые испорченные, преступные, ненормальные типы были, по мнению Нехлюдова, не что иное, как такие же люди, как и те, перед которыми общество виновато более, чем они перед обществом [...]" (*ibid.*, 312).

23 | "Кандыба был человек сильный, смелый и жестокий. О нем в острогах рассказывали чудовищные легенды. Рассказывали, что Кандыба многих засекал до смерти. [...] И еще рассказывали о нем, что однажды, находясь в бегах и заблудившись в тайге, он убил своего товарища и семь дней питался трупом убитого спутника. Такова была слава знаменитого сахалинского палача Кандыбы."

As the story proceeds, Kandyba's inner world opens up to the narrator and Kandyba gradually gains human/individual features. This re-humanising process culminates in the story's last scene, which depicts Kandyba in fetters running around the court yard and carrying Van'ka, the small child of an inmate, on his shoulders. Kandyba puffs, the child rejoices and the narrator, looking back, sums up:

> I can still clearly picture this scene and when I remember it now, I begin to understand how much wonder is hidden in the depths of the human soul (*ibid.*, 244).[24]

Crypto-criminal anthropological narrative models I: slum literature (V. A. Giliarovskii)

The *crypto*-criminal anthropological narrative model is a little more complex than the "confrontational" *anti*-model. The prefix *crypto-* indicates that this narrative model cannot be recognised immediately. Two genres are reminiscent of a criminal anthropological conceptualisation of the criminal: "slum literature" (*trushchobnaia literatura*) and the "degeneration novel." Vladimir A. Giliarovskii's sketches serve as an example of the genre of slum literature in the following analysis, while the degeneration novel is represented by Dostoevskii's *The Brothers Karamazov*.

In his sketches (*ocherki*) *People of the Slums* (*Trushchobnye liudi*, 1887), Giliarovskii designs spaces of criminal otherness in the centre of Moscow. Similar to other European literatures (Greenslade 1994, 47-64), the Moscow slums are portrayed as heterotopies of deviance amidst modern civilisation, enclosed spaces of biological/social regression.[25] Radicalising the literary tradition of the *trushchoby* (e.g. in V. Krestovskii's *Petersburgskie trushchoby*, 1864-1867; see Buckler 2005, 171-179), Giliarovskii designs a primitive counter-world, where crime forms part of everyday life – as in Lombroso's theory. Giliarovskii illustrates this regressive degeneration of spaces and people by the (crude) equation of slums and wilderness. In

---

24 | "До сих пор я отчетливо вижу эту сцену и, вспоминая о ней сейчас, начинаю понимать, сколько чудесного спрятано на дне человеческой души."

25 | For a similar conceptualisation of urban spaces of atavistic deviance in Russia, see Mechnikov 1878-1880.

doing so, he underlines the fascination felt by the reader as a "civilised person" that the anthropological otherness emanates:

> The lairs of the down-and-outs, those who have lost all human countenance, are derelict cellars, ruins, underground passages. Here, one cannot fall any deeper, the descent is irreversible. These people, like the predators of the forest, are afraid of the light, they are not seen during the day, but creep out of their dens at night. Midnight is when they come into their own. At midnight, they look to the night ahead, at midnight, they arrange their terrible orgies (Giliarovskii 1960, 80).[26]

His sketches often work according to the principle of sensation common in the adventure narrative: an observer from the civilised world, often a journalist, enters the dangerous world of the slums, crossing a semiotic border of restraint between the normal and the pathological, sometimes paying for this with his life. The plot requests that the radical diversity of the forbidden space be marked and results in recourse to criminal anthropological elements. The inhabitants of the slum appear to be a de-humanised and de-individualised dangerous mob, whose "natural" inclination towards criminality is not so much determined biologically or socially as spatially: their lives take place in dives close to the Khitrov market that bear names such as "Katorga" and "Sibir'" (*ibid.*, 88-94). Those are metonymies of criminal deviance, from which there is no exit, because the deportation to the real Katorga only means a transfer within a discrete space.

Crypto-criminal anthropological narrative models II: the degeneration novel (F. M. Dostoevskii)

The second variation of the *crypto*-criminal anthropological narrative model results from the integration of degeneration and atavism within the "degeneration novel." Degeneration novels emerge in European literature

26 | "Притон трущобного люда, потерявшего обличье человеческое, – в заброшенных подвалах, в развалинах, подземельях. Здесь крайняя степень падения, падения безвозвратного. Люди эти, как и лесные хищники, боятся света, не показываются днем, а выползают ночью из нор своих. Полночь – их время. В полночь они заботятся о будущей ночи, в полночь они устраивают свои ужасные оргии [...]."

between the 1880s and 1910s in the wake of Émile Zola's 20-volume family saga *The Rougon-Macquarts. Natural and Social History of a Family of the Second Empire* (*Les Rougon-Macquart. Histoire naturelle et sociale d'une famille sous le Second Empire*, 1871-1893). In degeneration novels, families and their hereditary disposition play an equally key part in a deterministic tale of decline, in which psychophysical diseases and other phenomena of deviance are the symptomatic manifestations of a progressively-developing process of disintegration. Examples of this trend can be found in the novels of Scandinavian authors such as Herman Bang's *Families Without Hope* (*Haabløse Slægter*, 1880/1884) and Bjørnstjerne Bjørnson's *The Heritage of the Kurts* (*Det flager i Byen og paa Havnen*, 1884); in Germany, Max Nordau's *The Malady of the Century* (*Die Krankheit des Jahrhunderts*, 1887) begins a tradition that leads us via Gerhard Ouckama Knoop's *The Decadents* (*Die Dekadenten*, 1898) and Thomas Mann's *Buddenbrooks* (1901) all the way to Eduard von Keyserling's *Twilight* (*Abendliche Häuser*, 1914); in Italy, Giovanni Verga's *I Malavoglia* (1881) and *Mastro don Gesualdo* (1888) perpetuate Zolaist project, which also finds approval in Portugal thanks to José Maria Eça de Queirós and in Spain as a result of Benito Pérez Galdós.

The context from which the early degeneration novels, above all Zola's cycle *The Rougon-Macquarts*, emerged is an interdiscursive field, in which literature and medicine (psychiatry) participate equally. The symbiosis of the two discourses was something towards which the naturalist movement in literature strove and which was made possible by participating in an interdiscursive knowledge regime (Gumbrecht 1978). The first Russian degeneration novels emerged as a direct result of engaging with Zola's epistemic poetics: Mikhail E. Saltykov-Shchedrin's *The Golovlev Family* (*Gospoda Golovlevy*, 1875-1880), Fedor M. Dostoevskii's *The Brothers Karamazov* (*Brat'ia Karamazovy*, 1879-1880), Dmitrii N. Mamin-Sibiriak's *The Privalov Fortune* (*Privalovskie milliony*, 1882) and Petr D. Boborykin's *From the New People* (*Iz novykh*, 1887) (Nicolosi 2006; 2008; 2010; 2015).

The narrative interweaving of degeneration, criminality and atavism is – according to my reading of the text – a central element of Dostoevskii's *The Brothers Karamazov*, not least because it takes place against the backdrop of grappling with Zola's naturalistic poetics. In *The Brothers Karamazov*, Dostoevskii poses one question with a frequency that seems downright obsessive: is *karamazovshchina* – understood as the totality of Fedor Pavlovich Karamazov's normatively deviant characteristics – genetically transmittable? Does it represent something biologically unconquerable, necessarily influencing the brothers in a negative way? The question of biological substance is the question of heredity and degeneration. In that light, it seems to me that Dostoevskii's last novel stands in discursive and intertextual relation to Émile Zola's cycle of degeneration novels *The Rougon-Macquarts.*[27]

Zola's family epic is tied programmatically to the medical discourse of his time. For Zola, the narrative schema of degenerate inheritance has a plot-forming function: the transmission and combination of negative qualities over five generations represents the family history's principle of macrostructural systematisation. At the same time, such inheritance represents a starting hypothesis, the scientific verification of which is undertaken by the author. Zola, in fact, views the experimental verification of concepts from the natural sciences as the very task of literature: the fictional world created by naturalist authors is meant to serve as a kind of laboratory for verifying scientific ideas concerning social and biological determination (Kolkenbrock-Netz 1981, 193-217).

It is well known that Dostoevskii was far removed from this sort of naturalistic idea of literature. *The Brothers Karamazov* is not concerned with verifying scientific concepts, nor at all with outlining a fictional world ruled by deterministic laws. Rather, running through the work on its fictional level is an unsettling suspicion that, in one's own world, deterministic laws – especially the law of heredity – prevail. What this involves is a transferal of the heredity question from the authorial level of French naturalism, where the author basically understands himself as a scientific observer and experimenter, to the level of the novel's acting figures, who observe both their own and alien genetic material and reflect on its potential influence on decisions and actions.

Dostoevskii's presentation of a fictional world infected by ideas of heredity would appear to represent a counter-experiment in the face of Zola's experimental cycle. Dostoevskii's own experimental hypothesis seems (put pointedly) to be as follows: how dangerous is it when human beings believe they function like naturalistic figures? Where Zola records the predetermined biological and social degeneration of a family during

27 | On intertextual links between *The Brothers Karamazov* and *The Rougon-Macquarts* see Reizov 1970, 147-158; Belknap 1990, 39-40. The first five volumes of *The Rougon-Macquarts* are recorded in the catalogue of Dostoevskii's personal library (Grossman 1922, 34).

France's Second Empire, the history of the Karamazov family is meant to show us that a bad hereditary disposition can, indeed, be overcome – and to make this point in terms of Christian regeneration. The disparity between the fates of the brothers, despite their common biological origins, is meant to demonstrate a responsibility for one's actions that is not biologically limited.[28] Nevertheless, a counter-meaning is also inscribed into Dostoevskii's text – one that appears to undermine the counter-experiment through the "tainted" blood of the Karamazovs: the novel has a surprising – no doubt unintended, but nevertheless clearly discernable – criminal anthropological dimension. As we shall see, the ambivalent figure of Smerdiakov plays a decisive role here.[29]

The first verbalisation of the idea of heredity in Dostoevskii's novel takes place in a dialogue between Alesha Karamazov and Rakitin, whom Dmitrii will characterise later in the novel as a "Russian Claude Bernard." The reference is no coincidence, since Claude Bernard was the author of *Introduction to the Study of Experimental Medicine* (*Introduction à l'étude de la médicine expérimentale*, 1865), which served as the basis for Zola's essay *The Experimental Novel* (*Le Roman Experimental*, 1880).[30] Following the simultaneously dramatic and carnivalesque gathering of the Karamazovs in the Starets Zosima's cell, Rakitin offers a first, remarkable explanation of the event – when Zosima went down on his knees in front of Dmitrii – in conversation with Alesha:

> To my thinking the old man really has a keen nose; he sniffed a crime. Your house stinks of it. [...] It'll be in your family, this crime. Between your brothers and your rich old father (Dostoevsky 2005, 81).[31]

---

28 | On Dostoevskii's experimental method see Paperno 1999, 161-167.

29 | See also V. Chizh's psychopathologic analysis of *The Brothers Karamazov* from 1885 (Chizh 2001, 290-293). Cf. Sirotkina 2002, 50-53.

30 | On Zola's theory of the experimental novel and its virulent reception in Russia see Nicolosi 2015.

31 | "– По-моему, старик действительно прозорлив: уголовщину пронюхал. Смердит у вас. [...] В вашей семейке она будет, эта уголовщина. Случится она между твоими братцами и твоим богатеньким батюшкой" (Dostoevskii 1976, Vol. 14, 73).

As a follow-up to his interpretation of Zosima's unusual gesture, Rakitin offers a kind of scientific explanation of the Karamazovian hereditary condition, which he sees – according to the law of nature – as also anchored in Alesha and Ivan:

[H]e [Dmitrii, R.N.]'s a sensualist. That's the very definition and inner essence of him. It's your father has handed him on his low sensuality. [...] In your family sensuality is carried to a disease. [...] You're a Karamazov yourself; you're a thorough Karamazov no doubt birth and selection have something to answer for. You're a sensualist from your father, a crazy saint from your mother. Why do you tremble? Is it true, then? [...] What is at the root of all you Karamazovs is that you're all sensual, grasping and crazy! (*ibid.*, 83-84)[32]

Rakitin's Darwinian vocabulary situates his remark in the context of a trivial/deterministic *Weltanschauung* in which qualities of character are exclusively a question of inheritance. As Rakitin sees things, if such a genetic constellation is present, as is the case with the Karamazovs, it will lead to murder, since it is insurmountable. On the one hand, as the bearer of such a world-view, Rakitin is morally discredited by Dostoevskii; but on the other, it seems that, having been verbalised, the idea of heredity, with all its deterministic implications, dominates the fictional world of *The Brothers Karamazov*. It is above all Dmitrii, Ivan, and Alesha who present thematically and problematise their pathology: at its core, they postulate an instinctive, pathological, border-crossing "violence/incontinence of passions" (*bezuderzh zhelanii*), a "lust brought to a white heat" (*dovedennoe do vospoleniia sladostrastie*; Dostoevskii 1976, vol. 14, 74). The development of the novel's plot, in particular the moral resurrection of Dmitrii, is meant to show that the Karamazovian nature possesses a "life thirst" (*zhazhda zhizni*), potentially a source of faith and Christian salvation.

---

32 | "– Он – сладострастник. Вот его определение и вся внутренняя суть. Это отец ему передал свое подлое сладострастие. [...] В вашем семействе сладострастие до воспаления доведено. [...] Ты сам Карамазов, ты Карамазов вполне – стало быть, значит же что-нибудь порода и подбор. По отцу сладострастник, по матери юродивый. Чего дрожишь? Аль правду говорю? [...]В этом весь ваш карамазовский вопрос заключается: сладострастники, стяжатели и юродивые!" (*ibid.*, 74-75).

The functions of the counter-experiment to Zola unfolding in *The Brothers Karamazov* can be illustrated with a comparison to Zola's *The Beast Within* (*La bête humaine*) – a classic example of the narrative interweaving of degeneration and atavism in naturalism. *The Beast Within* is a novel of sexual murder in which the deterministic effect of a diseased biological disposition on the actions of the protagonist, locomotive driver Jacques Lantier, is laid out in a very clear fashion. Lantier is thus the paradigmatic example of a naturalistic figure whose actions have been fixed, and whose struggle against his atavistic drives was lost from the start, due to endogenous factors nullifying any space of free choice. In his case, then, the "beast" will inevitably defeat the "human being." As Zola presents it, naturalistic man is dominated by impulses, emotions, dispositions, and influences of milieu, and can rarely leave the predictable path of degeneration.

In *The Brothers Karamazov*, Dmitrii, in particular, is unsettled by the idea of the possible effects on his actions of a pathological hereditary disposition, since he feels disgust at his father and fears the uncontrollability of his drives and impulses. Dmitrii especially hates his father's physiognomy, in the face of old Karamazov's pride in this very physiognomy, which he compares to that of a Roman patrician from the period of decline. What Dmitrii here focuses on intuitively in his father is the degenerative moment that, if hereditary, would also be part of himself. Dostoevskii here outlines a narrative situation that is typical for naturalism: his novel were a naturalist work, the "Karamazovian animal" would, self-evidently, predetermine his fate, with murder being the inevitable consequence. In actuality, it seems to be the basic point of the near-murder scene in which Dmitrii, standing in the garden, observes his father from the side while he peers far out of a window in the hope of seeing Grushen'ka:

The old man's profile that he loathed so, his pendent Adam's apple, his hooked nose, his lips that smiled in greedy expectation, were all brightly lighted up by the slanting lamplight falling on the left from the room. A horrible fury of hatred suddenly surged up in Mitya's heart: [...] It was a rush of that sudden, furious, revengeful anger of which he had spoken, as though foreseeing it, to Alyosha, four days ago in the arbor, when, in answer to Alyosha's question, "How can you say you'll kill our father?" "[...] I'm afraid he'll suddenly be so loathsome to me at that moment. [...] That's what I'm afraid of, that's what may be too much for me." [...]

This personal repulsion was growing unendurable. Mitya was beside himself, he suddenly pulled the brass pestle out of his pocket... (Dostoevsky 2005, 439).[33]

The scenario Dmitrii has feared thus concretises itself in precisely the way he anticipated, with the uncontrolled nature of his impulses setting in play an irrational chain reaction seemingly heading straight toward parricide. In Lantier's struggle with his own atavistic fantasies of murdering women, Zola shows us where drive-steered impulses lead in naturalist fiction: permanent observation and regulation of these drives does not save him from the compulsory deed – indeed, the process fails at the very moment that the sight of his beloved Severine's neck sparks a similar reaction to Dmitrii Karamazov's view of his father's hated profile:

She had finished by pressing him against the table, and he could no longer flee her; he looked at her in the vivid brightness of the lamp. He had never seen her like this, her blouse open, her coiffure so high, so that she was entirely naked, her neck bare, her breasts bare. He suffocated, struggling, already carried away, dazed by the tide of his blood, caught in the abominable thrill. And he recalled that the knife was there, on the table; he felt it, he needed only to extend his hand.[34]

33 | "Весь столь противный ему профиль старика, весь отвисший кадык его, нос крючком, улыбающийся в сладостном ожидании, губы его, все это ярко было освещено косым светом лампы слева из комнаты. Страшная, неистовая злоба закипела вдруг в сердце Мити [...] Это был прилив той самой внезапной, мстительной и неистовой злобы, про которую, как бы предчувствуя ее, возвестил он Алеше в разговоре с ним в беседке четыре дня назад, когда ответил на вопрос Алеши: 'Как можешь ты говорить, что убьешь отца?' [...] 'Боюсь, что ненавистен он вдруг мне станет своим лицом в ту самую минуту. [...] Вот этого боюсь, вот и не удержусь...' Личное омерзение нарастало нестерпимо. Митя уже не помнил себя и вдруг выхватил медный пестик из кармана [...]" (*ibid.*, 354-355)

34 | "Elle avait fini par l'acculer à la table, et il ne pouvait la fuir davantage, il la regardait, dans la vive clarté de la lampe. Jamais il ne l'avait vue ainsi, la chemise ouverte, coiffée si haut, qu'elle était toute nue, le cou nu, les seins nus. Il étouffait, luttant, déjà emporté, étourdi par le flot de son sang, dans l'abominable frisson. Et il se souvenait que le couteau était là, derrière lui, sur la table: il le sentait, il n'avait qu'à allonger la main." (Zola 1967, 268)

Lantier murders, Dmitrii does not; Lantier feels no remorse for his deed. On the contrary, he feels liberated because he has overcome the exhausting struggle with his own nature. Dmitrii feels rescued by God and acknowledges his guilt, in the end consisting of the sickness of his drives. As unfathomable as it may be, the decision not to murder, signifying an acceptance of individuality and responsibility, both restores his humanity and contradicts the thesis of mechanical drives.

Dostoevskii's experiment also contains a counter-test, meant to verify the initial hypothesis – in other words the decisive question for or against an ethical border-transgression in which irrational, unconscious, physiological forces are at play – through a similar experimental arrangement but with opposite results. The fate of Ivan, marked by a passive affirmation of evil leading to the realisation of evil by Smerdiakov, an incapacity for complete confession of guilt, and the eventual emergence of a grave nervous disease, is meant to show that reason and religious scepticism cannot overcome that which is biologically negative, but indeed make it stronger.

Can we consider Dostoevskii's counter-experiment a success? Although the present overview seems to suggest this, Dostoevskii's narrative experimental set-up contains a basic paradox that needs to be noted. Testing human free will in the face of evil demands border transgression, meaning murder. Without murder, the cathartic moment of the gospels' "dying of the wheat-grain" – the precondition for a resurrection in faith – would be absent. In Dostoevskii's fictional world, evil is more than a merely theoretical possibility: in his function as God's adversary and the seducer of human beings, the Devil is responsible for the eventfulness of the world, which consists in the fundamental struggle between good and evil for the human soul. But in having evil reveal itself through crime, Dostoevskii has to sacrifice someone to show divine triumph at work in a soul. In this manner, Dostoevskii seems to play in his experimental world the role that Ivan Karamazov polemically ascribes to God: that of an experimenter who creates human beings as "experimental beings" (*probnye sushchestva*; Dostoevskii 1976, Vol. 14, 238) in order to test himself in eternal struggle with evil.

And precisely this structural necessity of crime implies a hidden paradoxical motivation in *The Brothers Karamazov*, one that ultimately renders the conclusiveness of Dostoevskii's refutation of biological determinism problematic. Let us return to Rakitin's above-cited prediction of the parricide: "Your house stinks of it. [...] It'll be in your family, this crime. Between your brothers and your rich old father." The prediction is remarkably precise: it not only points to the shared moral guilt of the older brothers Dmitrii and Ivan, but to the actual murderer as well, Smerdiakov, his name phonetically evoked by use of the verb *smerdet'*, "stink." Despite Rakitin himself not being aware of this precision, it steers our attention towards deterministic premises finding their paradoxical confirmation in the figure of Smerdiakov. Allowing a differentiation of possible basic human attitudes towards evil, the fragmentation of the perpetrator's personality in *The Brothers Karamazov* renders Smerdiakov an instrument of the Devil, evil incarnate. The inescapability of Smerdiakov's fate, the developmental incapacity that makes him the novel's only sinner who cannot be saved,[35] is not only motivated by his structural function within the text's figural grammar but also by a biological determinism lending him the psycho-physical stigmata of degeneration and atavism.

In many respects, the figure of Smerdiakov thus corresponds to an image of degenerative illness with its necessary diachronic dimension in the chronic alcoholism of his grandfather Il'ia and the complete "idiocy" of his mother Elizaveta Smerdiashchaia. Within a synchronic perspective, Smerdiakov represents the endpoint of the progressive weakening of the Karamazovian life force. In line with the medical notions of the time, his epileptic fits serve as one of the best examples of non-healable destruction of the nerves, causing him to "age" prematurely, "shrivel up," and resemble someone "castrated."[36] Even as a child, Smerdiakov displays symptoms of pathological "moral insanity" that have a picture-book quality – a sadistic passion for "hanging cats and then burying them ceremoniously."[37] By carrying out the murder experiment, which promises him unlimited freedom of decision, Smerdiakov hopes to escape the inner-fictional determination of his fate that predestines him to be a delinquent figure in the criminal anthropological sense. Hence his atheistic axiom, "everything

35 | Michael Holquist (1977, 182) sees Smerdiakov "condemned always to be the helpless son."

36 | "Он вдруг как-то необычайно постарел, совсем даже несоразмерно с возрастом сморщился, пожелтел, стал походить на скопца" (Dostoevskii 1976, Vol. 14, 115).

37 | "В детстве он очень любил вешать кошек и потом хоронить их с церемонией" (*ibid.*, 114).

is permissible." That he in turn becomes not only an instrument but also a victim of that axiom casts an unsettling biologistic/deterministic shadow over Dostoevskii's last novel.

References

Abbott, H. P. 2002. *The Cambridge Introduction to Narrative.* Cambridge: Cambridge University Press.

Andriopoulos, S. 1996. *Unfall und Verbrechen. Konfigurationen zwischen juristischem und literarischem Diskurs um 1900.* Pfaffenweiler: Centaurus.

Becker, E. M. 2003. *Medicine, Law, and the State in Imperial Russia.* Budapest and New York: Central European University Press.

Becker, P. 2002. *Verderbnis und Entartung. Eine Geschichte der Kriminologie des 19. Jahrhunderts als Diskurs und Praxis.* Göttingen: Vandenhoeck & Ruprecht.

Beer, G. 1983. *Darwin's Plots. Evolutionary Narrative in Darwin, George Eliot and Nineteenth-Century Fiction.* London: Routledge & Paul.

Beer, D. 2008. *Renovating Russia: The Human Sciences and the Fate of Liberal Modernity.* Ithaca and London: Cornell University Press.

Beliakov, S. A. "Antropologicheskoe issledovanie ubiits." *Arkhiv psikhiatrii, neirologii i sudebnoi psikhopatologii* 4, no. 1, 19-48; no. 2, 12-52.

Belknap, R. L. 1990. *The Genesis of* The Brothers Karamazov. *The Aesthetics, Ideology, and Psychology of Making a Text.* Evanston: Northwestern University Press.

Bowler, P. J. 1988. *The Non-Darwinian Revolution. Reinterpreting a Historical Myth.* Baltimore and London: Johns Hopkins University Press.

Brown, J. V. 1981. *The Professionalization of Russian Psychiatry: 1857-1911.* Ph.D. Diss., University of Pennsylvania.

Buckler, J. A. 2005. *Mapping St. Petersburg. Imperial Text and Cityshape.* Princeton: Princeton University Press.

Campbell, J. A. 1997. "Charles Darwin: Rhetorician of Science." Harris, R.A. (ed.), *Landmark Essays on Rhetoric of Science: Case Studies.* Mahwah, NJ: Routledge, 3-17.

Chamberlin, J. E. and Gilman, S. L. (eds.) 1985. *Degeneration. The Dark Side of Progress.* New York: Columbia University Press.

Chekhov, A. P. 1978. *Polnoe sobranie sochinenii i pisem v tridcati tomakh*. Vol. 14-15 (*Iz Sibiri. Ostrov Sakhalin*). Moscow: Nauka.

Chizh, V. F. 1894. *Prestupnyi chelovek pered sudom vrachebnoi nauki*. Kazan': Tip. Imperatorskogo Universiteta.

Chizh, V. F. 1895. *Kriminal'naia antropologiia*. Odessa: Tip. Isakovicha.

Chizh, V. F. 2001. "Dostoevskii kak psikhopatolog." Chizh, V.F., *Bolezn' N.V. Gogolia. Zapiski psikhiatra*. Moscow: Terra, 287-384.

Depew, D. J. 2009. "The Rhetoric of the Origin of Species." Ruse, M. and Richards, R. J. (eds.), *The Cambridge Companion to the "Origins of Species"*. Cambridge: Cambridge University Press, 237-255.

Dril', D. A. 1884. *Maloletnie prestupniki. Etiud po voprosu o chelovecheskoi prestupnosti, ee faktorakh i sredstvakh bor'by s nei*. Moscow: A. I. Mamontov.

Dril', D. A. 1895. *Prestupnost' i prestupniki (ugolovno-psikhologicheskie etiudy)*. St. Petersburg: Ia. Kantorovich.

Dostoevskii, F. M. 1976. "Brat'ia Karamazovy." *Polnoe sobranie sochinenii v tridcati tomakh*. Vol. 14-15. Leningrad: Nauka.

Dostoevskii, F. M. 1980. "Sreda." *Polnoe sobranie sochinenii v tridcati tomakh*. Vol. 21 (*Dnevnik pisatelia* 1873). Leningrad: Nauka, 13-23.

Dostoevsky, F. 2005. *The Brothers Karamazov*. Trans. by C. Garnett. Minneapolis: Dover.

Dowbiggin, I. 1985. "Degeneration and Hereditarianism in French Mental Medicine 1840-90: Psychiatric Theory as Ideological Adaptation." Bynum, W. F. and Porter, R. (eds.), *The Anatomy of Madness. Essays in the History of Psychiatry. Vol. 1 (People and Ideas)*. London and New York: Routledge, 188-232.

Düwell, S. and Pethes, N. (eds.) 2014. *Fall. Fallgeschichte. Fallstudie. Theorie und Geschichte einer Wissensform*. Frankfurt and New York: Campus.

Engelstein, L. 1992. *The Keys to Happiness. Sex and the Search for Modernity in Fin-de-Siècle Russia*. Ithaca and London: Cornell University Press.

Ferri, E. 1926. "Polemica in difesa della scuola criminale positiva." Ferri, E., *Studi sulla criminalità*. 2nd ed. Turin: Bocca, 167-248.

Föcking, M. 2002. *Pathologia litteralis. Erzählte Wissenschaft und wissenschaftliches Erzählen im französischen 19. Jahrhundert*. Tübingen: Gunter Narr.

Foucault, M. 2002. *The Order of Things. An Archeology of the Human Sciences*. London and New York: Routledge.

Foucault, M. 2003. *Abnormal. Lectures at the Collège de France, 1974-1975*. London and New York: Verso.

Frank, S. K. 2001. "Dostoevskij, Jadrincev und Čechov als 'Geokulturologen' Sibiriens." Smirnov, I. P. et al. (eds.), *Gedächtnis und Phantasma. Festschrift für Renate Lachmann*. Munich: Sagner, 32-47.

Frigessi, D. 2000. "La scienza della devianza." Lombroso, C., *Delitto, genio, follia. Scritti scelti*. Frigessi, D. et al. (eds.), Turin: Bollati Boringhieri, 333-373.

Galassi, S. 2004. *Kriminologie im Deutschen Kaiserreich. Geschichte einer gebrochenen Verwissenschaftlichung*. Stuttgart: Franz Steiner.

Garofalo, R. 1884. "Di una nuova scuola penale in Russia." *Archivio di psichiatria, antropologia criminale e scienze penali* 5, 328-331.

Gibson, M. 2002. *Born to Crime. Cesare Lombroso and the Origins of Biological Criminology*. Westport (Conn.) and London: Praeger.

Giliarovskii, V. A. 1960. *Izbrannoe v trekh tomakh*. Vol. 1 (*Trushchobnye liudi. Moi skitaniia. Liudi teatra*). Moscow: Moskovskii rabochii.

Greenslade, W. 1994. *Degeneration, Culture and the Novel 1880-1940*. Cambridge: Cambridge University Press.

Grossman, L. P. 1922. *Seminarii po Dostoevskomu*. Moscow: Gos. izdatel'stvo.

Gumbrecht, H. U. 1978. *Zola im historischen Kontext. Für eine neue Lektüre des Rougon-Macquart-Zyklus*. Munich: Fink.

Holquist, M. 1977. *Dostoevsky and the Novel*. Princeton: Princeton University Press.

Huertas, R. 1992. "Madness and Degeneration, I. From 'Fallen Angel' to Mentally Ill." *History of Psychiatry* 3, 391-411.

Kolkenbrock-Netz, J. 1981. *Fabrikation – Experiment – Schöpfung. Strategien ästhetischer Legitimation im Naturalismus*. Heidelberg: C. Winter.

Kovalevskii, P. I. 1881. *Sudebno-psikhiatricheskie analizy*. 2nd ed. Khar'kov: Tip. M. Zil'berberga.

Kovalevskii, P. I. 1894. *Nervnye bolezni nashego obshchestva*. Khar'kov: Tip. M. Zil'berberga.

Kovalevskii, P. I. 1896. *Sudebnaia obshchaia psikhopatologiia*. Warsaw: Tip. VUK.

Kovalevskii, P. I. 1903. *Vyrozhdenie i vozrozhdenie. Prestupnik i bor'ba s prestupnost'iu*. 2nd ed. St. Petersburg: Tip. M. Akinfieva i I. Leont'eva.

Krafft-Ebing, R. v. 1898. *Über gesunde und kranke Nerven*. Tübingen: Verlag der H. Laupp'schen Buchhandlung.

Kurella, H. 1910. *Cesare Lombroso als Mensch und Forscher.* Wiesbaden: Bergmann.

Legrain, M. P. and Magnan, V. 1895. *Les dégénérés. État mental et syndromes épisodiques.* Paris: Rueff et Cie.

Lombroso, C. 1894. *Entartung und Genie.* Leipzig: Georg H. Wigand.

Lombroso, C. 1902. "Mein Besuch bei Tolstoi." *Das freie Wort* 1, 391-397.

Lombroso, C. 1910. *La nuova scuola penale.* Turin: Bocca.

Lombroso, C. 1911. "Introduction." Lombroso Ferrero, G., *Criminal Man According to the Classification of Cesare Lombroso.* New York and London: G.P. Putnam's sons, XI-XXI.

Lombroso, C. 2000. "Ritorno al primitivo." Lombroso, C., *Delitto, genio, follia. Scritti scelti.* Frigessi, D. et al. (eds.), Turin: Bollati Boringhieri, 426-457.

Magnan, V. 1892. *Psychiatrische Vorlesungen.* Vol. 2/3: *Über die Geistesstörungen der Entarteten.* Leipzig: Georg Thieme.

Mariani, C. E. 1901. "Appunti per uno studio sulla psicosi del genio in Tolstoi." *Archivio di Antropologia Criminale, Psichiatria, Medicina Legale e scienze affini* 31, 260-265.

Mazzarello, P. 1998. *Il genio e l'alienista. La visita di Lombroso a Tolstoy.* Naples: Bibliopolis.

McReynolds, L. 2013. *Murder Most Russian. True Crime and Punishment in Late Imperial Russia.* Ithaca and London: Cornell University Press.

Mechnikov, L. I. 1878-1880. "Iznanka tsivilizatsii." *Delo* (1878), no. 10, 89-132; no. 11, 181-222; (1880), no. 1, 49-84; no. 2, 99-137.

Mintslov, R. 1881. "Osobennosti klassa prestupnikov." *Iuridicheskii vestnik* 10, 216-246; 11, 355-418; 12, 577-606.

Möbius, P. J. 1900. *Über Entartung.* Wiesbaden: Bergmann.

Mogil'ner, M. 2008. *Homo imperii. Istoriia fizicheskoi antropologii v Rossii.* Moscow: Novoe literaturnoe obozrenie.

Montaldo, S. and Tappero, P. (eds.) 2009. *Cesare Lombroso cento anni dopo.* Turin: Utet.

Morel, A. B. 1857. *Traité des dégénérescences physiques, intellectuelles et morales de l'espèce humaine et des causes qui produisent ces variétés maladives.* Paris: J.B. Baillière.

Nicolosi, R. 2006. "Vyrozhdenie sem'i, vyrozhdenie teksta. Gospoda Golovlevy, frantsuzskii naturalizm i diskurs degeneracii 19-go veka." Bogdanov, K. et al. (eds.), *Russkaia literatura i meditsina. Telo, predpisaniia, sotsial'naia praktika.* Moscow: Novoe izdatel'stvo, 170-193.

Nicolosi, R. 2007. "Genealogisches Sterben. Zum wissenschaftlichen und literarischen Narrativ der Degeneration." *Wiener Slawistischer Almanach* 60, 137-174.

Nicolosi, R. 2008. "Das Blut der Karamazovs. Vererbung, Experiment und Naturalismus in Dostoevskijs letztem Roman." Schwartz, M. et al. (eds.), *Laien – Lektüren – Laboratorien. Wissenschaften und Künste in Russland 1850-1950*. Berlin: Peter Lang, 147-180.

Nicolosi, R. 2010. "Nervöse Entartung. Narrative Modelle von Neurasthenie und Degeneration im Russland des ausgehenden 19. Jahrhunderts." Bergengruen, M. et al. (eds.), *Neurasthenie. Die Krankheit der Moderne und die moderne Literatur.* Freiburg: Rombach, 103-138.

Nicolosi, R. 2015. "Eksperimenty s eksperimentami: Emil' Zolia i russkii naturalizm ('Privalovskie milliony' D.N. Mamina-Sibiriaka)." *Novoe literaturnoe obozrenie* 134, 202-220.

Nicolosi, R. 2017. *Degeneration erzählen. Literatur und Psychiatrie im Russland der 1880er und 1890er Jahre.* Paderborn: Fink (forthcoming).

Nye, R. A. 1984. *Crime, Madness, and Politics in Modern France. The Medical Concept of National Decline.* Princeton: Princeton University Press.

Orshanskii, I. G. 1910. *Atavizm i vyrozhdenie.* Moscow: I.N. Kushnerev.

Paperno, I. A. 1999. *Samoubiistvo kak kul'turnyi institut.* Moscow: Novoe literaturnoe obozrenie.

Pick, D. 1989. *Faces of Degeneration: A European Disorder, c. 1848-c. 1918.* Cambridge: Cambridge University Press.

Reizov, B. 1970. "K istorii zamysla 'Brat'ev Karamazovykh'." Reizov, B., *Iz istorii evropeiskikh literatur.* Leningrad: Izdatel'stvo Leningradskogo Universiteta, 129-158.

Roelcke, V. 1999. *Krankheit und Kulturkritik. Psychiatrische Gesellschaftsdeutungen im bürgerlichen Zeitalter (1790–1914).* Frankfurt a.M. and New York: Campus.

Salomoni, A. 2009. "La Russia." Montaldo, S. and Tappero, P. (eds.), *Cesare Lombroso cento anni dopo.* Turin: Utet, 249-261.

Schönert, J. 1991. "Bilder vom 'Verbrechermenschen' in den rechtskulturellen Diskursen um 1900: Zum Erzählen über Kriminalität und zum Status kriminologischen Wissens." Schönert, J. (ed.), *Erzählte Kriminalität. Zur Typologie und Funktion von narrativen Darstellungen in Strafrechtspflege, Publizistik und Literatur zwischen 1770 und 1920.* Tübingen: Niemeyer, 497-531.

Sikorskii, I. A. 1904. "Biologicheskie voprosy v psikhologii i psikhiatrii." *Voprosy nervno-psikhicheskoi meditsiny* 1, 79-114.

Sirotkina, I. 2002. *Diagnosing Literary Genius. A Cultural History of Psychiatry in Russia, 1880-1930*. Baltimore and London: The Johns Hopkins University Press.

Strasser, P. 1984. *Verbrechermenschen. Zur kriminalwissenschaftlichen Erzeugung des Bösen*. Frankfurt a.M. and New York: Campus.

Svirskii, A. I. 2002. *Kazennyi dom. Tiur'my, nadzirateli, arestanty*. Moscow: Eksmo-Press.

Tolstoi, L. N. 1936. *Polnoe sobranie sochinenii*. Vol. 32 (*Voskresenie*). Moscow: Khudozhestvennaia literatura.

Tolstoi, L. N. 1953. *Polnoe sobranie sochinenii*. Vol. 53 (*Dnevniki*). Moscow: Khudozhestvennaia literatura.

Tolstoy, L. N. 2005. *The Awakening*. Trans. by W.E. Smith. New York: Street & Smith Publishers. <http://intersci.ss.uci.edu/wiki/eBooks/Russia/BOOKS/Tolstoy/The%20Awakening%20Tolstoy.pdf> (last accessed 10 October 2016).

Troitskii, P. A. 1885. "Itogi kefalometrii u prestupnikov v sviazi s nekotorymi priznakami fizicheskogo ikh vyrozhdeniia (Materialy dlia sudebnoi psikhopatologii)." *Arkhiv psikhiatrii, neirologii i sudebnoi psikhopatologii* 5, no. 2, 1-93.

Velo Dalbrenta, D. 2004. *La scienza inquieta. Saggio sull'Antropologia criminale di Cesare Lombroso*. Padua: Cedam.

Villa, R. 1985. *Il deviante e i suoi segni. Lombroso e la nascita dell' antropologia criminale*. Milan: Franco Angeli.

Weingart, P. et al. 1988. *Rasse, Blut und Gene. Geschichte der Eugenik und Rassenhygiene in Deutschland*. Frankfurt a.M.: Suhrkamp.

Wetzell, R. F. 2000. *Inventing the Criminal. A History of German Criminology, 1880-1945*. Chapel Hill and London: The University of North Carolina Press.

Zola, É. 1967. *Œuvres complètes*. Ed. by H. Mitterand. Vol. 6. Paris: Cercle du Livre Précieux.

II. On the Treatment of Social Deviance and Criminals in the Late 1920s-early 1930s

Recidivism, Social Atavism, and State Security in Early Soviet Policing

David Shearer

In January 1933, several hundred delegates of the Communist Party of the Soviet Union gathered in Moscow, in the splendor of the Hall of Columns of the Central Trade Unions Building. They were gathered for a plenary session, or plenum, of the Party's Central Committee. Delegates were there, specifically, to hear their leader, Joseph Stalin, discuss the state of the Party and the progress of the Party's five-year revolutionary plan to industrialize and collectivize the country. The white columns, high gilt ceilings of the Hall provided an appropriate setting for this gathering, for there, Stalin declared to a jubilant plenary session that the fundamental victory of socialism had been accomplished in the USSR. The country had made the great leap forward out of capitalist retreat and onto the rails of full socialist construction. The allusion to railroads and rails was not casual. The Soviet leader reeled off the litany of "huge" successes of industrialization and collectivization during the previous several years. He cited Western "bourgeois" press accounts of stunning achievements. He declared that, despite hardships, despite hardened class resistance, and despite skepticism from many, the Party and the Soviet people had accomplished the "historic" tasks of the first Five Year Plan. Great factories had been erected and socialist farms had been organized. Soviet power ruled indisputably across the Soviet Union. Organized class resistance had been routed, Stalin declared, and in that lay a powerful victory. The remnants of the "dying" classes had been "knocked off balance." They had been "driven from industry and agriculture." They had been "scattered across the face of the USSR" (RGASPI,[1] f. 17, op. 2, d. 514, ll. 14-17). The first Five Year Plan, Stalin pronounced, was a triumph for socialism and the Party.

Stalin looked ahead to the tasks that lay before the Party in the coming period of socialist construction, but in doing so struck a note of alarm. Not all was well. Even as Stalin hailed the victory of socialism, he sounded a warning that the country faced perhaps its most serious challenge yet. The Party, said Stalin in 1933, could not yet rest because the class war continued – not in the organized, open form of opposition, but in the form of "quiet sabotage" (*tikhoi sapoi*), specifically in the form of crime and lawlessness. Stalin's remarks about criminality have since been obscured by the more sensational interest in political forms of opposition and repression during the 1930s. Yet Stalin devoted a substantial portion of his remarks to the 1933 plenary session to this new kind of class war. His descriptions of the dangers posed by crime and social disorder precipitated a major shift in perceptions of criminality and criminals and in policies of political and social kinds of policing. In fact, Stalin and other Soviet leaders worried less about direct political opposition in 1933 than they did about lawlessness and social disorder. This paper examines the realities and changing representations of crime and criminals from the 1920s to the 1930s, and the ways in which deviancy and marginality came to be politicized by Soviet leaders.

Crime as class war

In his remarks to the Central Committee's 1933 plenary session, Stalin laid out the dangers of criminality and social disorder. According to Stalin, remnants of hostile classes remained, even though organized class resistance had been broken. These hostile elements no longer had the force to engage in a direct attack against Soviet power, said Stalin, but they hated Soviet power and would attempt in any way possible to undermine the building of socialism. In Stalin's words, "they trick workers and collective farmers, they undermine Soviet power and the Party. [...] They burn warehouses and break machines. They organize sabotage [...]. They organize wrecking in collective and state farms [...]" (RGASPI, f. 17, op. 2, d. 514,

1 | Rossiiskii gosudarstvennyi arkhiv sotsial'no-politicheskoi istorii/Russian State Archive of Social-Political History, Moscow.

l. 15).[2] These kinds of direct wrecking activities amounted to anti-Soviet acts of sabotage, according to Stalin, but even these activities were not the main threat that the remnant capitalist classes posed to Soviet power. The most significant threat lay in the waves of pilfering and theft from factories, warehouses, freight trains, and farms, especially of such items as grain, coal, food, and other basic staple goods. Stalin made clear that he was talking about more than just a few desperate people. A single loaf of bread or some lumps of coal may not have amounted to much. Overall, however, this kind of theft occurred on a mass scale during the harsh years of the early 1930s. The cost to the Soviet economy ran into millions of rubles yearly. Here was the greatest danger, according to Stalin, repeating the litany: "Theft and pilfering from factories and enterprises, theft and pilfering from railroad cars and trade enterprises, theft and pilfering from warehouses, and especially from collective and state farms" (*ibid.*).[3]

Stalin gave no credence to the obvious – that those caught stealing were, for the most part, poor workers and peasants who had no other recourse to try to stay alive. Stalin attributed mass theft to a campaign of deliberate sabotage. According to Stalin, anti-Soviet "former people" (*byvshie liudi*) acted according to the "deepest class instincts," knowing that the basis of the Soviet economy, and of Soviet power, lay in the socialization of property. Thus, a strike against socialist property meant a strike against Soviet power. As a result, the main activity of these "former people" was to organize mass stealing and theft of socialist, cooperative, and collective farm property. Stalin chastised Party and local officials who turned a blind eye to pilfering, thinking that it amounted to petty crime and was unimportant in the overall scheme of priorities. On the contrary Stalin emphasized that protecting socialist property in all its forms lay at the heart of socialist construction and Soviet power. He compared the sanctity and protection of socialist property under Soviet socialism to that of private property under capitalist law. He declared that, just as capitalist societies meted out harsh punishment for violating private property, so

---

2 | "[…] единственное, что остается им делать, – это пакостить и вредить рабочим, колхозникам, Советской власти, партии. […] Поджигают склады и ломают машины. Организуют саботаж."

3 | "Воровство и хищение на фабриках и заводах, воровство и хищение железнодорожных грузов, воровство и хищение в складах и торговых предприятиях, – особенно воровство и хищение в совхозах и колхозах."

should socialist officials punish harshly even the slightest infraction against socialist property. Stalin defended the already infamous law of 7 August 1932, which made theft of socialist property, even petty pilfering, punishable by a long labor camp sentence and even by death. Socialist property theft, he repeated, was to be treated as seriously as any form of counterrevolutionary activity. To be indifferent to socialist property theft was tantamount to active cooperation in the destruction of Soviet power. He warned bluntly that it was the duty of "every communist, worker, and collective farmer" to enforce this law in its strictest application.

Socialist property theft on the scale that Stalin described amounted to more than the sum of individual acts, according to the Soviet leader. What the Soviet Union faced was not just crime, but a whole new and unanticipated stage of class war, and this new stage of class war required, in turn, a new and forceful response. Here, not for the first time, Stalin put forward his famous argument about the strengthening of the socialist state as society approached the realization of full socialism. Stalin declared:

> Some comrades understood the thesis about class destruction, about creation of a classless society, and the withering of the state as a justification for laziness and indifference, as a justification for the counterrevolutionary theory of the cessation of class struggle and the weakening of state power. It can only be said that such people have nothing in common with our Party. [...] The destruction of classes will be achieved not by a cessation of class struggle, but by its intensification. Withering of the state will not be achieved by weakening of state power, but through its maximal strengthening, which is necessary to beat down the remnants of the dying classes and to organize defense against capitalist encirclement, which is far from destroyed and which will not end soon (RGASPI, f. 17, op. 2, d. 514, l. 17).[4]

4 | "Некоторые товарищи поняли тезис об уничтожении классов, создании бесклассового общества и отмирании государства как оправдание лени и благодушия, оправдание контрреволюционной теории потухания классовой борьбы и ослабления государственной власти. Нечего и говорить, что такие люди не могут иметь ничего общего с нашей партией. [...] Уничтожение классов достигается не путем потухания классовой борьбы, а путем ее усиления. Отмирание государства придет не через ослабление государственной власти, а через ее максимальное усиление, необходимое для того, чтобы добить остатки умирающих классов и организовать оборону против капиталистического окружения, которое далеко еще не уничтожено и не скоро еще будет уничтожено."

As Stalin's comments show, his argument about strengthening the coercive power of the state did not result, initially, from fear of organized political opposition. Neither did it have much to do with the threat of capitalist encirclement. Stalin's reference to hostile external powers was a passing one. Stalin framed his comments about strengthening the state in the context of his concern about the destabilizing consequences of social disorder. Stalin focused his remarks specifically on the then widespread problem of theft and pilfering. Whether the Soviet leader had other types of criminal activity in mind is unclear, but his words carried exactly that import. Stalin's remarks placed the problem of criminality, and criminals, at the center of his address on reestablishing social order and building socialism in the country after the revolutionary upheaval of the previous three years. More than that, by linking class war and criminality, Stalin defined the latter not only as the central problem of social order, but social order as the central problem of state security. Beginning in 1933, in other words, the regime's officials, following Stalin, regarded criminality not as a social "anomaly," but as political opposition to the state. This new understanding deeply influenced civil and political police policies in the mid-1930s, and turned the fight against crime and social deviancy – indeed, any kind of social disorder – from a matter of social control into a political priority in defense of the state. Thus, Stalin's remarks politicized, or more accurately statized, criminality and criminals in a way uncharacteristic of the 1920s and the period after his death. This speech also justified an increase in state power, which was to be tied to increased policing for the specific purpose of quelling social disorder. That these pronouncements were occasioned by concern for domestic problems of criminality and social order highlighted all the more the link that leaders made between state security and social policing.

Other Soviet leaders repeated and expanded on Stalin's themes and on the threat that crime and criminals posed to the state and to the construction of socialism in the Soviet Union. These were no minor figures, but included the highest officials of the state and Party. A Supreme Court review from 1935 reiterated Stalin's January 1933 speech. The review's author, USSR Supreme Court Judge, Anton Antonov-Saratovskii, noted that Stalin's comments linking crime, social order, and class war provided the "starting point" (*iskhodnyi moment*) for all criminal policy since. Stalin's defense of socialist property had signaled the start of a sharp struggle "against thieves and wreckers in the economy, against hooligans and embezzlers of socialist property" (GARF,[5] f. 9474, op. 16, d. 79, l. 47ob).[6] Pavel Postyshev, a prominent Central Committee member, commented in a 1934 speech that

> At present, the criminal element in our country is comprised of various dekulakized elements and elements made up of escapees from labor, concentration camps, etc. […] We need to understand that, because the base of activities of the routed class enemy […] has been restricted, the class enemy all the more turns its gaze toward the criminal element, with which it is tied in its social origin (GARF, f. 8131, op. 37, d. 48, l. 7).[7]

A report of the USSR procuracy from the same year quoted Stalin's remarks about how professional and economic crimes were carried out by class enemies who had infiltrated into factories and enterprises, and who were hiding behind the mask of workers and collective farmers (GARF, f. 8131, op. 37, d. 48, l. 67).

In a 1935 speech to police officials, Genrikh Iagoda, then chief of the Commissariat of the Interior, the NKVD, made the specific link between class war, counterrevolution, and criminals. He reminded his audience that

> For us, the highest honor is in the struggle against counterrevolution. But in the current situation - a hooligan, a robber, a bandit - is he not the real counterrevolutionary? […] In our country […] where the construction of socialism

---

5 | Gosudarstvennyi Arkhiv Rossiiskoi Federatsii/State Archive of the Russian Federation, Moscow.

6 | "Революционная законность нашего времени направлена своим острием против воров и вредителей в общественном хозяйстве, против хулиганов и расхитителей общественной собственности."

7 | "Уголовный элемент сейчас в нашей стране комплектуется из разных раскулаченных, бежавших из трудовых, концентрационных лагерей, и.т.д. элементов. […] Надо учесть, что по мере того как база для деятельности остатков классового врага […] суживается, он все больше обращает свой взор к уголовному элементу, с которым его связывает к тому же своего рода социальное родство."

has been victorious [...] any criminal act, by its nature, is nothing other than an expression of class struggle (GARF, f. 9401, op. 12, d. 135, doc. 119).[8]

We might reasonably assume that Iagoda was engaging in a bit of hyperbole in order to inflate the morale of his audience of policemen. Yet, according to his later critics, the NKVD chief emphasized similar priorities even in his communications with the state security organization, the GUGB, the successor agency to the OGPU political police, responsible not for social order but for the political security of the state and its leaders. According to Leonid Zakovskii, a senior OGPU/GUGB official under Iagoda, the latter stressed protection of state property as the foremost concern for OGPU operational and territorial organs in the struggle against counterrevolution. According to Zakovskii, Iagoda laid out this priority in one of his first directives as head of the NKVD in August of 1934. Zakovskii, as well as other critics such as Iakov Agranov, Iagoda's assistant chief, claimed that Iagoda maintained this emphasis in his operational administration of the GUGB throughout the 1930s.[9]

By in large, Iagoda's critics were correct. Throughout the 1930s, Iagoda, as well as other high officials, understood social and economic order as the primary task of the NKVD in defending the political interests of the Soviet state. As such, criminals became a special focus of attention for the political police. At a 1932 conference of OGPU operational heads, one OGPU official confirmed that agents saw the hand of the counterrevolution behind all forms of organized criminal activity (GARF, f. 9415, op. 5, d. 475, ll. 6-7). Writing in 1935, a leading specialist on crime and law, A. Shliapochnikov, echoed this assessment. Writing in a collection of articles on crime, Shliapochnikov provided one of the most articulate and detailed presentations of the new perceptions of criminals and of the argument that crime amounted to a new form of assault against the state. He offered a litany of stories and statistics on

8 | "Для нас высочайшая честь это борьба против контрреволюции. Но в теперешней ситуации – хулиган, грабитель, бандит – это ли не настоящий контрреволюционер? [...] В нашей стране [...] победного строительства социализма – каждое преступное действие это по своей природе ничто иное как выражение классовой борьбы."

9 | Cf. RGASPI, f. 17, op. 2, d. 598, ll. 12, 41-43, respectively. GARF, f. 9401, op. 12, d. 135, doc. 31, l. 4.

professional-economic crime, banditry, crimes of speculation, of stealing state property, and of hooliganism. Although much had been done to combat crime, in general, wrote Shliapochnikov, the state's response remained "weak" and "*ad hoc*" (*samotek*), especially against these "most dangerous" and "pervasive" kinds of crimes (Shliapochnikov 1935, 99). More to the point, according to Shliapochnikov, the problem of crime was no longer simply a matter of individual criminal activities. The rise in crime rates represented a dangerous alliance between traditional criminal elements and the state's enemies, the lower middle-class strata (*melkoburzhuaznyi sloi*). "An essential reason for the growth of a whole range of crimes," wrote Shliapochnikov, "is the merging of the class enemy with the criminal element [...] which characterizes [...] the class struggle at the present stage" (*ibid.*, 75).[10] Pilfering and theft had become transformed, in Shliapochnikov's words, from a petty criminal activity into the "chief activity of class-dangerous elements [as well as] backward elements of the working class" (*ibid.*, 95). In this new stage of class war, he continued, police repression needed to be strengthened; the purpose of law and policing, and of repression in general, had to be redefined – to "repress disobedience" *(anarkhichnost')* in general, and not just to be tougher on criminals (*ibid.*, 99).[11]

A new taxonomy of crime

Organized political opposition to the Stalinist state was impossible, of course, but in officials' perceptions, crime became its social equivalent, and criminals became the new state enemy. Soviet officials considered the waves of crime that swept the country in the early and mid-1930s as more than the sum of individual criminal acts. This is not to say that all criminals were motivated by anti-Soviet sentiments or ideologies. The kinds of crime, and crime on the broad social scale that occurred in the 1930s, bear witness more to mass social disobedience than to conscious

10 | "Одной из существенных причин этого роста ряда преступлений является смыкание классового врага с уголовным элементом [...] характеризуя своеобразие классовой борьбы на данном этапе."

11 | Cf. Krylenko 1935, 21, 23; Volkov 1935b, 74; Vyshinskii 1935, 35; L. Kaganovich: Speech, 23 August 1932, to a Moscow police conference (RGASPI, f. 81, op. 3, d. 151, ll. 1-17).

resistance to the state or the regime. Still, officials perceived crime, and more broadly, social disorder, as the social expression of a new kind of class war and as a threat to the security of the state. The highest Party and state officials believed crime and lawlessness posed a danger to the country's social and economic order, and even to the stability of the regime. But, did crime and, more broadly, social disorder, threaten the very foundations of the state, as Stalin and other leaders claimed? How bad was criminality and social disorder during the early and mid-1930s? Was it as bad as authorities claimed or feared? Who committed crimes, what motivated criminals in their activities, and what kinds of crimes were most prevalent? What kinds of crimes most worried the regime's leaders, and did those crimes reflect a real state of social breakdown or deep-seated anti-Soviet opposition? These are pertinent questions, given the near hysteria about crime and social disorder expressed by local and national authorities, but they are also difficult to answer, since Stalin's speech in January 1933 not only politicized crime but also the ways in which officials categorized and talked about crime, and about criminals. As a result, official discourse from the 1930s tells us more about leaders' priorities and their understanding of state security than about the social dynamics of crime.

The way officials categorized criminals changed from the 1920s to the 1930s, and the following reports reflect that change. A 1930 report, for example, was one of the last to reflect a traditional reading of crime. The report, which ran to nearly two hundred pages, was prepared by the police for the head of the then Russian republic NKVD, Vladimir Tolmachev. Based on incidents of police investigations, the report detailed crime trends during the last five years of the 1920s. The report contained no politicized language, no references to anti-Soviet elements, and the categories of crimes were laid out in a straightforward, literally descriptive manner. Crimes were grouped by the statutes covering them and organized as a compendium that would have been recognizable to professional policemen anywhere in Europe. No crime or set of crimes was given special attention for ideological or strategic reasons of state security. Each group was analyzed, first of all, according to incidence of occurrence – whether on the rise or declining – then by age group, region, season, and other such criteria. The "professions" of prostitution and panhandling were listed along with crimes of hooliganism, conditions of alcoholism, and child homelessness as "social anomalies" requiring the attention of social organizations as well as police. The report described banditry and bandits as a criminal problem, not as a form of political counterrevolution (GARF, f. 393, op. 84, d. 4, l. 21; GARF, f. 5446, op. 55, d. 1532, l. 1).

The 1930 crime report represented a traditional nineteenth-century professionalized approach to policing as a nonpoliticized fight against statutory violations of law. It reflected the separation, characteristic of the 1920s and again of the post World War II era, between ordinary criminal and policing activities and opposition policing carried out by the political police. The report contained no language about recidivism, or about predisposed biological or social origins of criminality. Tolmachev, of course, was soon removed from his position and the Russian NKVD was abolished as Stalin carried out his purge of the police and then merged it under centralized control of the political police. For a time, after the merger, some police officials attempted to maintain professional independence and, by implication, a separation between "ordinary" and political kinds of criminals. A police official at a 1931 conference reiterated that, despite subordination to the OGPU, police operations should "under no circumstances" be politicized, nor should "objects" or "persons" of police attention be placed in a "political light" (*politosveshchenie*) (GARF, f. 9415, op. 5, d. 475, l. 38). The subordination of police to the OGPU was already well underway, however, and Stalin's comments in early 1933 gave official sanction to the process of politicizing crime and other social "anomalies." Iagoda's comments from 1935, as well as others, cited above, show the extent to which criminality and criminals became politicized.

The process of politicizing, or statizing, crime altered the way officials categorized threats to society and the state. Crime reports from the 1930s no longer organized crimes according to statute and frequency of occurrence. Officials ranked crimes according to their perceived danger to the strategic policies of the state, or by the level of danger they posed to the fulfillment of state policy campaigns. State crimes (*gosudarstvennye prestupleniia*), and crimes against administrative order became the most dangerous of crimes, in addition to outright political crimes adjudicated under the infamous statute 58 of the criminal code. Consequently, those who committed crimes listed as state crimes were regarded as the worst of counterrevolutionaries. Political crimes were included in the same discussions as other crimes, and the language of counterrevolution and anti-Soviet "elements" permeated all discussion of criminality and social order. Thus, a procuracy report on crime, written in 1935, started with a long section on the trend in political crimes, terror acts against state and Party officials, and crimes of wrecking. "Crimes of speculation" (*spekulatsiia*) came next. In contrast, the 1930 crime report, noted above, did not discuss political crimes, and it did not group crimes under vague headings such as speculation – a reference to profiteering – but listed crimes under their separate criminal statutes.

In the 1935 procuracy report, the section on speculation was followed by categorical discussion of crimes against the governing order (*prestupleniia protiv poriadka upravleniia*). This category included, first and foremost, incidents of mass disorder, such as rioting or illegal strike activity (*massovye besporiadki*). Banditry and "resistance to and disrespect of [Soviet] power" also fell within this category. This last category also included short discussions of avoidance of military service, theft from and abuse of nationalized forest and land, violations of moonshine laws, and incidents of labor indiscipline. With the rapid extension of state monopoly, "occupational" crimes (*dolzhnostnye prestupleniia* or white-collar crimes) became a major category of concern in the 1930s, especially as rapid and nearly unchecked bureaucratization followed inevitably from increasing state control over the economy. The procuracy's report devoted a lengthy section to these categories of crimes, which included bribery, embezzlement, illegal trade within state procurement and trade and banking organizations, and other kinds of graft and organizational corruption (GARF, f. 8131, op. 37, d. 48). During the 1930s, officials extended the state's monopoly over crime and social disorder as they extended the state's monopoly over economic and social processes. Crime and criminals, in other words, became statized and were administered as a state monopoly, just as the economy. Crimes against persons and property together with hooliganism made up the last three categories discussed in the procuracy's 1935 crime report, but even here, the author's language politicized, or more to the point, statized, what had been previously regarded as nonpolitical, or nonstate, spheres of criminality. The author of this report discussed the dynamics of these types of crimes in terms of class-enemy influence, but also as a direct and increasing threat to the state. Incidents of hooliganism, he noted, were decreasing from their highs during the late 1920s, but acts of hooliganism were beginning to take more dangerous forms than in previous years. No longer characterized by individual insults or rowdiness, hooliganism was characterized increasingly as a group form of disorder, which included physical beatings and other kinds of physical injury and, most disturbing, organized theft and other illegal activities that "cross over into outright banditry and counterrevolutionary crimes." The report accounted for this transformation by the supposed increase in numbers of recidivists and "declassed and class-harmful elements" that engaged in criminal activities (GARF, f. 8131, op. 37, d. 48, l. 227). In general, according to the procuracy report, courts needed to pay more attention to these types of crimes, not because they were on the increase, but because they were directed toward the disruption of production and cultural-educational work, and disorganization of the new Soviet way of life. These were dangerous crimes not because they occurred often, but because they threatened state interests. The report concluded this section with a reminder to the courts – not that they do more to fight statutory crime, but that they not underestimate the importance of their function to protect the state and to struggle against capitalist remnants (GARF, f. 8131, op. 37, d. 48, l. 228).

A draft report from May 1937 for a new criminal code also ranked crimes explicitly according to their perceived threat to the state. The report was written over the signature of I. A. Akulov, then head of the Central Executive Committee, TsIK, of the Soviet Union. In Akulov's summary, counterrevolutionary crimes came first, especially crimes of treason. Immediately behind in order of danger were crimes against socialist property, since, as Akulov wrote, the constitution and the law of 7 August 1932 viewed "pilferers" (*raskhititeli*) of socialist property as enemies of the people. In third place were especially dangerous crimes against "state order," that is, *protiv gosudarstvennogo poriadka*. Interestingly, crimes in this category, such as hooliganism, illegal strikes, and other illegal gatherings, had traditionally been categorized under crimes against administrative order, or *protiv poriadka upravleniia*. By 1937, "administrative order" had turned into "state order." All three categories of crimes were considered "state crimes," and were ranked as the most dangerous. A second section included crimes against defense of the Fatherland (*otechestvo*), such as avoidance of military duty. Only in a third section did Akulov include crimes against persons, or that threatened the life or health of Soviet citizens. In Akulov's reading, protection of the state came first, then defense of the Fatherland, then, and finally, the protection of citizens (GARF, f. 3316, op. 64, d. 1523, l. 103).

From a-social to anti-Soviet

Stalin's declaration in 1933 about the victory of socialism in the USSR altered the definitions of and approaches to deviancy, criminality, and other forms of anti-social behavior. If crime and deviancy could be accepted and even tolerated as part of the compromise with capitalism of the 1920s, such tolerance was no longer possible after Stalin's announcement of socialist victory. Social disorder could be explained as nothing else but class hostility toward the new Soviet order, and as sabotage of Stalin's grand project to build socialism. As Iagoda and numerous other officials repeated, criminals could no longer be seen as social deviants, but as counterrevolutionary agents acting against the Soviet state and against the construction of socialism (Hoffmann 2003, 177-178).

This shift in perception led to a consequent and dramatic change in how regime officials and specialists came to view the social status of criminals. During the 1920s, most specialists viewed crime and criminals as a product of capitalist conditions. As such, they saw only a fine line between the criminal strata and the working class. These categories were quite porous, and the two strata were considered close to each other in their social relations to capitalist laws about private property. With the "victory of socialism," however, this perception changed. Even in the early 1930s, the common criminal was no longer positioned in the social order close to the working class, as had been the case in the 1920s. Perceptions of the criminal strata were now seen as compromised by the infiltration of that strata by remnants of anti-Soviet lower middle-class elements. This shift occurred suddenly and dramatically when the "victory" of socialism drove the counter-revolutionary elements underground to infiltrate, exploit, and subvert the criminal world to the goals of counter-revolution. This change of perception turned criminals of all sorts from a-social elements into anti-Soviet elements. Consequently, this shift made the fight against criminality not just a matter of civic order but of state security. If, in the 1920s, criminals were seen as "close" to the working classes, now, they were seen to have merged with the counter-revolutionary strata. Even the working class could not be trusted, since, as Stalin declared, enemies of socialism could and did easily hide behind the mask of the worker or the farmer. This meant that, essentially, no one could be trusted.

Recidivism

Recidivism presented an interesting category within this shift of perceptions. Soviet criminologists, of course, rejected many of the prevailing European explanations of recidivist criminal activity as biologically rooted or as the result of general sociological deformations. M. N. Gernet, the great Russian and then Soviet criminologist, wrote vehemently against the biological cum racial theories of Cesare Lombroso, the Italian phrenologist who so influenced thinking on recidivism and deviance in the late nineteenth century. Gernet proposed a "sociological" explanation of crime, as a function not of biology, but of social conditions, a theory compatible with but not dependent on a Marxist class analysis (Gernet [1924], 135; Nye 1984; Pick 1989). G. I. Volkov, a Soviet procuracy official and specialist on criminality, agreed, and went further, arguing that even general improvement of social conditions would not, alone, solve problems of crime. In Marxist fashion, Volkov wrote that the elimination of crime from society required a change in social relations of whole classes to political power and production (Volkov 1935a; 1935b). Thus, only Soviet socialism provided the conditions for the complete eradication of crime and recidivism. As a result of these kinds of ideas, many social theorists as well as government figures encouraged the promotion of skilled training and job placement for criminal convicts as a way to integrate them into a healthy socialist society. The corrective labor camp system, as well as the labor colony system, was supposedly based on this principle of social redemption through work under conditions of Soviet socialism.

Iagoda paid lip service to this social-determinist view and often made reference to the rehabilitating function of labor camps and colonies. At the same time, Iagoda pointed to statistics showing that many crimes were committed by individuals with former convictions. How, then, was recidivism to be explained under Soviet conditions of socialism? Iagoda minced no words. He reviled recidivists. He believed, as did many other European criminologists and policemen, that recidivism was an atavistic trait and that repeat offenders constituted a class of unredeemable people. Iagoda believed, however, that recidivism was socially not biologically rooted. The majority of severe crimes in the country, he argued in a 1936 report, were committed by a hard core of criminals, but these criminals also fit the category of socially harmful elements, specifically the déclassé element (GARF, f. 9401, op. 12, d. 135, doc. 31, l. 3). Iagoda explained criminal recidivism, in other words, as the expression of an anti-Soviet social orientation. As such, according to Iagoda, recidivist criminals were incorrigible because they were inherently hostile to Soviet power, and they could never be rehabilitated (Werth and Moullec 1994, 44).

Iagoda's brand of social atavism was based on his experience within the punitive organs of Soviet power. There is no evidence that he read or was familiar with, let alone influenced by, any of the neo-Lombrosian writings of the 1920s. As a number of writers have noted, continuation of the so-called anthropological school in Soviet criminology came primarily through the medical and psychiatric professions, and was limited mainly to those journals, or disputes and discussions, within the criminological institutes of the time, especially within the Institute for the Study of Crime and the Criminal (*Institut po izucheniiu prestupnosti i prestupnika*) (Gernet [1945], 608-610; Ivanov and Il'ina 1991). Some of the members of that institute worked in the practical organs of jurisprudence or the procuracy, such as Gernet, E. G. Shirvindt, G. I. Volkov, Aaron Sol'ts, and others. These officials and academics were the foremost proponents of anti-Lombrosian trends, proponents of the Marxist or sociological school of criminology. As head of the Commissariat of Health, N. A. Semashko was one of the few neo-Lombrosian proponents in the Institute who also worked directly with social agencies. Even so, the academic discussions within the criminological professoriate were far removed from the world of working police organs. Semashko, for example, and another major proponent of the anthropological school, S. V. Poznyshev, published often in the medical-psychiatric journal *Korsakov Journal of Neuropathology and Psychiatry* (*Zhurnal nevropatologii i psikhiatrii im. Korsakova*). Police officials did not read these kinds of journals, and rarely participated in these kinds of debates. As procuracy officials often complained, the great majority of civil as well as political police had never read the Soviet criminal and criminal procedure codes, let alone any theoretical or research material about crime and criminals. Even high police officials boasted that they had never opened the criminal code, and did not need to know any theory (RGASPI, f. 671, op. 1, d. 118, l. 34; Plotnikova 2000).

Categorical imperatives

Iagoda took his cues not from academic literature, but from Stalin, to whom he was directly responsible. And Iagoda, as well as other officials, both in the police and in the juridical field, espoused Stalin's idea of criminals and marginal populations as the new class enemy. As such, police and security officials were not interested in the psyche or biology of individual criminals, but in practical measures of categorical social prophylactics, that is, in being able to identify whole groups of anti-Soviet "elements," and to isolate and neutralize them on a mass scale. As I discuss below, this approach was not contrary to atavistic typing. Categorical kinds of policing in fact reinforced essentialism in police thinking about different social groups. But, that kind of atavistic thinking did not stem from medicalized ideas about individual criminal types. Police approaches to prophylactic kinds of mass policing were directly at odds with the anthropological approach. M. I. Voevoda, a leading proponent of Lombrosian ideas addressed this point in a speech from the 1920s, declaring that "We are not interested in the question of criminal prophylactics; we talk only about individual cures, and primarily about diagnosis of the individual criminal psyche" (Ivanov and Il'ina 1991, 166).[12]

To police, the danger that anti-Soviet groups posed was a categorical not an individualized danger, and was associated with categories of class, not defined by property, but class as defined by productive contribution or service to the state. Consequently, and as attitudes hardened toward deviant or marginal groups, Iagoda urged local police and GUGB officials to intensify their campaigns against socially harmful elements, based on the infamous NKVD operational order 00192. That order, from May 1935, officially recognized "socially dangerous elements" as a fundamental threat to Soviet order. The substance of the instructions categorized who was to be considered a socially harmful element, and shows the extent to which the definition of socially harmful elements had broadened. In the 1920s, police defined these elements narrowly as people with a criminal record. While they were suspect, they were generally not subject to summary arrest simply because of their socially deviant or marginal

12 | "Мы отбрасываем вопрос о профилактике преступлений и говорим лишь об индивидуальном лечении и в первую очередь об индивидуальном диагнозе психики правонарушителя."

background. According to the new 1935 directive, however, socially harmful elements fell into one of several categories: persons with previous criminal convictions and "continuing uncorrected ties" to the criminal world; and persons with no criminal convictions, but with no definite place of work and ties with the criminal world. Other categories also included "professional" beggars, persons caught repeatedly in urban areas without proper residence permits, persons who returned to places where they were forbidden to live, and children over the age of twelve caught in a criminal act. All of these types of people were to be regarded as socially harmful. They were now subject to summary sentencing by the extrajudicial troikas of the NKVD for up to five years in corrective labor camps (GARF, f. 8131, op. 38, d. 6, l. 61).

As NKVD order 00192 showed, police approaches to criminals became increasingly categorical, but the criteria for including any person in a criminal category was based on social status and social relations, not on anthropological or medical considerations. Campaigns against socially harmful elements were most often carried out through implementation of passport and residence laws. With the implementation of order 00192, head of the police Passport Department, Fokin, and the assistant police commissar, Markar'ian, issued instructions to apply exile orders categorically, and in retrospect. All former *lishentsy* – those who had lost civil rights privileges – were to be deported from regime cities, regardless of their current circumstances, even if they had had their rights restored. This was to be applied also to any category of socially dangerous elements (GARF, f. 9401, op. 12, d. 135, doc. 31, ll. 3-4).

There were several reasons why police adopted a categorical approach to social typing. Administrative processing of large numbers of people had become ingrained in OGPU practice during the dekulakization and border cleansing campaigns of the early 1930s. That kind of counterinsurgency policing proved resistant to change, and carried over from OGPU practice to influence the operational culture of civil police and then the NKVD. As a result, police continued to use campaign and administrative methods of repression during the so-called "social defense" campaigns of the mid-1930s. As it turned out, such methods were also the most effective way that authorities could utilize scarce resources. Throughout the 1930s, despite increases in budgets and personnel, civil police officials found themselves hard pressed. Lack of staff, lack of training, and lack of discipline, among other problems, continued to hamper policing efforts to react to and prevent crime and to maintain social order. Campaign-style cleansing operations in cities, regions, rail depots, marketplaces, and other areas compensated for the ineffectiveness of routinized policing methods. In many localities, sporadic and intensive policing campaigns became a norm rather than an exception. Finally, the very language of description of the population, with its broad categories of socially near, socially alien, and socially dangerous elements lent itself to mass types of policing methods. Description influenced practice as police turned increasingly to repression of categories – of whole groups of people – rather than of individual offenders. This categorical imperative came to characterize Stalinist policing culture during the 1930s and reinforced a strong tendency to fix segments of the population with atavistic characteristics (Hagenloh 2009; 2000; 2001; Shearer 1998; 2001; 2009).

In Iagoda's reckoning, prophylactic policing according to social categories was justified in order to rid the country simultaneously of anti-Soviet and hard-core criminal elements. In his view, these two categories were one and the same. Such social incorrigibles, according to Iagoda, had to be removed from socialist society permanently and not allowed the possibility of reintegration. Despite the official line about rehabilitation through labor, Iagoda made it clear that, once exposed to the underside of Soviet life, anti-socials and criminals could not return to normal society. As a result, Iagoda instructed local camp officials in 1935 not to allow repatriation of detainees outside of their regions of exile, even if they had completed their sentences (GARF, f. 9479, op. 1, d. 30, ll. 14-15). Procuracy officials complained repeatedly about violations of this kind, apparently to little effect, but also, and importantly, even after Iagoda's removal in late 1936, which indicates that this kind of practice pervaded police culture and was not peculiar to Iagoda. In July 1937, the procuracy official and Sovnarkom member Leplevskii reported to Molotov that the commission reviewing the criminal codes was stalled over the issue of allowing ex-convicts back into major cities and industrial cities. He pointed to the leading NKVD member on the commission, Berman, who insisted that they should be kept out. Leplevskii criticized this position, noting the large number of laws allowing many ex-criminals access to regime areas (GARF, f. 5446, op. 22a, d. 69, l. 31).

Vyshinskii, among others such as Leplevskii, opposed such categorical policies, and soon after Iagoda's removal in late 1936, the chief procurator tried to revive policies of social reintegration for recidivist criminals. In the early months of 1937, Vyshinskii established a program, in cooperation with the NKVD, to amnesty recidivists and to place them in socially useful work if they would give themselves up to police. In a report to Sovnarkom and to Stalin, Vyshinskii claimed that his commission, working in conjunction with the police, had found work for over six hundred recidivists. As proof of the effectiveness of his program, the chief procurator produced letters from several municipal government heads supporting his initiative. In addition, he proffered testimonials from self-described "recidivist-thieves." Each spoke well of his former "profession" and its supposed code of honor, but each expressed gratitude for the chance to "work honestly." One repeated his pleasure at having been issued a legal passport, along with receiving regular pay and a place to live (GARF, f. 5446, op. 22a, d. 69, ll. 2-13).

N. I. Ezhov, Iagoda's successor, proved somewhat more flexible in his policies toward recidivists. Ezhov supported Vyshinskii's project and cooperated in the amnesty and placement program. Ezhov went so far as to make recommendations to Sovnarkom in April 1937 for establishment of a commission, run by trade union councils, to take over the placement program. In a memorandum to Sovnarkom and to Stalin, however, Ezhov could not help but underscore what he believed to be the social danger posed by repeat offenders. Using arrest and conviction statistics from 1936, Ezhov emphasized that a significant proportion of serious crimes were committed by what he described as the "contingent" of recidivist criminals. According to Ezhov, criminals with prior convictions often made up the core leadership "cadre" of criminal gangs. Each month, he wrote, over 60,000 criminal offenders were released from confinement at the end of their sentences, but the NKVD could place only six to seven thousand of these in jobs immediately after release. "The rest," warned Ezhov, "disperse across the country and, without work, begin to commit crimes again, even on the very road out of the camp" (GARF, f. 5446, op. 22a, d. 69, l. 46).[13] Ezhov acknowledged that many former convicts could not find work because of prejudice against them, but many, he argued, simply did not want to work honestly, even if offered jobs. Ezhov quoted one thief, still serving time in a labor camp, who arrogantly proclaimed (apparently to a prisoner informant): "I don't want to work when I get out

13 | "Остальные разъезжаются по союзу искать работу, начинают совершать преступления даже по дороге от лагеря."

of here. I like to travel around to different cities and rob. I love the sun, the open air, and the campfire. I will sit here only until summer, then, absolutely, I will take off" (GARF, f. 5446, op. 22a, d. 69, l. 45).[14] Ezhov warned that, given such attitudes, it was necessary to keep recidivists under strict control, even as he supported Vyshinskii's placement program. Ezhov proposed that Sovnarkom allow camp sentencing boards to extend sentences of recidivists automatically for up to three years should they engage in the slightest tendency toward disobedience or "hooliganism."

Vyshinskii opposed this recommendation, as did his deputy, G. Leplevskii (also a Sovnarkom member), and the head of the justice commissariat, N. Krylenko. All three argued that any individual had to be sentenced for a specific crime, not for something so vague as "disobedience," and in any case, such sentencing authority should belong to special judicial boards, not to the NKVD troikas. Leplevskii, in addition, noted in his letter to Molotov (as head of Sovnarkom) that NKVD officials continued to insist that all ex-convicts, regardless of crime and number of convictions, be barred from residency in regime cities and industrial areas. Referring to the August 1936 reforms of passport laws, Leplevskii complained that such a demand was unconstitutional, since only those convicted of the most serious crimes were now forbidden from regime zones. Leplevskii's letter revealed the extent to which attitudes of essentialism pervaded police and other NKVD practices toward former criminals and other social marginals (GARF, f. 5446, op. 22a, d. 69, l. 31).

Comparisons

As with much in Soviet history, Soviet attitudes and policies toward criminals and marginals both fit and did not fit into general trends in the rest of Europe. On the one side, Soviet officials and most criminologists accepted and furthered the arguments of the opponents of Lombroso and the idea of born criminals. In France, the work of progressive reformers such as Edouard Gauckler and Emile Garçon laid the groundwork in the 1880s for policies that stressed social reform as a means to combat crime. Even French anthropologists in the 1880s were moving away from a physiological to a cultural orientation. They, along with other reformers

14 | "Я не хочу работать, когда освобожусь. Я езжу по городам и ворую. Я люблю солнце, воздух и костры. Сидеть буду только до лета, потом обязательно убегу."

– the German Franz von Liszt, the Belgian Adolphe Prins, and the Dutch reformer G. A. van Hamel – helped to mobilize opposition to Lombroso's biological determinism. At the same time, as Robert Nye argues, the process of medicalization, and pretensions toward scientific theory, helped turn the work of the French "social school" increasingly toward a biological orientation in the 1890s and early 1900s (Nye 1984, 97-99, 111). The ideas of pathological degeneration, espoused by Valentin Magnan in the 1890s was crucial in this regard, and led many French criminologists to adopt a view of the habitual criminal that fell somewhere between the advocates of a social milieu-rehabilitative approach and the biological determinism of Lombroso. According to Magnan, pathological syndromes arose as a result of dysfunctional social environments, but those environments could also lead to pathological and habitual criminal behavior through physiological weaknesses in certain individuals. That weakness could proceed in stages to a final state of hopeless criminality, but it could also be arrested, and a person could be reformed through social and medical intervention (Nye 1984, 124-125; Pick 1989).

This intermediate theory of the habitual criminal fits closely with the so-called anthropological school of the early Soviet work at the Institute for the Study of Crime and the Criminal. Much like French psychiatrists and doctors, advocates in the Soviet Institute such as Voevoda and Poznyshev espoused a combination of sociological and medicalized treatment for criminals. They believed that crime could be habitual, and certain people could be predisposed toward crime, given certain conditions, but they did not accept the idea of a born criminal. The latter distinguished them from Lombroso, despite the charges that they were followers of the Italian school. Criminological theories of the Soviet anthropological school did not have the complete pessimism of Lombrosian thinking.

On the other hand, Soviet policing practices, while officially based on the idea of rehabilitation, bore striking similarities to biologically and racially determined policing practices in National Socialist Germany. The NS law against "dangerous habitual criminals" from November 1933 gave police the authority to incarcerate "habitual" criminals permanently. That law, which set policies for the 1930s into the 1940s, in fact culminated determinist trends that had gained prominence in Germany even in the 1920s, during the Weimar era, and which resulted from the waves of criminality associated with harsh economic times, depression and unemployment, and the impoverishment of much of the working population (Wachsmann 2001, 166). The definition of habitual was based on the criterion of three convictions, which was the same definition used in the Soviet Union beginning in the late 1920s to define recidivism. In addition, police organs in Germany gained extra-judicial sentencing authority over habitual criminals in the late 1920s, while in the Soviet Union, police gained that jurisdiction beginning in the early 1930s, mainly from 1933 on, in association with the introduction of internal passport and residence laws. In the Soviet Union, as well, police dealt with recidivism in slightly different and more varied ways than in NS Germany. Soviet police organs had the authority to ban habitual criminals from living and working in certain cities, but they did not have the legal authority to incarcerate them permanently, except in the still rare cases where anti-social criminals were committed to asylums. Soviet police could sentence a-socials or recidivists for up to five years. At the same time, as noted above, Iagoda took it on himself in 1935 to issue executive orders forbidding recidivist criminals – indeed anyone incarcerated in a camp or exile colony – from leaving the region of incarceration or exile, even after fulfillment of a penal sentence. Ezhov sought, but failed, to have the law formally changed to allow police boards in camps to sentence convicts to extended terms for infractions of discipline or disorderly behavior under the rubric of "hooliganism." Judicial and procuracy officials were able to quash this attempt, and to keep sentencing power within the jurisdiction of courts and sentencing boards for specific violation of laws rather than vague criteria of unruliness (Shearer 2009, 267-268).

It is not surprising that police focused their attention on many of the same kinds of groups in NS Germany and the Soviet Union. These included, first and foremost, the unemployed, the homeless, beggars and tramps (*Landstreicher* and *gastroliruiushchie*, respectively), professional prostitutes, and homeless children (Ayaß 1995, 180-186). There were two exceptions to these similarities. In the Soviet Union, officials perceived theft and thieves as an especially dangerous threat, since they supposedly posed a direct danger to the economic strategies and policies of the regime. Theft of state property was a counterrevolutionary act, whereas in NS Germany theft most often affected private property. Petty criminals were certainly held in permanent custody in Germany as a-socials, but they were not targeted with such ferocity as in the Soviet Union. Conversely, German police and officials targeted Roma and Sinti populations as both racially inferior and as a-socials (Ayaß 1995, 196). In the Soviet Union, while police worried about the semi-itinerant culture of the *tsygane*, officials did not actively target them for isolation or deportation.

The most striking similarity with NS Germany lay in the mutual radicalization of policies toward habitual criminals, from confinement to extermination. In this case, it was the Soviets who took the lead with the now infamous mass operations of the late 1930s based on the NKVD executive order 00447. As Marc Junge, and many others have now shown, this order launched a wave of state violence that led to the arrest of nearly 800,000 people, and the execution of some 370,000, many of them criminals or former convicts or social marginals.[15] Radicalization of NS policies began in the late 1930s, also, with the transfer of authority over criminals from civil police to the SS for work in strategic factories or incarceration in concentration camps (Wachsmann 2001, 176). In 1943, Hitler initiated a policy of outright extermination of habitual criminals and a-socials, motivated by a fear of negative natural selection. As increasing numbers of "healthy" Germans were dying at the front, according to Hitler, the proportion of degenerates in the population would grow, and possibly lead to conditions of rebellion, as had occurred in 1918, at the end of the Great War (Wachsmann 2001, 179; Wachsmann 1999, 628-629).

Hitler's motivation was remarkably similar to the motivation that many historians ascribe to Stalin in his decision to pursue policies of extermination toward "anti-Soviet elements." Scholars still debate whether Stalin was motivated by fear of invasion and possible rebellion by organized criminal populations, or whether he reacted to pressure from regional Communist Party leaders about a growing threat of hostile "elements" to the Soviet system. Likely, the explanation involves a mixture of motivations. In either scenario, however, and especially in the first one, Stalin, like Hitler, rationalized his exterminatory policies because of the threat that he perceived from hostile populations at a time of danger to the official order.

At least three important differences separated Soviet and NS policies toward habitual criminals. The first was a difference in scale. In Germany in 1938 about 13,000 people designated as habitual criminals were being held in permanent custody, while the numbers in the Soviet Union, either in camps or colonies, in jails, or scratching out existence under some kind of discriminatory regime ranged in the hundreds of thousands.

15 | The best summary analysis remains Junge and Binner 2003, 122-136.

Moreover, in Germany, from 1942 on, 20,000 criminals were slated for transfer to concentration camps to be exterminated by *Vernichtung durch Arbeit*, "annihilation through labor." According to the historian Nikolaus Wachsmann, some two-thirds of those died in the camps, but this is a number that stands in sharp contrast to the nearly 370,000 exterminated in the Soviet Union during the mass operations of 1937 and 1938 (Wachsmann 1999, 627).

The second difference involved how criminals and a-socials were selected for extermination. In the German case, Ministry of Justice officials traveled to various penal institutions. There they examined individual files, and even prisoners, to determine if the latter were reformable or should be transferred to the SS for killing (Wachsmann 1999, 639-640). This was an enormously time consuming process, but the judicial organs managed to maintain control over this process, not the police. In the Soviet extermination campaigns, such decisions were made by the police, almost without challenge. Procuracy officials were supposed to sit on the sentencing boards, the *troiki*, set up to adjudicate cases during the mass operations of the late 1930s. Their presence, however, was mainly a fiction, and the Procuracy General at the Time, Andrei Vyshinskii, made it clear that state officials should not challenge the work of the security police. In addition, many of the arrests and killings that occurred under order 00447 were done by category, or list. Many victims were never interrogated or faced any police or court officials. This was especially true as pressure built in late 1937 and early 1938 to intensify the pace of operations. NS and Soviet approaches to habitual criminals were both exterminatory, but the Soviets conducted their extermination campaigns categorically rather than individually (Hagenloh 2009; Leibovich 2006; Shearer 2009; Tepliakov 2008; Vatlin 2004).

This mass approach no doubt contributed to the extraordinarily high numbers of victims in the Soviet case. Indeed, as Wolfgang Ayaß argues, there existed no "overall" plan for a "final solution" to the "social problem" in NS Germany. Regime officials made it a goal to eliminate entirely social illnesses such as poverty and criminality. This was part and parcel of fascist theory. The movement toward extermination, however, was cumulative and carried out on a case-by-case basis (Ayaß 1995, 219-220). In the Soviet Union, by contrast, and with a certain bitter historical twist, the anti-Soviet campaigns of 1937 and 1938 fit very much a "final solution" scenario. Operational order 00447, after all, culminated nearly a decade of policies intended to identify and isolate socially dangerous populations. According to Ezhov, those policies had failed, and the problem of socially dangerous "elements" had only gotten worse. The new campaign was specifically designed to solve forever the problem of those elements. It was to accomplish this goal simply by killing those who fell into the categories of a-socials, or by removing them permanently from society. "[O]nce and for all time" (*raz i navsegda*) was the phrase Ezhov used in the instructions that launched the mass operations.[16]

The third major difference in Soviet and NS extermination policies revolves around perceptions of the habitual criminal. As a number of scholars have noted, NS attitudes and even dominant criminological attitudes in the 1920s, toward criminality, were grounded in biological ideas of degeneration (Ayaß 1995, 13-18). To Nazi racial scientists, there was such a thing as a born criminal, and born as well as habitual criminals suffered a biological disease that could not be cured. They represented a threat – as in the infamous reference to *Schädling*, or vermin – in the national body, the *Volkskörper*, or to the national community, the *Volksgemeinschaft*. Such criminals had to be either permanently removed from society, or, in the extreme, exterminated.

Soviet ideology, in contrast, remained grounded in theories of social origin and milieu, although it is clear that many officials believed in the existence of permanently hostile class aliens. To officials such as Iagoda and Ezhov, incorrigible criminals and anti-Soviet elements were one and the same. These groups posed a threat to society, either as socially dangerous, *sotsial'no-opasnyi*, or socially harmful, *sotsial'no-vrednyi*. However, Soviet officials and police used neither the language of bodies nor nation to describe the threat posed by criminals and a-socials. In the end, though, and regardless of the regime and the reasons, it came to the same thing: permanent punishment and then extermination.

Soviet essentialism

There are interesting parallels in the evolution of Soviet official attitudes toward criminality and notions of ethnicity and nationality. As other historians have noted, the attitudes of Soviet leaders about ethnicity

16 | Cf. *Izvestiia TsK KPSS*, 1989, no. 10, 81-82; *Trud*, 4 June 1992, 4; Zolotov 1996, 766-780; Vert and Mironenko 2004, 267-275.

hardened in the 1930s into definitions of primordial beginnings and inherent national traits. As Terry Martin and Amir Weiner, among others, have shown, deportations of ethnic groups began even in the early and mid 1930s, although such campaigns – such as cleansing western border areas of those with Polish backgrounds – were not categorical (Martin 2000, 2001; Weiner 2001). Deportation policies became increasingly categorical during and after World War II. During the ethnic expulsion campaigns of the 1940s, it was not just a few Chechens, Tatars, Ingushets, and others who were deported; Lavrentii Beria, Stalin's head of the NKVD, gave orders that the whole of the population should be removed to thwart the potential of anti-Soviet collaboration or rebellion. In Terry Martin's phrase, these populations were regarded immutably as enemy nations.

This kind of categorical approach already permeated police practice toward social groups beginning in the late 1920s, and then hardened around the intractable and anti-Soviet traits of criminality, recidivism, and marginality, but not around biological markers. The trend toward atavistic thinking culminated in and made possible the mass operations of the late 1930s, not just of criminals, but of national groups, as well. Whatever the origins, such attitudes were certainly abetted by the categorical ways in which the regime dealt with the population. They so believed in sociological approaches that these became hardened into historical "facts" rather than malleable evolutionary tendencies. In the end, then, police and other Soviet officials rejected the biological basis of determining social deviance, which had so fascinated other European and American observers. Yet Soviet officials believed, nonetheless, in a social and ethnic kind of atavism that produced recidivist criminals, incorrigibly harmful social elements, and enemy nations even within Soviet borders. That brand of atavism provided police, or so they believed, with the means to identify, separate and, if necessary, to exterminate, not just potentially dangerous individuals, but whole groups.

References

Ayaß, W. 1995. *Asoziale im Nationalsozialismus.* Stuttgart: Klett-Cotta.

Ayaß, W. 2009. "Schwarze und grüne Winkel: Die nationalsozialistische Verfolgung von Asozialen und Kriminellen – ein Überblick über die Forschungsgeschichte." Diercks, H. (ed.), *Ausgegrenzt: "Asoziale" und "Kriminelle" im nationalsozialistischen Lagersystem: Beiträge zur*

Geschichte der nationalsozialistischen Verfolgung in Norddeutschland, Heft 11. Bremen: Edition Temmen, 16-30.

Bakirov, E. A. et al. 1997. *Butovskii poligon, 1937-1938 gg.: kniga pamiati zhertv politicheskikh repressii*. Moscow: OOO Panorama.

Gernet, M. [1924] 1974. "Predislovie k rabote *Prestupnyi mir Moskvy (1924)*." Gernet, M. *Izbrannye proizvedeniia*. Moscow: Iuridicheskaia literatura, 401-437.

Gernet, M. [1945] 1974. "Izuchenie prestupnosti v SSSR. Istoricheskii ocherk (1945)." Gernet, M. *Izbrannye proizvedeniia*. Moscow: Iuridicheskaia literatura, 595-613.

Hagenloh, P. 2000. "'Socially Harmful Elements' and the Great Terror." Fitzpatrick, Sh. (ed.), *Stalinism: New Directions*. London and New York: Routledge, 286-308.

Hagenloh, P. 2001. "'Chekist in Essence, Chekist in Spirit': Regular and Political Police in the 1930s." *Cahiers du Monde russe* 42, no. 2-4, 447-476.

Hagenloh, P. 2009. *Stalin's Police: Public Order and Mass Repression in the USSR, 1926-1941*. Baltimore: John Hopkins University Press.

Hoffmann, D. 2003. *Stalinist Values: The Cultural Norms of Stalinist Modernity, 1917-1941*. Ithaca: Cornell University Press.

Iunge [Junge], M. and Binner, R. 2003. *Kak terror stal "bol'shim." Sekretnyi prikaz No. 00447 i tekhnologiia ego ispolneniia*. Moscow: AIRO-XX.

Ivanov, L. V. and Il'ina, L. 1991. "Bor'ba s neolombrozianstvom." Ivanov and Il'ina, *Puti i sud'by otechestvennoi kriminologii*. Moscow: Nauka, 155-176.

Krylenko, N. 1935. "Proekt ugolovnogo kodeksa Soiuza SSR." *Problemy ugolovnoi politiki*. Vol. 1. Moscow: OGIZ, 3-25.

Leibovich, O. (ed.) 2006. *Vkliuchen v operatsiiu. Massovyi terror v prikam'e, 1937-38 gg*. Perm: Permskii gosudarstvennyi tekhnicheskii universitet.

Martin, T. 2000. "Modernization or Neo-Traditionalism? Ascribed Nationality and Soviet Primordialism." Fitzpatrick, Sh. (ed.), *Stalinism: New Directions*. London and New York: Routledge, 348-367.

Martin, T. 2001. "Ethnic Cleansing and Enemy Nations." Martin, T. *Affirmative Action Empire: Nations and Nationalism in the Soviet Union, 1923-1939*. Ithaca, NY: Cornell University Press, 311-343.

Nye, R. 1984. *Crime, Madness, and Politics in Modern France*. Princeton, NJ: Princeton University Press.

Pick, D. 1989. *Faces of Degeneration: A European Disorder, c. 1848-c. 1918.* Cambridge: Cambridge University Press.

Plotnikova, N. 2000. "O deiatel'nosti osobogo soveshchaniia pri NKVD SSSR." Zdanovich, A. et al. (eds.), *Istoricheskie chteniia na Lubianke.* Vyp. 3. *Otechestvennye spetssluzhby v 1920-1930-kh godakh.* Moscow: FSB, 51-55.

Shearer, D. 1998. "Crime and Social Disorder in Stalin's Russia: A Reassessment of the Great Retreat and the Origins of Mass Repression." *Cahiers du Monde russe* 39, no. 1-2, 119-148.

Shearer, D. 2001. "Social Disorder, Mass Repression, and the NKVD during the 1930s." *Cahiers du Monde russe* 42, no. 2-4, 505-534.

Shearer, D. 2009. *Policing Stalin's Socialism: Repression and Social Order in the Soviet Union, 1924-1953.* New Haven: Yale University Press.

Shliapochnikov, A. 1935. "Prestupnost' i repressiia v SSSR." *Problemy ugolovnoi politiki.* Vol. 1. Moscow: OGIZ, 75-100.

Tepliakov, A. 2008. *Mashina terrora. OGPU-NKVD Siberii v 1929-1941 gg.* Moscow: Novyi Khronograf.

Vatlin, A. 2004. *Terror raionnogo masshtaba: "Massovye operatsii" NKVD v Kuntsevskom raione Moskovskoi oblasti 1937-1938 gg.* Moscow: Rosspen.

Vert [Werth], N. and Mironenko, S. V. (eds.) 2004. *Istoriia stalinskogo gulaga. Konets 1920-kh – pervaia polovina 1950-kh godov. Sobranie dokumentov v semi tomakh.* Vol. 1: *Massovye repressii v SSSR.* Moscow: Rosspen.

Volkov, G. I. 1935a. "Kritika burzhuaznykh teorii prestupleniia." Volkov, G. I. *Klassovaia priroda prestuplenii i sovetskoe ugolovnoe pravo.* Moscow: OGIZ, 115-170.

Volkov, G. I. 1935b. "Nakazanie v Sovetskom ugolovnom prave." *Problemy ugolovnoi politiki.* Vol. 1. Moscow: OGIZ, 40-74.

Vyshinskii, V. 1935. "K reforme ugolovno-protsessual'nogo kodeksa." *Problemy ugolovnoi politiki.* Vol. 1. Moscow: OGIZ, 26-39.

Wachsmann, N. 1999. "Annihilation Through Labour: The Killing of State Prisoners in the Third Reich." *Journal of Modern History*, 3, 624-659.

Wachsmann, N. 2001. "From Indefinite Confinement to Extermination: 'Habitual Criminals' in the Third Reich." Gellately, R. and Stoltsfus, N. (eds.), *Social Outsiders in Nazi Germany.* Princeton, NJ: Princeton University Press, 165-191.

Weiner, A. 2001. *Making Sense of War: The Second World War and the Fate of the Bolshevik Revolution.* Princeton NJ: Princeton University Press.

Werth, N. and Moullec, G. 1994. *Rapports secrets soviétiques 1921-1991: La société russe dans les documents confidentiels.* Paris: Gallimard.

Zolotov, Iu. M. (ed.) 1996. *Kniga pamiati zhertv politicheskikh repressii.* Ulianovsk: Dom Pechati.

Cesare Lombroso and the Social Engineering of Soviet Society

Marc Junge

Why were certain groups, namely petty criminals, beggars, nomads, the unemployed, prostitutes, hooligans, and other social deviants, systematically and collectively punished by the state during the Great Terror in the Soviet Union? How were disproportionally long sentences and, in many cases, death sentences for these groups legitimized by the state? An examination of the harsher sentences assigned to criminals and social deviants is necessary because these groups were considered in theory, ideology, and practice, to be a "socially near element" of Soviet society (i.e. they were considered to be quasi workers that had been relegated to the margins of society by structures of the capitalist system). What motivated this persecution? Are there political-historical roots for these courses of action that can be revealed through further study?

In our previous work on the subject, Rolf Binner and I have clearly established that the biological models of explanation for the causes of criminality and/or social deviance articulated by Cesare Lombroso and others had no place in the Soviet context. In fact, our work demonstrates that social deviance and criminality were not viewed as a biologically determined phenomenon in the Soviet Union and that Soviet institutions had already abandoned biological and anthropological models for researching criminality and social deviance by the 1920s (Junge 2010b, 209-244; Junge 2010a, 215-275).

Further complicating matters, it was during the 1930s that criminality and social deviance were no longer considered to be a purely social phenomenon, although this had been the dominant explanatory model in the early Soviet Union until approximately 1929 (Rozanov 1924).

From the 1930s onward it was no longer possible to view the criminal as an innocent victim of his/her social circumstances because the social structures associated with capitalism, which were assigned responsibility for corrupting the individual, were meant to be completely abolished now.

At the beginning of the 1930s, it became increasingly difficult to designate the Soviet society as a transitional society and, in particular, to research the causes of criminality. Specifically, it was no longer possible to prioritize micro-social and explanatory models, especially those that were rooted in the pre-revolutionary past (Gernet 1974a, 410, 437). As a result, the prohibition against exploring the causes of criminality within the socialist society from the mid-1930s onwards makes it difficult for scholars to ascertain from official statements or scientific reports how the state attempted to deal with the explosion of crime that occurred as a result of forced collectivization and industrialization processes. Even an examination of the state-directed execution and incarceration of criminals fails to provide scholars with clear statements regarding the legitimization of these actions.

According to penal policy in the 1930s, under the Soviet state the individual had only two possibilities: to integrate him or herself into the new society or to place oneself outside of it. Social deviants – often those who refused to integrate themselves – fell into the latter category. In these cases, the state assumed the right to isolate, and even to kill, these persons. For example, beginning in the 1930s, the *Police Troika* and the Special Counsel (*osoboe soveshchanie*) in the Ukraine assumed the task of enforcing policies of isolation and execution. However, from 1937 onwards, the *Police Troika* lost the right to issue death sentences and this role was taken over by the *Kulak Troika* until the end of 1938 (Junge 2016, 244-333).[1]

As a result of these changes, new life was once again injected into the classical theory of criminality based on free will and/or the individual's freedom of choice in the Soviet Union. The result of this process was that by the end of the 1930s, the criminal had mutated from a "socially near element" into a "socially hostile/harmful element" or a "socially dangerous element" (*ibid.*). The remainder of this paper will test the explanations for the severe suppression of criminality and other deviance that transpired

1 | The *Troikas* were designated as the main extrajudicial sentencing board during the so-called mass operations against "socially alien elements" (*Police Troika*) and Kulaks, criminals and petty political enemies of the Bolsheviks (*Kulak Troika*).

in the 1930s. By re-examining the sources used in our previous work, it will be possible to understand the rationale for these procedures across three sites of analysis: the elites, the penal bodies, and the Soviet society.

Lombroso and the Young Soviet Union

Up until the October Revolution of 1917, Cesare Lombroso's populist and pseudo-scientific explanation of the biological roots of criminality and social deviance held credence in certain pre-revolutionary scientific sectors in Russia. The first indications of this can be found in Daniel Beer's work, *Renovating Russia: The Human Sciences and the Fate of Liberal Modernity, 1880-1930* (Beer 2008). In a review of the book written by Benjamin Zajicek, Beer's argument is summarized as follows:

> [...] that Russian psychiatrists and criminologists at the turn of the twentieth century, like their Western European counterparts, were deeply engaged in trying to explain social problems as functions of mental illness, hereditary "degeneration", and the inherently unequal ability of different individuals to use reason (Zajicek 2008).

Accordingly, it is interesting for us to examine, whether the ideas of Lombroso were carried over into the young Soviet Union and, if so, whether they played a role in influencing scientific investigations of criminality or state policies related to the penal bodies. Of particular interest to our study is the fact that in 1923, under the leadership of V.L. Orleanskii who was the head of the administrative Department of Councillors at this time, a commission of criminologists, psychiatrists, anthropologists, and statisticians was formed. Many of the members of this commission were a part of the sociological school that identified social and economic conditions as the main cause of criminality. After the formation of this committee, every person arrested was to be examined by experts (Gernet 1974a, 407).[2] This procedure took place first in Moscow and was subsequently expanded to other larger cities within the Soviet Union. Based on contemporary research in Soviet journals it is clear that, through these examinations, experts not only gathered the usual information on

2 | A comprehensive investigation was begun in Moscow; however, anthropologists were hardly involved due to a personnel shortage.

such things as arrests, previous convictions, and other personal data, but they also conducted psychiatric evaluations that included asking questions about the individual's social milieu. In some cases, individual criminals even went through comprehensive examinations involving evaluations of their domestic environments in a specially set up psychiatric clinic (*ibid.*, 410). Since the material, on which the published statistics and short analyses were based, was never made publicly available due to ideological reasons, it is unclear whether these examinations contained approaches and questions that sought to determine biological and anthropological understandings of criminality.

In 1929, the aforementioned commission was absorbed by the State Institute for the Study of Crime and the Criminal. This Institute was founded in 1925 by the People's Commissar for Internal Affairs (NKVD). Being now placed under the jurisdiction of the NKVD (Gernet 1974b, 609) – the state's secret service – meant that the commission operated under strict secrecy and control. The institute itself was divided into four divisions: 1) the social-economic 2) the penal 3) the bio-psychological and 4) the criminal section. According to Mikhail Gernet, a leading Soviet criminologist, the bio-psychological section was particularly interested in exploring the mental capacity of the criminal; whereas, the penal section of the commission, focused on the struggle against crime and the organization of institutions of imprisonment. Within the fourth division of the commission, disclosure techniques were the main focus (*ibid*). The documents of this Institute, which was likely dissolved in the mid-1930s, were "confiscated" by the NKVD and remain under lock and key today at the Central Archive of the FSB of the Russian Federation.[3] The fact

3 | In a letter of inquiry, access to the following materials and funds was requested. The letter argued that the following material should be examined for explicit mentions of biological explanations of social deviation: the funds of the commission of the Central Control Commission of the Communist Party of the Soviet Union for the suppression of criminality; the materials of the All-Russian Cabinet for researching the personality of criminals and criminality; the materials of the Moscow Department for health care (*zdravookhraneniia*); the materials of the administrative Department of the All-Russian Central Executive Committee (VTsIK), which dealt with problems of criminality; the materials of the commission of the OGPU-NKVD, which concerned itself from 1925 until 1934 with criminals and criminality. Moreover, a letter of inquiry was sent to the archive of the security that these sources are not publicly available at this time makes an analysis of the influence of anthropological and biological approaches in pre-war USSR precarious at best.

Without having access to these documents, contemporary scholars can still begin to investigate the biological and anthropological approaches to understanding criminality by examining the texts of scientists' writing in the 1920s. Literary works, also from the post-revolutionary periods, can also be understood to be a reflection of the broader understandings of social deviance.

Lombroso and Recidivist Perpetrators

There is one additional reason to depart from our position, which is that until the end of the 1920s the Soviet Union viewed crime as an exclusively social phenomenon. Specifically, many Western criminologists and police forces in the 1920s and 1930s believed that the majority of crimes could be traced back to a small, homogenous group of offenders that could not be re-socialized. This group was defined as being "professional criminals," "repeat offenders," or "habitual offenders." According to this line of thinking, if the core criminal group could successfully be defeated, then it would be possible to significantly decrease the crime rate (Wagner 2002; Baumann 2006). It is worth noting here that in the 1920s in the Soviet Union, there was already a focus on the repeat offender (*ugolovnik-/prestupnik-retsidivist*).

On July 19, 1927, the All-Russian Central Executive Committee (VTsIK) and the Soviet People's Commissariat (SNK) implemented a resolution entitled, *On the penal policy and the conditions of the prisons* (*O karatel'noi politike i sostoianii mest zakliucheniia*). This resolution stated: "One must recognize the necessity of carrying out strict measures exclusively against the class enemy and the declassed professional criminals and repeat offenders" (Petrov 2004, 612).[4] Furthermore, on July 14, 1935, the People's Commissar for Internal Affairs, Genrikh Iagoda, submitted

---

service of the Ukraine with the request for access to the equivalent materials of the cabinet for researching the personality of criminals and criminality in Odessa.

4 | "Признать необходимым применять суровые меры репрессии исключительно в отношении классовых врагов и деклассированных преступников – профессионалов и рецидивистов."

a report entitled, *On the mistakes in the performance of the judicial bodies* (*O nedostatkakh v rabote sledstvennykh organov*) to Stalin and Molotov. In this report, Iagoda writes: "It appears to me that it should be clear to all, including the co-workers of the courts, that the repeat offenders are first and foremost in need of isolation" (Vert 2004, 231).[5]

The position taken by his successor, Ezhov, further clarifies Iagoda's oft-cited opinion of April 9, 1937 regarding the work provisions for the nearly 60,000 prisoners released every month from the Corrective Labour Camps (*ispravitel'no-trudovye lageria, ITL*), Corrective Labour Colonies (*izpravitel'no-trudovye kolonii, ITK*), and prisons. Ezhov argued that the NKVD could provide a maximum of 6-7000 ex-prisoners a place of employment because other state companies and agencies generally refused to employ former camp detainees. He also believed that both the labour unions and Communist Party were guilty of ignoring the needs of these employees, refusing to grant advanced payments for food or provide adequate housing.

Among the released prisoners, Ezhov identified a group of "unremedial repeat offenders" (*neispravimye retsidivisty*) who refused the work offered to them by the state and remained involved in criminal activity. According to Ezhov, a disproportionate number of serious crimes, including robbery, murder and burglary, were committed by former offenders upon their release from custody. In the Soviet Union in 1936, criminal convictions consisted of the following: 45.3% for armed robbery, 46.7% for unarmed robbery, 30.5% for cattle thievery and 46.5% for break-ins. That same year, 42% of all arrested robbers, thieves and cattle thieves were repeat offenders, of whom the majority had just recently been released from camp. According to Ezhov, repeat offenders were particularly significant because not only did they constitute the cadre of gangs dedicated to robbery and theft, but many were considered to be mentally unstable as well. Along with a host of practical proposals for the integration of large numbers of released prisoners into the work world, Ezhov recommended that the *retsidvisty* who had served out their criminal sentences, but had not proven to be re-socialisable in camp, not be released but rather sentenced by camp court or *Police Troika* to an additional three years imprisonment. All of

5 | "Казалось бы, что всем, в том числе и работникам суда, должно быть ясно, что преступники-рецидивисты подлежат изоляции в первую очередь." For more detailed information on Iagoda cf. Shearer 2004, 860-862.

the recommendations contained in Ezhov's letter were initially agreed to by Vyshinskii. However, on July 7, 1937, Vyshinskii – affirming the sense of his March campaign in the *Izvestiia* in which criminals were allowed to publicly disassociate themselves from their deeds – distanced himself from Ezhov's letter (Sheinin 1937).

Ezhov's fixation on repeat offenders as the most dangerous criminal group was already reflected in the list of "contingents who are again subject to repression" (*kontingentov podlezhashchikh repressii*) under Order No. 00447 *About repression of former kulaks, criminals, and other anti-Soviet elements* (*O repressirovanii byvshikh kulakov, ugolovnikov i drugikh antisovetskikh elementov*). This preoccupation would become increasingly evident in Circular No. 61,[6] drafted by Ezhov's deputy, M.P. Frinovskii, who was the main person responsible for the planning and implementation of Order No. 00447. This circular was disseminated to all leaders of the regional secret service and police on August 7, 1937.

The circular not only gave detailed directions for both combatting crime in a broader sense and for implementing Order No. 00447, it also reiterated which kind of offenders should be targeted by the *Troikas*. The targeted offenders included the following groups: 1) Felons who had committed armed and violent robbery; 2) Recidivous (habitual) criminals involved in cattle theft, street robbery, or the handling of stolen goods, as well as operators of gin palaces; 3) Recidivists and criminals who had escaped from a prison; 4) Recidivists and other criminals without a permanent residence who were not performing any useful work, and who, even if not charged with a specific crime, maintained contact with the criminal subculture. The third point outlined in the circular called for the transfer of charged persons from the *Police Troikas* to the *Kulak Troikas* and is an almost literal reproduction of paragraph 2 of Iagoda's and Vyshinskii's previously cited *Police Troika* instructions of May 9, 1935.

Through the implementation of the instructions contained within Circular No. 61, some of the sentences that had previously been handled by the *Police Troikas* were transferred to the newly established *Troikas* against Kulaks and other "counterrevolutionary elements." With this transfer came a drastic intensification of sentences, as the *Police Troikas* had only been permitted to issue sentences for convicted criminals of up to five

6 | The Cirkular No. 61 was published for the first time in Ivanov 1995, 52-53. Cf. Junge et al. 2008, 174-175.

years. Frinovskii's directive also recommended that the police implement constant raids (*oblavy*) in the rayons and conduct meticulous examinations of the personal belongings of captured persons so that repeat offenders could not avoid identification. The leader of the Moscow district NKVD, S. F. Redens, brought the consequences of all this into focus in his report on the successes of the Kulak operation when he insinuated the following in his reflections on a conversation between two Kolkhoz peasants from the Riazan' rayon:

Dmitriev (Village of Kanishchevo): These thieves can't be reformed, they need to be liquidated. The bodies of the NKVD have recently assumed the actual purging of thieves from the villages.
Krysanov (Village of Nedostoevo): In our village there are completely unremedial thieves like Aleksandrov, the brothers Zacharov, Mishin and others. These persons can't live without committing a crime. They must be imprisoned for life or liquidated (Junge et al. 2008, 182).[7]

As an explanation for the severe punishment of repeat offenders, Daniel Beer emphasizes that by the end of the 1920s the biological-social discourse of the 19th century had influenced the emergence of the concept of the "socially hostile element" within the Soviet Union (Beer 2008, 164-204). Is it possible that the more frequent occurrence of the term "socially hostile element" in Soviet penal documents in the 1930s and the extreme fixation on the repeat offender during the Great Terror indicate a connection between Lombroso's biological model and the penal policies instituted by the USSR? To this end, sources including the protocols of the extra-judicial bodies of the *Troikas, Dvoikas,* and the *Special Council* warrant further examination by scholars. These documents must also be

7 | "Колхозник д. Канищево Дмитриев заявил: 'Этих воров не исправишь, их надо просто уничтожать. Органы НКВД последнее время действительно взялись за очистку деревни от воров'. Колхозник д. Недостоево Крысанов заявил: 'У нас в деревне есть совершенно неисправимые воры, как Александров, братья Захаровы, Мишин и др. Эти люди не могут жить, не совершая преступления. Их необходимо все время держать в тюрьме, или уничтожать'."

examined alongside sources from the regular judicial bodies, as well as larger-scale evaluations of societal crime trends.[8]

Lombroso after Stalin's Death

In order to come to any meaningful conclusions about the use of a biological model of understanding crime in the Soviet Union, it is necessary to examine the policies of the state in its fight against crime and social deviance after Stalin's death in 1953 (Zubkova and Zhukova 2010; LaPierre 2012). As such, the thesis of this paper can be expanded to argue that in the phase of Nikita Khrushchev's liberalization policy, biological explanations of crime once again gained momentum. An analysis of scientific literature, archival material, and literary works from the period after Stalin's death can provide important insight for scholars on this subject.

Until now, Rolf Binner and I have only concerned ourselves with the literary works written about criminals in the camps by Aleksandr Solzhenitsyn and Varlam Shalamov. Both authors describe professional criminals who, isolated from the mainstream social environment, formed a secret order within the camp with a special code of honour and endogamous recruiting. Antisocial and prepared to fight, they harass the "politicals" in the camp.[9] The Russian philosopher Mikhail Ryklin has also analyzed these influential works by focusing on their portrayal of criminals (Ryklin 2007, 107-124). It is interesting that Ryklin, despite his reservations about the description of the criminal world as impenetrable and homogenous, accepts the basic structure of the position taken by

---

8 | *Kulatskaia troika* and *Natsional'naia troika*: An extra-judicial committee-of-three formed in the capital and in all large administrative units of the USSR, presided over by the respective head of the secret service, the NKVD. Members were the corresponding prosecutors and party secretaries. *Dvoika* is an extrajudicial commission-of-two, which was composed of the federal, regional or local state prosecutor and the current head of the NKVD. *Militseiskaia troika* (*Police troika*): The chairman was usually the local, regional or federal head of the NKVD or his representative, the other members being the corresponding state prosecutor and the leader of the administration of the civil police (*militsiia*), as well as the leader of the responsible departments of the police.

9 | Shalamov 1998; Shalamov 1998a; Solzhenitsyn 1974, 404, 408-427.

Shalamov and Solzhenitsyn and, more specifically, the strict dichotomy between the criminal world and that of the "politicals." In fact, Ryklin strengthens this division and uses it to construct his own thesis of the "affinity of the [Stalinist] regime with the world of criminals" (*ibid.*, 111-112, 117; Solzhenitsyn 1974, 231, 299-300, 408-427).[10]

In establishing the evidence required for his thesis, Ryklin refers to the critiques offered by Shalamov and Solzhenitsyn of Soviet writers such as I. Babel, V. Kaverin, L. Leonov and I. Il'f und E. Petrov, who idealise criminals. Ryklin contends that, out of this long literary tradition, the concept of the criminal as a "socially accepted element" by the working class came into being. With this conceptualization of the criminal, re-education and reformation of these individuals was considered to be possible. Ryklin further asserts that the "massive social upgrading of criminals was a constituent part of Soviet policy" and "the rapprochement of Soviet ideology with this milieu [of criminals] and its idealised exaggeration was no misunderstanding but was inherent in this ideology" (Ryklin 2007, 113, 123; Solzhenitsyn 1974, 408-427). However, it is necessary to point out that Ryklin's understanding of the criminal has a clear weakness. Specifically, the policy of *perekovka* (re-forging) was completely shut down in early 1937 with the closing of the camp newsletter of the same name. The "socially accepted" had long since mutated into the "socially hostile element." A close reading of these texts indicate that Solzhenitsyn, Shalamov, and Ryklin demonized criminals in their descriptions of the Stalinist period. Furthermore, as Binner and I have argued in previous work, it is through the almost hopelessly negative characterization of the criminal world in the work of both Solzhenitsyn and Shalamov that the ideas of social deviance under Stalinism can be identified (Junge 2016).

It is also useful to examine whether the rhetoric of scientists and writers of this time period include biological explanations of the behaviour of criminals in camps, as well as how these writers depict the way that criminality was treated under Stalinism. Through a sample of the materials produced by post-Soviet scientists, literary figures, and representatives of the penal bodies, it is possible to identify praise for the state's fight against criminals and criminality during the Great Terror.[11]

10 | On Solzhenitsyn's position cf. Rittersporn 1991, 231-232.

11 | The former Deputy Police Chief from the city of Ivanovo writes in his 1960s memoirs the following: "While the Society people found themselves in

How is this praise to be explained? Can this dubious compliment for the Stalinist regime be traced back to the authoritarian thought patterns of Stalinism in scientists' and writers' minds or do biological explanations also play a role in their interpretation?

Without Lombroso

In this section, we will further expand upon the reasons that we have excluded biological thinking as a basis for the mass-scale persecution of criminals and social deviance. The forced introduction of socialism had a tremendous impact on rural life, including the disappropriation and deportation of the so-called Kulaks (large-scale farmers), the abolishment of private property, and the forced reorganization of individual agricultural production into large-scale collectives. These changes led to an explosion in crime and social deviance. While there are no supporting statistics published from this time period, the escalation in crime is demonstrated by the fact that Iagoda made fighting crime his top priority – even ahead of fighting the state's political enemies (Shearer 1998, 119-148; Shearer 2009). The class enemy – considered to be a remnant of the "old" society

---

the iron grasp of Ezhov, confined in camps and relentlessly annihilated, they had in fact committed fewer and fewer criminal offenses." "Советский народ, жестко схваченный в 'ежовые' рукавицы, посаженный в лагеря и беспощадно уничтожаемый, действительно все меньше и меньше совершал уголовных деяний" (Shreider 1960, 95-96). In the memorial book from the area of Tver', historian V. A. Smirnov writes: "One must recognize the administration [of the Kalinin's region NKVD] had implemented decisive measures for 'cleansing' our region of criminal elements, that were not even once brought to justice for banditry, armed robbery, murder, theft, or other crimes." "Надо признать, что управление [НКВД по Калининской области] приняло решительные меры по 'отчистке' нашего региона от уголовно-преступных элементов, неоднократно преследовавшихся за бандитизм, кражи и другие преступления уголовного характера" (Kravtsova 2001, 27). In his work, Omsk Historian V. M. Samosudov gives the impression that criminals have accidentally fallen into the politically targeted groups for mass persecution (Samosudov 1998, 67). Solzhenitsyn spread the rumour that "in 1937 the true goniffs, the pillars of the underworld had all been shot." "Главные-то подлинные воры, головка воровского мира, все расстреляны в 37-м году" (Solzhenitsyn 1974, 422).

that supposedly resurfaced during periods of societal reconstruction – was blamed for the misery caused by the socialist transformation. How can we explain the change from the regime's typical interpretation of social deviance to the relentless combat of criminality during the Great Terror? In our research to date, we have focused on the unsuccessful fight of the People's Commissar of Internal Affairs (Iagoda) and the failure of the re-forging policy (*perekovka*) toward the "socially near elements." We would like to now add another line of argumentation. Specifically, at the beginning of the 1930s, a phase of "nationalisation" (*ogosudarstvlenie*) was already underway. This process was governed by a strong, unifying, and ideologically oriented process, which was transferred to state institutions and was symbolized by the *Short History of the VKP(b)* (*Kratkii kurs istorii VKP(b)*) of 1938. As a consequence, the Soviet state, which had become increasingly entangled with the state party, regulated the economy and society through the use of state institutions from the beginning of the 1930s.

With regard to combatting crime, these changes paved the way for the leader of the Extraordinary Commission, the infamous Cheka, Felix Dzerzhinskii, to implement his own approach. Already in 1924, Dzerzhinskii had characterized the attempt to rehabilitate and re-educate criminals as a "liberal silver strangling wire" (*liberal'nye kaniteli*; Petrov 2004, 582-583).

At that time, Dzerzhinskii was already opposed to a "class bonus" for criminals. He understood punishment as protection for the power of the workers and peasants, rather than as a corrective exercise. From his point of view, the Soviet republic could not invest large sums of money in dealing with its criminals. These individuals, according to Dzerzhinskii, were to remain separated from the general population in remote locations. To counter crime, he advocated a "method of short, crushing blows" (*po metodu korotkikh, sokrushitel'nykh udarov*; *ibid.*, 582-583). It can be argued, then, that Dzerzhinskii took a more classically conservative position on crime.

At first glance it appears that the biological viewpoint plays no role here. However, with a closer and more systematic investigation it can be argued that the policy laid out by Dzerzhinskii can be characterized as a vehicle through which biological thinking in Russia was transported from the 19th into the 20th century.

Without the Criminal

There is yet another way by which an attempt can be made to explain both the biological and the sociological approach to understanding crime and other social deviance. In this approach, the criminal is explicitly classified among the *political* opponents of the Bolsheviks. This particular approach to understanding criminality denies that the struggle of this group bears social-technological features or that the Soviet state from the beginning could not sufficiently distinguish between *social* and *political* deviance. To this end, David Shearer argues that there was a politicization of the struggle against social deviants.

In our previous work Rolf Binner and I agree with the approach taken by Arch Getty, Gabor Rittersporn, and Viktor Zemskov (Junge 2016). In their work, these three scholars argue that the system works, "to separate ordinary criminality from genuine opposition to the system as well as from other reasons for which people were subjected to penal repression" (Getty et al. 1993, 1033). This perspective suggests the value of investigating whether, and, if so, how and why, the regime distinguished between political and non-political offenders. With reference to state sources, these authors establish that an important function of the camp system was, along with fending off real and imagined opposition, to suppress social deviance (*ibid.*, 1034, 1035, 1044).

Summary

The goal of this paper was to revisit the work of Rolf Binner and myself and to explore the validity of our previous inclusions using new archival material. In doing so, we hope to open a new forum for discussion about whether biological thought systems could have influenced the treatment of social deviance during the Great Terror in the Soviet Union. According to the evidence presented here, official positions on the subject cannot be relied upon and so further attention must be given to the activities of the penal bodies during this time period. Within recent scholarship, there have already been a few attempts to investigate the biological heredity of "class" (McDonald 2011; Viola 1993). Therefore, it appears legitimate to test whether state policies, with respect to criminals and social deviants, were also influenced by biological thinking in criminology and/or in the penal bodies (e.g. secret service, police, justice). Even in the face of the extreme deterioration of the social situation and in spite of the changes in the official discourses on crime, it is possible that biological thinking could have shaped state policies.

In addition to questions about the meaning of biological models of explanation in the fight against crime and social deviance in the Soviet Union, it is also important to take note of the interpretations of Stalinist persecution policy during the Great Terror that emerged in the 1990s. Influenced by conceptions of National Socialism and, on the basis of weak empirical investigations of mass persecutions between 1937 and 1938, some scholars believe that an "ethnicisation of penal policy in Stalinism" and even racist and genocidal structure can be identified (Baberowski 2012, 345, 352; Weitz 2002b, 6). Such far-reaching biological assessments are not very convincing, however, since such policies could only have been realized with the assistance of state structures and its attendant ideology.

The fundamental issue that scholars face in a discussion regarding the persecution policies of the Soviet Union is that the motives of the penal policies must be uncovered solely from their outcomes. This problem is caused by the fact that there exists no data or documents that outline (even at a theoretical level) the ways in which the party, the state, and/or penal bodies, legitimized policies related to social deviance. Additionally, it is also necessary for scholars to consider that biological explanations of crime do not necessarily require racist approaches. This is also true for an interest in the psychology of the criminal, or what today would be referred to as social pathology and psycho-pathology.

Our objective with the renewed focus on the investigation of the influence of anthropological, biological, and sociological approaches to the phenomenon of crime and other social deviance in the era of Soviet enlightenment in the 1920s and 1930s is to overcome a general impasse.

Subject of future work will be to focus on three aspects of the debate about the treatment of criminality during the Great Terror: the discourse on crime, penal practice, and penal bodies. The interplay between these three domains should be explored through a comparison between the Soviet Union and its western and southern border regions – and part of the empire – and the Soviet Union with Ukraine, Belorussia and Georgia.

Three strands in the formation of knowledge and definitions on and of crime stand in the foreground: a) philosophical-intellectual statements; b) social-theoretical and political theories; c) legislative deliberations (jurisprudence and the establishment of laws) and the executive forces (criminology, criminalistics, police, and secret police) on crime and social deviance. In order to anchor theory in practice and/or to test its impact on society, we have included the history of the sanctions on crime. We ask, in what ways and how severely were crime and social deviance punished and how has that changed? What influence have debates and theoretical deliberations had on strategies of marginalisation and punishment? Through examining the theory and the penal practices related to criminality and social deviance, it is clear that special attention to the handling of crime is necessary.

References

Baberowski, J. 2012. *Verbrannte Erde. Stalins Herrschaft der Gewalt.* Munich: Beck.

Baumann, I. 2006. *Dem Verbrechen auf der Spur. Eine Geschichte der Kriminologie und Kriminalpolitik in Deutschland 1880-1980.* Göttingen: Wallstein.

Beer, D. 2008. *Renovating Russia: The Human Sciences and the Fate of Liberal Modernity, 1880-1930.* Ithaca and London: Cornell University Press.

Ennker, B. 2014. "Sovetskii narod, stalinskii rezhim i konstitutsiia 1936 goda v politicheskoi istorii Sovetskogo Soiuza: issledovatel'skie podkhody i predvaritel'nye vyvody." *Soviet History Discussion Papers,* 3. <http://www.perspectivia.net/publikationen/shdp/ennker_narod> (last accessed 18 January 2016).

Gernet, M. 1974a. "Izuchenie prestupnosti v SSSR. Istoricheskie ocherki." Gernet, M., *Izbrannye proizvedeniia.* Moscow: Iuridicheskaia literatura, 595-613.

Gernet, M. 1974b. "Predislovie k rabote 'Prestupnyj mir Moskvy'." Gernet, M., *Izbrannye proizvedeniia.* Moscow: Iuridicheskaia literatura, 401-437.

Getty, J. A. et al. 1993. "Victims of the Soviet Penal System in the Pre-war Years." *American Historical Review* 98, no. 3, 1017-1049.

Hagenloh, P. M. 1999. "'Socially Harmful Elements' and the Great Terror." Fitzpatrick, Sh. (ed.), *Stalinism. New Directions.* London: Routledge, 286-308.

Hirsch, F. 2002. "Race without the Practice of Racial Politics." *Slavic Review* 61, no. 1, 44-53.

Ivanov, V. A. 1995. *Organy gosudarstvennoi bezopasnosti i massovye repressii na Severo-Zapade v 30-50-ye gody.* Sankt Peterburg.

Junge, M. et. al. 2008. *Vertikal' bol'shogo terrora. Istoriia operatsii po prikazu NKVD N° 00447.* Moscow: AIRO XXI.

Junge, M. 2010a. "Delo 'ugolovnikov'. Sledstvennoe delo na invalidov P. i T. (dokumenty)." Binner, R. et al. (eds.), *Massovye repressii v Altaiskom krae 1937-1938.* Moscow: ROSSPEN, 215-275.

Junge, M. 2010b. "Sotsial'no-technologicheskii aspekt prikaza N° 00447." Junge, M. et al. (eds.), *"Cherez trupy vraga na blago naroda." Kulatskaia operatsiia v Ukrainskoi SSR 1937-1941.* Vol. 2: *Vtoroi etap repressii. Zavershenie Bol'shogo terrora i vosstanovlenie "sotsialisticheskoi zakonnosti".* Moscow: ROSSPEN, 209-244.

Junge, M. 2016. "Repression of the Social Body." Junge, M. *Stalin's Mass Repression and the Cold War Paradigm.* New York: Kindle e-book.

Kravtsova, E. I. (ed.) 2001. *Kniga pamiati zhertv politicheskikh repressii Kalininskoi oblasti. Martirolog 1937-1938,* vol. 1. Tver': Gosudarstvennyi memorial'nyi kompleks "Mednoe".

LaPierre, B. 2012. *Hooligans in Khrushchev's Russia: Defining, Policing, and Producing Deviance during the Thaw.* Madison: The University of Wisconsin Press.

Leimon, A. 2002. "Without a 'Concept'? Race as Discursive Practice." *Slavic Review* 61, no. 1, 54–61.

McDonald, T. 2011. *Face to the Village: The Riazan Countryside under Soviet Rule, 1921-1930.* Toronto: University of Toronto Press.

Petrov, N. (ed.) 2004. *Istoriia Stalinskogo GULAGa.* Vol. 2: *Karatel'naia sistema. Struktura i kadry.* Moscow: ROSSPEN.

Rimmel, L. A. 2000. "A Microcosmos of Terror, or Class Warfare in Leningrad. The March 1935 Exile of 'Alien Elements'." *Jahrbücher für Geschichte Osteuropas* 48, no. 4, 528-551.

Rittersporn, G. 1991. "From the GULAG of the Memorial to the History of Penal Policy in the Soviet Union. 1933–1953." Rittersporn, G. *Stalinist Simplifications and Soviet Complications. Social Tensions and Political Conflicts in the USSR. 1933–1953.* Chur: Harwood Academic, 229-318.

Rozanov, Ia. S. (ed.) 1924. *Problema prestupnosti.* Kiev: Gosudarstvennoe izdatel'stvo Ukrainy.

Ryklin, M. 2007. "Der 'verfluchte Orden'. Šalamov, Solženicyn und die Kriminellen." *Osteuropa* 57, no. 6, 107-124.

Samosudov, V. M. 1998. *Bol'shoi terror v Omskom Priirtysh'e 1937-1938.* Omsk: Omskii gosudarstvennyi universitet.

Sheinin, L. 1937. "Iavka s povinnoi." *Izvestiia,* 15.03., 4.

Shalamov, V. 1998. "Krasnyi krest." Shalamov, V. *Sobranie sochinenii v chetyrekh tomakh,* vol. 1. Moscow: Khudozhestvennaia literatura, Vagrius, 141-148.

Shalamov, V. 1998a. "Ocherki prestupnogo mira." Shalamov, V. *Sobranie sochinenii v chetyrekh tomakh,* vol. 2. Moscow: Khudozhestvennaia literatura, Vagrius, 7-100.

Shearer, D. 1998. "Crime and Social Disorder in Stalin's Russia. A Reassessment of the Great Retreat and the Origins of Mass Repression." *Cahiers du Monde russe* 39, no. 1-2, 119-148.

Shearer, D. 2004. "Elements Near and Alien. Passportisation, Policing and Identity in the Stalinist State, 1932-1952." *The Journal of Modern History* 76, 835-881.

Shearer, D. 2009. *Policing Stalin's Socialism: Repression and Social Order in the Soviet Union, 1924-1953.* New Haven: Yale University Press.

Solomon, P. 1996. *Soviet Criminal Justice under Stalin.* Cambridge: Cambridge University Press.

Solzhenitsyn, A. 1974. *Der Archipel GULAG. 1918-1956. Versuch einer künstlerischen Bewältigung, Folgeband.* Bern: Scherz.

Shreider, M. P. 1960. "Zapiski chekista-operativnika." Archiv NIPTs "Memorial-Moscow".

Vert, N. et al. (eds.) 2004. *Istoriia Stalinskogo GULaga.* Vol. 1: *Massovye repressii v SSSR.* Moscow: ROSSPEN.

Viola, L. 1993. "The Second Coming. The Class Enemies in the Soviet Countryside." Getty, J. A. and Manning, R. Th. (eds.), *Stalinist Terror. New Perspectives.* Cambridge: Cambridge University Press.

Wagner, P. 2002. *Hitlers Kriminalisten. Die deutsche Kriminalpolizei und der Nationalsozialismus zwischen 1920 und 1960.* Munich: Beck.

Weiner, A. 2002. "Nothing but Certainty." *Slavic Review* 61, no. 1, 44-53.

Weitz, E. D. 2002b. "Racial Politics without the Concept of Race. Re-evaluating Soviet Ethnic and National Purges." *Slavic Review* 61, no. 11, 1-29.

Yekelchyk, S. 1998. "The Making of a 'Proletarian Capital.' Patterns of Stalinist Social Policy in Kiev in the mid-1930s." *Europe-Asia Studies* 50, no. 7, 1229-1244.

Zajicek, B. 2008. "Review – Daniel Beer, Renovating Russia: The Human Sciences and the Fate of Liberal Modernity, 1880-1930." <http://historypsychiatry.com/2010/08/10/review-daniel-beer-renovating-russia-the-human-sciences-and-the-fate-of-liberal-modernity-1880-1930-ithaca-cornell-university-press-2008/> (last accessed 2 February 2016).

Zubkova, E. Iu. and Zhukova, N. Ju. (eds.) 2010. *Na "kraiu" Sovetskogo obshchestva. Sotsial'nye marginaly kak ob''ekt gosudarstvennoi politiki. 1945-1960-e* gg. Moscow: ROSSPEN.

Concepts of the Criminal in the Discourse of "Perekovka"

Anne Hartmann

In the first half of the 1930s in the Soviet Union the slogan *perekovka* (re-forging) was used to propagate a successful re-education of lawbreakers by the Soviet penal system. Borrowed from the vocabulary of steel industry, the concept was very much in the spirit of the time. Just like nature was supposed to be subdued and transformed by Stalin's five-year plan, so people, too, were to be moulded according to a master design. "Criminal prisoners" were to turn into "dedicated believers and practitioners of Soviet ideology" (Draskoczy 2012, 30-31). In practical terms, the process was taking place in the so-called correctional labor camps for adults (*ispravitel'no-trudovye lageria*, ITL) as well as labor colonies for children and adolescents. Both systems were operated by the Joint State Political Administration (OGPU), which meant Chekists would double as guards and as educators.

A newspaper for the Belbaltlag, the labor camp complex whose inmates were working on the construction of the White Sea-Baltic Canal (the Belomor Canal), was actually called *Perekovka*, while similar publications in other institutions bore the titles *The Voice of Perekovka* (*Golos perekovki*), *Perekovka Beyond the Polar Circle* (*Zapoliarnaia perekovka*), *Perekovka at the Construction Front* (*Perekovka na fronte stroitel'stva*) and so on.[1] The then famous, now infamous *History of the Construction of the White Sea-Baltic Canal* (*Belomorsko-Baltiiskii kanal imeni Stalina. Istoriia stroitel'stva* [henceforth *BBK*], 1934), edited by Maksim Gor'kii, Leopol'd Averbakh and Semen Firin, drew its entire educational pathos from the idea of

1 | On camp newspapers, see Gorcheva 1996; Fischer von Weikersthal 2011; Hedeler 2011.

re-forging. Anton Makarenko[2] and Matvei Pogrebinskii[3] developed the idea practically in their work in communes for homeless adolescents and juvenile delinquents, and theoretically in their writings. The term also found its way into the official discourse on crime policy. It was a key concept in what became "a sort of bible of Soviet penal philosophy" (Draskoczy 2014, 44) – Ida Averbakh's treatise *From Crime to Labor* (*Ot prestupleniia k trudu*, 1936). Andrei Vyshinskii, Prosecutor General of the USSR, also mentions the term in his introduction to the book.

Perekovka as a Flagship-Project

As a theoretical concept and as practice, *perekovka* is associated with that short time span in which the Gulag was presented insistently as a showcase of the Soviet correctional system to the public both at home and abroad.[4] Films, posters, documentaries, poems and theater plays were produced, celebrating the "correction" and social rehabilitation through labor. The glossy magazine *USSR in Construction* (*SSSR na stroike*), published in several languages, even dedicated a whole issue to the topic (12/1933). The highlight of this publicity campaign, however, was without a doubt the *History of the Construction of the White Sea–Baltic Canal*.[5] The Belbaltlag

2 | Makarenko claimed to have "reforged around three thousand people" (Makarenko 1958, 466). On Makarenko's educational views and his attitude to the discourse around the Belomor Canal project see Dobrenko 2007, 183-207.

3 | The Bolshevo commune, managed by Pogrebinskii, was a showpiece of the Soviet propaganda (Hillig 2006; Gladysh 2004), aimed in particular at foreign visitors. It was mentioned in a complimentary tone by many renowned intellectuals, for example Henry Barbusse, Martin Anderson-Nexø, George Bernard Shaw, Gustav Regler, Oskar Maria Graf, André Malraux, André Gide (David-Fox 2012, 169-70; Hartmann 2012a, 101-102).

4 | An additional purpose of the campaign was to work against Western sanctions. The USA and Great Britain in particular threatened with the boycott of Soviet produce made by camp inmates or forced laborers (Applebaum 2003, 97-99; Klein 1995/96, 55-56).

5 | A shorter version of the book appeared also in English: The White Sea Canal. Being an Account of the Construction of the New Canal Between the White Sea and the Baltic Sea (1935).

labor camp was the model example of a re-forging of inmates – but also of writers.[6]

In August 1933, a brigade of 120 writers was sent to Karelia in order to witness the success of the canal construction and of the re-socialization of criminals.[7] 36 of them, including such well-known authors as Aleksei Tolstoi, Mikhail Zoshchenko, Vsevolod Ivanov, Valentin Kataev, Vera Inber and Viktor Shklovskii, became contributors to the *BBK* chronicle. Just like the construction of the waterway, the writers' collective work was finished in record time, and a deluxe edition was presented to the delegates of the 17th Congress of the Communist Party of the Soviet Union in January 1934. A less pretentious edition saw light a few months later. Most of the illustrations were by the avant-garde photographer Aleksandr Rodchenko, who had been sent to the site a few months earlier, as it were, "on probation." Other intellectuals submitted requests to be included in the trip to the northern site for the simple reason that for them, participation in the *perekovka* project offered a chance to clean their own biographies. Such, for example, was the case of the young Konstantin Simonov, whose ambition at the time was to renounce his aristocratic background and to create a new identity for himself as a proletarian writer.[8] Nikolai Ustrialov, having returned to the USSR from emigration in 1935, saw *perekovka* as a chance to fulfil the personal duty to re-educate himself, so as to make sure his consciousness was in line with the policy of the party (Goldt 2005, 58).

There was something special about the writers' brigade of 1933. The journey was part of the measures aimed at transforming the literary field after the dissolution of literary groups in 1932 (Chartreux 2006, 175-180).

---

6 | The practice of *perekovka* had supposedly been tested in numerous labor colonies and communes of the GPU, but it was only at the construction of the Belomor Canal that it was realized "so boldly, on such a grand scale" (*BBK*, 12).

7 | Delegating writers to production sites and major construction projects of the country was part of the five year plan. What was distinct about this particular project is the hereto unheard-of magnitude.

8 | Following the publication in 1934 of a poem about the re-education of camp inmates the publisher agreed for Simonov to spend four weeks at the Belomor Canal, where he was a contributor to the journal *Perekovka* (Figes [2]2008, 299-303). Many writers, for example Andrei Platonov, had no luck with their requests to be sent to the site (Epelboin 2009, 261), while others, like Mikhail Bulgakov, categorically rejected participation in such initiatives (Bulgakova 2004, 149).

The 120 writers were supposed to leave behind past feuds and become a collective (Avdeenko 1989, 13). As Gor'kii explained in his address before the shock workers of the Belomor Canal project, they were expected to encourage the writers to become part of the work process and to overcome personal aberrations, which in its turn would have a positive effect on the fruit of their literary labor:[9]

> You've lifted the spirits of some hundred men of letters who visited the Canal and saw your work. You pushed them into this stream of living labor, brought them closer to the work process, clearly showed them both yourselves and what you had done. I think that many of these comrade writers, those of them who were hesitating in the fog of incomprehension or else had no wish to understand what is happening in our country, I hope that having been introduced to the Canal [...], these writers will have acquired something, too, and what they have acquired will find a vivid expression in literature (Gor'kii 1953d, 74).[10]

The writers fell captive to the discursive machinery of *perekovka*, which at the same time they were supposed to serve with their writings. The purpose of the collectively authored volume was to both document and shape the new consciousness. It appeared in the series *The History of Factories and Plants* (*Istoriia fabrik i zavodov*), whose editor-in-chief Gor'kii was and which was set up in order to immortalize the achievements of the new regime, to raise reality to a new level, and to set standards for the future by historicizing the present (Klein 1995/96, 73-76; Zhuravlev 1997; Clark 2004).[11]

---

9 | The address was also cited in the book (*BBK*, 595-597). On the "reformation" of Soviet writers in the 1920s-1930s see also Shubinskii 2006.

10 | "Вы подняли настроение сотки литераторов, которые были на канале и видели вашу работу. Вы вдвинули их в этот поток живой работы, приблизили их к трудовому процессу, воочию показали им и себя и то, что вами сделано. Я думаю, что многие из тех товарищей литераторов, которые колебались в тумане непонимания или не имели желания понять происходящее в нашей стране, после знакомства с каналом [...], писатели тоже что-то приобретут, и это приобретение ярко отразится в литературе."

11 | On the principle of "pious fraud," heroization, and revolutionary romanticism in Gor'kii, see Günther 1993, 39-40, 104-108; Heller 1975, 124-127. The

It is no coincidence that socialist realism, with its idea that the writers' function and purpose was to be "engineers of the human soul," was introduced at around the same time – and also under Gor'kii's guidance. When the authors at the First All-Union Congress of Soviet Writers (1934) were entrusted with the task of "transforming the human consciousness in the spirit of Socialism" (*peredelki soznaniia liudei v dukhe sotsializma*; Zhdanov 1934, 5), this meant that they were virtually assigned the roles of Chekists. At the same time, Gor'kii called OGPU officers "engineers of the re-forging of human souls" (*inzhenerami perekovki dush*; Gor'kii 1953d, 74), thus comparing them, in a kind of mirror gesture, to true writers (Dobrenko 2007, 158). Tellingly, Gor'kii conceptualized *perekovka* in aesthetic categories, as an "epic of the proletariat" (*eposom proletariata*; Gor'kii 1953b, 509).

Ultimately, *perekovka* can be regarded as a model for the whole society, because the project of a mental transformation applied to all Soviet citizens, just as coercive labor (*prinuditel'nyi trud*) and labor coercion (*prinuzhdenie k trudu*) were two sides of the same coin in the 1930s. In terms of the labor organization, the distribution of privileges, the management of cultural life and even the layout of the newspapers, the camp was functioning as a double of the Soviet world outside. According to Jacques Rossi, it was an "exact embodiment of the state, which created it."[12] Seen from a different angle, the camp as a "factory of human beings" and a "school of work" was paradigmatic for the entire country.

---

collection on the labor commune in Bolshevo *Members of the Bolshevo Commune* (*Bolshevtsy*, 1936) also appeared in the series *The History of Factories and Plants*.

12 | "[...] советскии ГУЛАГ был [...] самым точным воплощением создавшего его государства" (Rossi 1994, 178). In the words of Ivan Solonevich "there was little difference between the camp and 'free life' outside. [...] Whatever is happening in the camp, is also happening out there. And the other way around." "Ничем существенным лагерь от 'воли' не отличается. [...] Все то, что происходит в лагере, происходит и на воле. И наоборот" (Solonevich [1938], 8). Cf. Geller 1994, 111-112.

Political Police and Literature

The metaphor of *perekovka* is as catchy as it is vague. In any case, its persuasive potential must have been remarkable because it encompassed literary, pedagogical, and technological beliefs of the first five-year plan, from the writers and Chekists as engineers to the delinquents as "human raw material" (*chelovecheskoe syr'e*) (*BBK*, 609) which was being remolded from scratch in the camps. However, as the author Mikhail Prishvin noted in his diary in 1933, thieves and petty criminals would have interpreted the metaphor differently, namely in the word's more direct sense of a re-shoeing of horses whose old shoes make them limp. The new shoes might make the horse run faster, but it is still the same horse (Prishvin 2009, 205).[13]

The coining and distribution of this metaphor predominantly through writers (and OGPU members with literary ambitions) is no coincidence. Since his spectacular visit at the Solovetskii Islands labor camp in 1929 (Guski 2009; David-Fox 2012, 142-174), Gor'kii had been downright obsessed with the idea of being able to defeat the untamed, hostile nature, including human nature, through labor and discipline. Gor'kii, who found the idea of "educating people in camps through labor remarkably healthy and beautiful,"[14] was a friend and patron of the pedagogue Anton Makarenko (after whom a labor colony was actually named) and of Matvei Pogrebinskii, head of the OGPU labor commune at Bolshevo, which bore the name of the secret police chief Genrikh Iagoda.[15]

Although Gor'kii did not take part in the writers' trip to the White Sea-Baltic Canal, he was nevertheless the initiator of, and the mastermind

13 | Even though he was not included in the writers' team, Prishvin went to the north of his own initiative. However, his proposed contribution to the *BBK* chronicle was rejected by Gor'kii as too long and (ideologically) vague (Prishvin 2009, 929-930).

14 | "[...] идея перевоспитать людей в лагерях трудом – замечательно здоровая и красивая" (Gor'kii 1953c, 63). Here Gor'kii quotes approvingly the autobiography of a former delinquent.

15 | Gor'kii also wrote the introduction to Pogrebinskii's *The OGPU Labor Commune* (*Trudovaia kommuna OGPU*, 1928) and reviewed the collection *Members of the Bolshevo Commune* (Literaturnaia gazeta, No. 46, 1936). On Pogrebinskii, see David-Fox 2012, 160-173; Podurets 2013.

behind, the idea of the book project as well as of the conceptualization of *perekovka*. The most senior official in charge of the practical implementation of re-forging in the camp was Semen Firin, since 1932 Chief of Construction of the Canal; later he was appointed head of the Dmitlag at the Moskva-Volga Canal and deputy head of the Gulag.[16] Firin, who in the words of Romain Rolland was inspired by a "police-like idealism" (*l'idéalisme policier*; Rolland 1992, 181), saw himself as a connoisseur of literature and promoted artistic talents in the camp.[17] Leopol'd Averbakh, the third publisher of the book, may not have been a particularly renowned writer, but he was well known – and dreaded – as a RAPP official. His sister Ida Averbakh, who authored the above mentioned book on the reeducation of delinquents through labor, was married to Genrikh Iagoda, who in turn was in close contact with Gor'kii, not least because he was chasing after the writer's daughter-in-law 'Timosha' (Nadezhda) Peshkova. The interconnection between political police and literature is greatly symptomatic of the *perekovka* project in general, beyond this biographical association.

Social and Biological Determinism

One might regard *perekovka* as a euphemistic or even as a cynical term used to gloss over the exploitation of inmates in inhuman working conditions. One might also feel tempted to follow the example of Aleksandr Solzhenitsyn in his groundbreaking *Gulag Archipelago* in condemning the writers who stooped to such glorification of slave work.[18] Solzhenitsyn's merciless settlement of accounts with the "misanthropic fantasies"

16 | On Firin see, in particular, N. Fedorov's contributions.

17 | Cf. Firin's report to the Communist Academy (1934) and the obituary he wrote for Gor'kii (1936).

18 | Solzhenitsyn's monumental work can even be read as a direct response to the Belomor collection (Chartreux 2006, 170) - after all, he writes in the preface: "Material for this book was also supplied by thirty-six Soviet writers, led by Maksim Gor'kii, authors of the disgraceful book on the White Sea Canal, which was the first text in Russian literature to glorify slave labor" (Solzhenitsyn 1973b, XII). "Материал для этой книги также представили тридцать советских писателей во главе с Максимом Горьким – авторы позорной книги о Беломорканале, впервые в русской литературе восславившей рабский труд" (Solzhenitsyn 1973a, 11).

(*chelovekonenavistnicheskie legendy*) of the master ideologues of the canal construction (Solzhenitsyn 1974, 80) has been taken up in numerous works of scholarship, often "without the researchers first reading the text [of the *BBK*]" (Draskoczy 2014, 13). Since the appearance of Solzhenitsyn's scorching critique more differentiated analyses have seen light, addressing the authors' motivations as well as the process of the book's production and its function.[19] The creation and development of Soviet prison camps, as well as their reorganization according to economic principles in 1928/29, have also been analyzed in depth.[20] But while scholars were focusing mostly on the ideological and aesthetic aspect (*perekovka* as propaganda and fiction), or on the historic dimension (Belbaltlag, Dmitlag and other camps as settings for, or phases in, the history of the Gulag), other aspects have remained neglected. For example: How did the officials in charge explain the fact that crime persisted in the socialist society? Where did the contemporaries stand on the "nature versus nurture" debate? In how far were these perspectives new, and to what extent were they a development of more traditional perceptions? And what understanding of the criminal was actually behind the label *perekovka*?

Addressing these questions necessitates taking a closer look at earlier Russian and Soviet debates on criminal behavior. In retrospect, it is remarkable that around the turn of the century the debates on outlaws and criminals were being conducted in Europe at such a high international level and that the engagement with these topics was so intense. Especially influential were the theories of the Italians Cesare Lombroso and Enrico Ferri. Their impact on criminology and criminal anthropology in Russia was unquestionably significant, as has been shown by Daniel Beer, Marina Mogil'ner and others. However, in Russia the biologistic emphasis of the Italians was not as popular; there, more emphasis was

19 | On the writers' delegation and the collected volume see especially Carleton 1994; Klein 1995/96; Günther 1996; Ruder 1998. On the Canal as a goal of travel and pilgrimage cf. Balina 2000, 902-904; Frank 2009, 256-258. On *perekovka* as a socialist realist master plot in the autobiographic narratives of the inmates who wrote about their transformation from delinquents to good Soviet people cf. Draskoczy 2012; 2014, 20-75.

20 | On the particularities and the most important stages of the Soviet camp system see especially Stettner 1996; Ivanova 2001; Applebaum 2003; Jakobson and Smirnow 2006; Scherbakowa.

placed on the significance of social factors in the development of criminal tendencies. According to Daniel Beer, "the majority of Russian clinicians accepted the existence of physical stigmata among criminals; they simply disputed Lombroso's interpretation of their origins" (Beer 2008, 113). In their view, the stigmata pointed less to an atavistic stage of development and were more indicative of the deformities of the body social, and the fact that socioeconomic conditions can be changed was the foundation of the Russian school's belief in the "reformability of the deviant." In Beer's words, "the Russian commitment to social reform extended to the fervent belief that virtually no criminals were immune to healing influences, coercive or otherwise" (*ibid.*, 129).

Hence the confidence that crime could be defeated (Binner and Junge 2010, 214; Beer 2008, 121), a conviction which after the October Revolution was to turn into an optimistic prognosis that in the new social conditions, with the abolition of the corrupting capitalist system, crime would become totally extinct and the society would soon be able to do without prisons at all. But first, criminal law had to be reformed. This was soon done. The RSFSR Criminal Code and the Correctional Labor Code (introduced in 1922 and 1924, respectively) were quite a progressive set of laws that had been prepared over a relatively short time period. The Commissariat of Justice (Narkomiust / NKIu) in particular,[21] whose influence, however, was gradually weakening,[22] promoted "re-education" or "improvement" as the goal of criminal punishment.

In opposition to the West, which according to Soviet officials focused exclusively on making prisoners feel the full power of vengeance and retaliation, on subjecting them to suffering and humiliation, in Russia, it was all about re-socialization. Terms such as 'crime' and 'expiation'

---

21 | Numerous "bourgeois specialists" were still working there (Ivanova 2001, 28). See also Dallin and Nicolaevsky 1948, 134-143; Solomon 1980, 195-201.

22 | In the 1920s the domains of responsibility of penal authorities were redefined multiple times, and turf wars would sometimes erupt. In the competition between Narkomiust and NKVD concerning the management of penal institutions NKVD came out the winner (Stettner 1996, 43-87; Jakobson and Smirnow 2006 3-17; Scherbakowa, 591-596). Another pillar of the system of penal institutions were the camps managed by the Cheka and its successors GPU and OGPU, where from the very beginning the system's concern was not with "improvement," but with the isolation and concentration of political opposition.

vanished from the official vocabulary. Instead, there was talk of "protection" or of the "social defense of the proletarian state" (Shirvindt and Utevskii 1927, 63-69; ²1931, 16). It was not just a matter of changing labels. Those very people who had suffered for their convictions under the old regime, wanted to do away with "the old courts and laws, [...] prisons and katorgas" once and for all (Dallin and Nicolaevsky 1948, 136). Consequently, the attributes of the tsarist penal practice – solitary confinement, handcuffs, chains and food deprivation – were outlawed. According to the visions of the Bolshevist judiciary, "socially near" individuals who had gone to the bad under the influence of their environment were supposed to be re-formed into useful members of society. In this, the most important instrument was the so-called "correctional labor" (*ispravitel'nyi trud*). As early as in 1919, in a declaration made at a congress of the Communist Party, labor was proclaimed to be "a universal remedy that reforms and educates" (*ibid.*, 137).

Until the end of the New Economic Policy rather progressive opinions prevailed in the Soviet judiciary (though not where political prisoners were concerned – we will return to this point later).[23] According to Evsei Shirvindt, head of the NKVD's Central Directorate of Prisons, the treatment of law breakers in prisons, labor colonies and other places of confinement had to be based on principles of lenience, differentiation, and individualization (Shirvindt 1925). The severity of penalties was downgraded.[24] Now, besides prison sentences, there were also fines or the option of continuing to be employed at the same work place for a lower wage. In 1923, only one out of every four convicted delinquents was sent to prison. Once in prison, the delinquents who proved their enthusiasm for labor could be eligible for parole. In addition, courses in general education and literacy were developed and inmates had opportunities to join a professional apprenticeship program. Early release and release on amnesty were common practices, though the reasons were less humanitarian and had more to do with the chronic overcrowding and underfinancing of the prisons (Ivanova 2001, 29-30; Applebaum 2003, 68).

It might seem as if Lombroso's influence had been definitely overcome by that time. In any case, there was hardly an essay or treatise that did

23 | On the coexistence of terror and penal pedagogy see Hartmann 2012b, 12-15.

24 | For a discussion of individual measures, see Solomon 1980, 197-198.

not critically distance itself from his theories.[25] And yet, as Daniel Beer emphasizes, sociological and biological theories of deviance are by no means mutually exclusive. They have in common the ideas of hygiene and contamination (and thus isolation) as a basis to the ordering of society (Beer 2008, 189-191), as well as the denial of free will (*ibid.*, 177). The actions of a human being are considered to be determined by factors beyond his or her conscious control, be it through the environment and/or through biopsychic factors. A collection of essays that appeared in 1925 clearly stated the following:

As our approach is grounded in scientific determinism, and since we reject the so-called "free will," being convinced instead that each step, each thought are a result of a complex interworking of influences, both social and biological, on our body, we cannot, of course, look at a delinquent as if he were guided by an evil will [...]. Rather, we see in him, in his personality and in his actions, a product of the environment, of the conditions of individual development etc., all of which together are determined, of course, by the existing social-economic relations (Meditsinskaja inspektsiia, 3).[26]

Thus, combined with Marxian sociology, Lombroso's criminology lived on in various studies and documents,[27] and especially in the remarkable institution of the Cabinets for the Study of Crime, whose ambition was

25 | The authors of the *History of the Belomor Canal* also distanced themselves from Lombroso very clearly: "It is wonderful that Lombroso's teaching is being for the first time practically refuted in the country." "Замечательно, что Ломброзо впервые практически опровергается в стране" (*BBK*, 594-595).

26 | "Поскольку мы стоим на почве научного детерминизма, отрицая так называемую 'свободу воли', считая, что каждый наш шаг, каждая мысль является результатом сложного взаимодействия влияний, социальных и биологических, на наш организм, мы не можем, конечно, смотреть на преступника, как на носителя злой воли [...] а видим в нем, в его личности и поступках, продукт среды, условий индивидуального развития и т. д., что в сумме обусловливается, конечно, существующими общественно-экономическими отношениями."

27 | The "influence of Lombrosian and hereditarian theories" was apparent even in official papers, for example, in a 1924 circular of the People's Commissariat of Justice (Berman and Hunt 1950, 642).

to analyze criminality in order to annihilate it altogether.[28] Such "Crime Cabinets" (under slightly different designations)[29] were established already in the early 1920s in some larger cities such as Petrograd/Leningrad (where the first steps in this direction were taken in 1918), Moscow, Saratov, Rostov-on-Don, Minsk, Khar'kov, Kiev, Odessa, Baku, Tbilisi. A branch was opened even at the Solovki prison camp (Lichatschow 1997, 80-92). The State Institute for the Study of Crime and the Criminal under the auspices of the NKVD was founded in Moscow in 1925 for a coordination of different fields of research. The Institute brought out statistical reviews in four languages, and the researchers of some of the "Crime Cabinets" contributed actively to the scholarly press of the time, so that their activities are well documented. Their interdisciplinary and holistic approach is remarkable. The delinquents would be examined by a whole team of experts with the purpose of establishing their sociological, psychiatric, psychological, physical, biochemical and medical characteristics (Krasnushkin 1925, 33). The "criminological-anthropological profile" thus created was supposed to serve the penal institutions as a basis for an individually adjusted treatment of the criminal (Ivanov 1925, 87).

The Moscow "Cabinet," accountable to the Institute of Health in the capital (Moszdravotdel), was especially famous for its bio-psychological profiling (Makepeace 1980, 126). In the collected volumes brought out in 1926 and in 1927 by Evgenii Krasnushkin and his colleagues under the title *The Criminal and the Crime (Prestupnik i prestupnost')*, Lombroso's thesis of the "born criminal" was explicitly refuted, with the authors claiming that if this were true, a criminal would be doomed by nature to commit acts of crime and would not have a chance to redeem his ways (Krashnushkin 1927, 8). Yet, quite a few articles in the volumes are based on the belief that criminal acts are, in fact, biologically determined, in

28 | Also in statistical departments, especially in the sections for "moral statistics," criminological research was conducted ("Razvitie kriminologii v 20-kh - 30-kh gg.").

29 | For example, in Saratov there was the "Cabinet for Criminal Anthropology and Forensic Medical Expertise" (*Kabinet kriminal'noi antropologii i sudebno-meditsinskoi ekspertizy*), while in Moscow a similar institution was called "Cabinet for the Study of the Criminal Personality and Crime" (*Kabinet po izucheniiu lichnosti prestupnika i prestupnosti*).

particular when it is a case of "epileptoid symptoms" (Rapoport 1927) or causative psycho-pathological factors.[30]

S. Ia. Bulatov, author of *The Revival of Lombroso in Soviet Criminology* (*Vozrozhdenie Lombrozo v sovetskoi kriminologii*, 1929), subjected the work of the Moscow "Crime Cabinet" to trenchant criticism, reminding his readers that Lombroso himself would have subscribed to this broader view. Bulatov was of the opinion that just rejecting the "born criminal" label was not enough to overcome the influence of Lombroso's ideas as long as his methodological assumptions were still retained. Bulatov further remarked that in the Moscow research group sociology gave way to psychiatry, because the concept of "a social disease" was understood literally, as a bio-psychological anomaly (Bulatov 1929, 46). Social conceptions were biologized, crime was pathologized and individuals were classified according to psycho-physical criteria, that is, outside of their social environment and the historical period (*ibid.*, 48, 49, 56).

Bulatov's harsh, but professionally grounded critique was by no means a singular instance. The work at the "Crime Cabinet" in Rostov-on-Don, for example, was also criticized – in general, because the team tended to "biologize social problems," and in particular, because of the medical experiments on inmates conducted by Aleksei Brailovskii, head of the "Cabinet." The decision of the authors of a collected volume brought out by the Rostov "Cabinet" (Sborniki 1927) to accord Enrico Ferri a prominent place in their contributions attracted criticism, too (N.N. 1928, 162-163). In a debate conducted in 1929 at the Section on the General Theory of State and Law at the Communist Academy chaired by Evgenii Pashukanis some scientists, primarily psychiatrists, were accused of promoting Lombrosianism.

Deprofessionalization/Politicization

The "Crime Cabinets" were now blamed for "ideological distortions" and an "infiltration of bourgeois theories" (Shikhantsov 2001; Makepeace 1980, 126). Their end was nearing. With the beginning of the 1930s they shared the fate of the Department of Moral Statistics at the Central Statistical

30 | See Krasnushkin 1926; Shneider 1927. Over a period of two years the Moscow "Cabinet" collected material on over 3.600 delinquents who were examined by the doctors.

Administration, which is to say they were, one after another, either getting closed down, or else reorganized. Research on the "personality of the criminal" (*lichnost' prestupnika*) and the origins of crime was to be put on hold for decades, until the second half of the 1950s. It was a full swing from the interest in biopsychic factors, which defined the 1920s, to the opposite extreme: criminal acts were now considered to be rooted only in social conditions.

Now, however, this approach was no longer grounded in the claim that one should look for reasons of criminal behavior in the disadvantageous environmental factors that determined the life of an individual. Instead, it was about belonging to a certain class or social group. Accordingly, it was not the crime committed, but the affiliation with, or attribution to, a certain social type – *kulak*, NEPman, *byvshie liudi* etc. – that marked an individual as a "socially dangerous element" (*sotsial'no opasnyi element*). As David Shearer pointed out, one was dealing with "essentialized identities" and "contingents" (Shearer 2009, 260, 268). Sheila Fitzpatrick calls this process "ascribing class," emphasizing that it went together with the stigmatization of all those who were defined as *lishentsy*, generally disfranchised, superfluous people (Fitzpatrick 1993, 755-758). Significantly, the term "criminal" was now used rather reluctantly, if at all. Instead, one preferred to speak of "human material" (*liudskoi material*), "elements who are hostile towards Socialism" (Averbakh 1936, 3), and – in the context of the camps – of "inmates" (*zakliuchennye / zeki*) or "canal soldiers" (*kanaloarmeitsy*). The non-specific designations are significant, as they signal a lack of precision in the legal language, with the convicts losing individual features.

The categories of "socially alien" or "socially harmful" were introduced soon after the October Revolution. In September 1918 the "Decree of the Council of People's Commissars on Red Terror" legitimized executions, mass terror and detention of suspects. Class enemies were isolated by the Cheka in "concentration camps" outside of cities, in order to "force them to cooperate with the Soviet system, to humiliate and to penalize" (Stettner 1996, 45). As is well known, the camp on the Solovetskii Islands became the foundation stone of the later Gulag system. But while in the 1920s the camp was still an exception, in the subsequent years the camp network grew enormously, with the secret police expanding its power to include more and more elements of the penal system. The starting signal was given by the decree of the Council of People's Commissars of 11 July

1929 "On the Use of Common Criminals as a *Workforce*," which officially authorized the OGPU to set up so-called correctional labor camps (ITL) in order to "colonize remote regions" and to "exploit their natural resources" (Jakobson and Smirnow 2006, 15).[31] The forced labor of hundreds of thousands was used at gold- and coal pits, for wood logging, but primarily at large-scale construction projects: canals and railways.

The system of the OGPU camps was growing fast, covering large parts of Northern Russia, and the number of inmates increased sharply, especially after more acts were defined as criminal following the forced collectivization. Simultaneously, the introduction of the new taxonomy of crime penalties meant that 'old' criminal acts were now penalized much harsher, or else the old law was applied in a new fashion (Stettner 1996, 99-193; Solomon 1980, 214). Sentencing now occurred mostly without court hearings, but even in cases when the defendants were sentenced in court, by 1932 the number of convictions had grown four times compared to 1929. As David Shearer showed, this marked an end of the "traditional reading of crime" (Shearer 2009, 26). On the one hand, the category of the "socially harmful" was now expanded to include a broad "range of socially marginal or deviant groups of people" (*ibid.*, 57-58). On the other hand, criminality and social deviancy were politicized to a so far unknown extent. Banditry, for example, was no longer treated as a criminal problem, but as a form of political counter-revolutionary activity (*ibid.*, 26), an accusation that was also applied to farmers who resisted the forced collectivization. Alcoholics, prostitutes, and hooligans, who in the 1920s were still considered to be "suffering from a social disease" and therefore curable (Lebina 2015, 407-417), were often also sentenced under article 58 of the Criminal Code as "counterrevolutionaries" and "class enemies." Likewise, a more forceful regime of punishment was introduced to resolve the problem of homeless and unsupervised children. Starting from 1935, even twelve-year olds were considered adults from the judicial point of view and could therefore even be sentenced to death.[32]

Passportization and residence restrictions led to a criminalization of further demographic groups. Essentially, everyone could turn out to be an enemy, whereas, to quote David Shearer again, "it fell increasingly to the police rather than to civil authorities to define who was 'near'

31 | On the goals and aftermath of this decree see Baron 2001, 628-633.

32 | See the justification of this measure in Averbakh 1935.

(*blizko*) [sic] and who was 'alien' (*chuzhdoi*) [sic], who was a loyal citizen and who was a socially dangerous element" (Shearer 2009, 63). With the universalization of the term "enemy" the political police was able to extend its power to large parts of the penal system, while at the same time the importance of civil jurisdiction was being reduced significantly. The lawyer was superseded by political officials or Chekists – just as was the forensic psychiatrist. The supporters of a progressive penal policy such as Shirvindt,[33] Isaev, and Poznyshev now faced the accusation of having a "sentimental-liberal" or "extremely soft" attitude towards criminality (Vyshinskii 1936, VI; Estrin and Trachterev 1934, 20). There were no more discussions of international research on the topic; at the same time, the Western penal system was stereotypically cast in dark tones. Citations from Marx, Lenin and mostly Stalin replaced references to professional literature. The differentiated, field-specific, academic argumentation gave way to a one-size-fits-all political jargon, as the following example from Ida Averbakh's *From Crime to Labor* shows:

> Remnants of the crashed class enemy, déclassé segments, and unsteady delinquent elements from the proletarian milieu are all re-forged in the forge of conscious productive labor which is combined with all forms and methods of cultural and educational work (Averbakh 1936, 5).[34]

The new rhetoric was dominated by the spirit of class struggle, in full accordance with Stalin's dictum from 1928 that in the course of the transition to socialism, class struggle would grow in intensity rather than weaken, as the classes doomed to extinction would not be prepared to renounce their place of their own free will. Seen from this perspective, criminality could indeed be regarded as a social phenomenon which had originally resulted from the division of classes in society. This made it possible to explain why the crime rates, far from going down, were increasing, and also why the measures against all types of delinquent

33 | Shirvindt lost his position in 1932; in 1938 he was arrested, and years in prison (until 1948) were followed by exile until 1954.

34 | "В кузнице сознательного производительного труда, соединенного со всеми формами и методами культурно-воспитательного воздействия, перековываются остатки разгромленного классового врага, деклассированные элементы и совершившие преступления неустойчивые элементы из среды трудящихся."

behavior had to be so strict. According to Andrei Vyshinskii, "a merciless suppression of any rebellion initiated by the enemies of the working class" was necessary.[35] The application of pressure and force, however, had to be dialectically combined with efforts at persuasion and re-education (Vyshinskii 1936, VI; Vyshinskii 1934, 8) in order to achieve "the reform of the re-formable" (*ispravlenie ispravimykh*) (Estrin and Trachterev 1934, 22).

Social and soul-engineering

But who was re-formable? It seemed easiest to exercise influence on the "socially close" individuals, that is, delinquents from the proletarian milieu. However, the aspirations went further: "class-alien elements" were also to leave the camps as "socially renewed" (*sotsial'no-obnovlennye*). They, too, had to be made able "to work consciously for the socialist society," because the "class-determined attitude" (*klassovaia ustanovka*) could be transformed by the process of re-forging (Averbakh 1936, 15, 31). At the same time, the relationship between class-related determinism and the possibility of rehabilitation remained a mute point. Vyshinskii explained that the challenge was to educate not just "unstable elements from the proletarian milieu," but also "those elements from the milieu antagonistic to the proletariat who appear to be in the right state to absorb the educational influence of institutions of corrective labor, as a result of which they will become part of the working class."[36] He (and not only he) remained, however, silent on how exactly this was to happen.

The "most dangerous déclassé criminal" (as the phrase went) was the persistent repeat offender, who had internalized criminal behavior and thus posed special methodological problems. According to Iagoda, "recidivist criminals were incorrigible because they were inherently hostile to Soviet power, and they could never be rehabilitated" (Shearer

35 | "[…] необходимость беспощадного подавления всякого рода сопротивления врагов рабочего класса" (Vyshinskii 1936, VII).

36 | "[…] перед пролетарским государством стоит […] задача воспитательного действия, с одной стороны, на неустойчивые элементы из среды трудящихся […], и с другой, на те элементы из враждебной пролетариату среды, которые оказываются в состоянии воспринять воспитательное влияние исправительно-трудовых учреждении и в результате этого воздействия стать в ряды трудящихся" (Vyshinskii 1934, 8).

2009, 264-265). However, his wife Ida Averbakh saw no problem with reforming the "professional criminal," claiming that, while "psychiatrists and anthropologists tried consistently to present crime as an inevitable result of the behavioral mechanisms of a repeated offender," in fact,

> the social side of biologically determined mechanisms of behavior can be reversed by the determined and skillful labor of re-forging; just like one can reverse the flow of the Volga, one can also reverse the social significance of biological mechanisms, mobilize them for the benefit of socialist construction, for the benefit of the people transforming nature and themselves together with it, first by coercion, then by inner conviction (Averbakh 1936, 32).[37]

The objective was unequivocal and one-sided: transforming the "bad human material" into "full-fledged, active and conscious builders of socialism" (Averbakh 1936, 4).[38] Hereby, labor functioned both as a means and as a goal of education; it was, according to Vyshinskii, "that magical force which [...] transformed human beings from non-existence and nothingness into heroes" (Vyshinskii 1934, 10)[39] The emphasis was no longer on therapy, but on disciplining and productivity. The socio-economic goal corresponded exactly to the principles which, in the spirit of the Stalinist project of engineering both the social environment and the souls of the people (Gestwa 2009), extended to all of the Soviet society. The daring utopia of a completely "new man," which emerged in the revolutionary era (Groys and Hagemeister 2004), was now reduced to striving for an impeccable functioning of the individual as a small screw in the machinery of the state (Geller 1994, 10). While in the 1920s diverse

37 | "[...] биологически однозначные механизмы поведения могут быть со своей социальной стороны повернуты напряженной и умелой работой по перековке в прямо противоположную сторону; как, поворачивая течение Волги, удается повернуть и социальную значимость биологических механизмов, мобилизовать их на пользу социалистического строительства, на пользу людям, переделывающим природу и с ней себя, сначала по принуждению, а потом по внутренней необходимости."

38 | "Превращение самого скверного людского материала в полноценных, активных и сознательных строителей социализма [...]."

39 | "Труд [...] является тем чародеем, который из небытия и ничтожества превращает людей в героев."

pedagogical experiments were still conducted and a variety of psychological or psychoanalytic views were still being debated in an attempt to promote the transformation of humans from the inside (Etkind 1996), now all these contesting views had been silenced by the omnipresent discourse of disciplining. There was no room for "excesses in the realm of desires, thoughts and behavior" (Rüting 2002, 153),[40] everything disturbing and disturbed was to be done away with by means of purposeful conditioning.

The vision of the possibility of a total disciplining was complemented by that of doability,[41] which referred to a comprehensive guidance by the party and its functionaries, so that empathy and attention to the development of an individual was replaced by regulatory measures and commands from external and superior bodies (Ushakin 2005). Such being the case, it is not surprising that of all people it was Chekists, "the sword and shield of the party," who were celebrated as the best educators in the labor colonies and camps of the OGPU, as an embodiment of the spirit of leadership, "steel-like logic and discipline" (*metallicheskaia logika i distsiplina*; *BBK*, 330), those who had to, and could, force others "who could not re-educate themselves" to "live a Soviet life, pushing them until they can do it of their own free will" (*ibid.*, 116).[42] "The GPU-people know how to reconstruct human beings. Indeed, they can do that!", Gor'kii confirmed (Gor'kii 1953d, 74).[43]

However, what about those who were not "re-formable," all those who had been hopelessly corrupted by their earlier life? Gor'kii, who can be considered a chief ideologist of that period, had a categorical answer to this question, too:

40 | Rüting shows how Pavlov's discoveries and theories on conditional reflexes in dogs made their way from the lab into the society and colonized "the territory of psychological discourses" (Rüting 2002, 109).

41 | On the contradiction between the Marxist vision of class-related causation and the voluntaristic belief in the controllability of historical processes see Dobrenko 2007, 156.

42 | "Мы в лагерях принуждаем людей, не способных самостоятельно перевоспитать себя, жить советской жизнью, толкаем их до тех пор, пока они сами не начинают делать это добровольно."

43 | "Люди из ГПУ умеют перестраивать людей. Умеют!"

> The Soviet power has a legally justified right to punish and even annihilate bandits, robbers, thieves, but only in those increasingly rare cases when these are people suffering from an untreatable disease, completely deformed by the petit bourgeois, wolfish life (Gor'kii 1953b, 510).[44]

The enemies who got in the way had to be eliminated in order to win the fight against man's arch nemesis – nature and its elemental forces (Gor'kii 1953d, 76). In his writings from the 1930s, Gor'kii indulges freely in fantasies of extermination. One had to eliminate mice, rats, insects, which threatened the products of people's labor, the harvest; but the same held true for human pests, particularly the petty philistines with their "parasitic way of living" as well as the "incurably degenerated" bourgeoisie and other "human monstrosities." By dehumanizing them, Gor'kii cleared the way for the extermination of the enemies, who were now nothing more than microbes, lice, tapeworms, snakes, spiders or cockroaches. The "other" was, once again, biologized (or rather – zoologized), but this time it was not in order to comprehend his individual physical and psychological profile. In Gerd Koenen's opinion, Gor'kii's attitude can be described as a form of "social racism" (Koenen [2]1992, 99; Koenen 2000, 284).

In the volume on the Belomor Canal, similar attacks on degeneracy, rottenness, and "two-legged animals" (*dvunogie zhivotnye*; *BBK*, 609) can also be found; however, they are downplayed as the success story is given more weight. With catchwords such as "pride," "fortune," "glory," "honor" and "heroism," the volume celebrates the message of victory and successful "recovery." Again and again, labor is evoked as the universal medicine for the cure of the socially diseased, even though not in the sense of a gentle, individualized therapy. Rather, the delinquent would be "forced to become a different person" (*on obiazan stat' drugim; ibid.*, 603) and to leave all private desires or unorthodox life projects behind. "The zoologically individual has been shattered by the truth of collective labor," proclaimed Gor'kii proudly in one of his contributions to the volume

44 | "Советская власть вполне обладает законно обоснованным правом наказывать и даже уничтожать бандитов, грабителей, воров, но только в тех всё более редких случаях, когда это неизлечимо больные люди, совершенно изуродованные мещанской, волчьей жизнью."

(*ibid.*, 17).[45] Also in their future endeavors, on the new construction sites, the former inmates wanted, or had, to "preserve their collective face of the Belomor constructors" (*ibid.*, 568).[46]

The process of the transformation was described in the text as "re-education" (*perevospitanie*) or "re-birth" (*pererozhdenie*), and this second term is especially remarkable. Being reborn into the new life and accepting its values presupposes the death of the old nature of the individual and an annihilation of the past (Draskoczy 2014, 36). Tellingly, the "resurrection" could only be achieved if the inmates "forgot themselves" (*zabyt' sebia*) and internalized "state meanings" (*gosudarstvennye smysly*) of labor (*BBK*, 19), through which they were being trained to transform their negative energies into productive ones and to "fight against the rock, the swamp, the river" (*ibid.*, 15).[47] To cite Marx, by transforming nature these men were transforming themselves (*ibid.*, 318).

The inmates may have had a personal background – as kulaks, saboteurs etc. – but no biography.[48] Accordingly, it is impossible to find a clear psychological explanation of what triggered their transformation into Heroes of Labor. Rather, the re-birth of "lawbreakers [as] ideal human beings" (*ibid.*, 494)[49] happens abruptly, almost miraculously (as suggested by the overused prefix *pere-*) (*ibid.*, 589). *Perekovka* becomes an act of conversion through which the delinquent finds his "faith" in the project and it is as a reformed, indeed "born anew," human being that he is released back into normal life. Once the criminal has atoned for his "guilt before the country" (*svoiu vinu pered stranoi*; *ibid.*, 73), he can be pardoned and granted a new life. In the words of contributors to the volume, "the biographies of these people have been corrected,

45 | "[…] правда коллективного труда пошатнула зоологическое индивидуальное."

46 | "Мечтая о будущей работе, они хотят и там, на новых стройках, сохранить свое коллективное беломорстроевское лицо […]."

47 | "[…] его озлобление против людей обращается на борьбу с камнем, болотом, рекой."

48 | Even though the literature on successful re-forging is primarily based on (auto)biographic reports, the focus is not on the individual, original life story, but – like in Christian hagiography – on the typical, whereby the collective biography was to serve, in a way, as a sketch for the private one.

49 | Сделать из "правонарушителей идеальных людей […]."

purified, completed" (*ibid.*, 582).[50] In a corresponding tone of religious exaltation, the OGPU appears as an institution which "does not only punish but also saves" (*OGPU ne tol'ko karaet, no i spasaet*; *ibid.*, 587). The Chekists are representatives of "a collectively organized reason" (*kollektivno organizovannyi razum*; *ibid.*, 608), and as such, they possess not only unlimited knowledge, phenomenal memory, and unheard-of working capacity, but super-human, downright god-like abilities. They are able to look into human souls: "Chekists untied the knots, spoke the unspoken, came to know that which was most secret – they've been doing it for thirteen years now, they've mastered their trade" (*ibid.*, 96).[51] Here, connections to *bogostroitel'stvo* become very apparent (Draskoczy 2014, 29-33).[52] Once again, Gor'kii's influence is noticeable, and via him – that of Nietzsche.

The mythical narrative did not brave reality. The miracle of *perekovka* turned into its protagonists' nightmare. On March 28, 1937, Narkom Iagoda was arrested. Ida and Leopol'd Averbakh, Semen Firin and 218 people close to him (Fedorov 1997, 7, 27, 140-141), employees and inmates of the Bolshevo commune (Gladysh 2004, 168-172) and many others were caught up in this maelstrom of arrests. These events marked an end of the practice of, and discourse on, *perekovka* which, put in a nutshell, was a hybrid of an aestheticization and politicization of judicial discourse and an expression of a transitional period. Its concept of the criminal ranged from determinateness to changeability, from oppression to improvement,[53] from belief in purposeful influence to belief in miracle, from social and biological essentialization to medicalization. However, it still contained,

50 | "Биографии этих людей исправлены, очищены, дополнены."

51 | "Чекисты распутали узлы, досказали недосказанное, дознались о самом скрытом – они тринадцать лет этим занимаются, научились."

52 | One can draw here a parallel with the magical promise of Trofim Lysenko, who claimed it was possible to change the nature of an organism by means of external influences.

53 | Even the early Soviet utopian vision of a total disappearance of crime was again taken up: "We will make sure there are no delinquents in the Soviet Union. Time will come and we will see a congress where the OGPU will announce: there are no more criminals." "Мы добьемся того, что у нас не будет правонарушителей в Советском союзе. Мы еще увидим съезд, где ОГПУ скажет: нет больше преступников" (*BBK*, 587).

in whatever outlandish way it might have been, the promise of a rebirth and return to everyday life. Shortly thereafter, the victims of the Great Purge would have to let go of any hope whatsoever.

References

Applebaum, A. 2003. *Der Gulag*. Berlin: Siedler.

Avdeenko, A. 1989. "Otluchenie." *Znamia*, no. 3, 5-73; no. 4, 78-133.

Averbakh, I. L. 1936. *Ot prestupleniia k trudu*. Moscow: OGIZ.

Averbakh, I. L. 1935. "Zakon 7 aprelia i prestupnost' nesovershennoletnikh." *Za sotsialisticheskuiu zakonnost'. Organ prokuratury SSSR*. 8, August, 10-15.

Balina, M. 2000. "Literatura puteshestvii." Giunter, Ch. [Günther, H.] and Dobrenko, E. (eds.), *Sotsrealisticheskii kanon*. St. Petersburg: Akademicheskii proekt, 896-909.

Barnes, St. A. 2011. *Death and Redemption. The Gulag and the Shaping of Soviet Society*. Princeton and Oxford: Princeton University Press.

Baron, N. 2001. "Conflict and Complicity: The Expansion of the Karelian Gulag, 1923-1933." *Cahiers du Monde russe* 42, no. 2-4, 615-648.

Beer, D. 2008. *Renovating Russia. The Human Sciences and the Fate of Liberal Modernity, 1880-1930*. Ithaca and London: Cornell University Press.

Berman, H. J. and Hunt, D. H. 1950. "Criminal Law and Psychiatry: The Soviet Solution". *Stanford Law Review* 2, 635-663.

Binner, R. and Junge, M. 2010. "Vom 'sozial nahen' zum 'sozial feindlichen Element'. Kriminelle in der sowjetischen Gesellschaft 1918-1938." Binner et al. (eds.), *Stalinismus in der sowjetischen Provinz 1937-1938. Die Massenaktion aufgrund des operativen Befehls No. 00447*. Berlin: Akademie-Verlag, 161-216.

Bolshevtsy. Ocherki po istorii Bolshevskoi im. G.G. Iagody trudkommuny NKVD. 1936. Moscow: OGIZ.

Bulatov, S. Ia. 1929. "Vozrozhdenie Lombrozo v sovetskoi kriminologii." *Revoliutsiia prava* 1, 42-61.

Bulgakova, E. 2004. "Roman nuzhno okonchit'. Dnevnik E. S. Bulgakovoi i pis'ma M. A. Bulgakova." Bulgakovy, M. and E., *Dnevnik mastera i margarity*. Moscow: Vagrius.

Carleton, G. 1994. "Genre in Socialist Realism." *Slavic Review* 53, no. 4, 992-1009.

Chartreux, F. 2006. "*Le canal mer Blanche-Baltique Staline* (1934), pratiques d'écriture collective et transformation du champ littéraire soviétique." *Temporalités* 3, 163-180.

Clark, K. 2004. "The History of Factories as a Factory of History: A Case Study on the Role of Soviet Literature in Subject Formation." Hellbeck, J. (ed.), *Autobiographical Practices in Russia*. Göttingen: V & R Unipress, 251-278.

Dallin, D. J. and Nicolaevsky, B. I. 1948. *Zwangsarbeit in Sowjetrußland*. Wien: Verlag Neue Welt.

David-Fox, M. 2012. *Showcasing the Great Experiment. Cultural Diplomacy and Western Visitors to the Soviet Union, 1921-1941*. Oxford et al.: Oxford University Press.

Dobrenko, E. 2007. *Politekonomiia sotsrealizma*, Moscow: Novoe literaturnoe obozrenie.

Draskoczy, J. 2012. "The *Put'* of *Perekovka*: Transforming Lives at Stalin's White Sea-Baltic Canal." *The Russian Review* 71, 30-48.

Draskoczy, J. 2014. *Belomor: Criminality and Creativity in Stalin's Gulag*. Boston: Academic Studies Press.

Epelboin, A. 2009. "Platonov und Mittelasien." Kissel, W. St. (ed.), *Flüchtige Blicke. Relektüren russischer Reisetexte des 20. Jahrhunderts*. Bielefeld: Aisthesis, 261-284.

Estrin, A. and Trakhterev, V. 1934. "Razvitie ispravitel'no-trudovoi politiki kak chasti sovetskoi ugolovnoi politiki." Vyshinskii, A. (ed.), *Ot tiurem k vospitatel'nym uchrezhdeniiam*. Moscow: Gosudarstvennoe izdatel'stvo sovetskoe zakonodatel'stvo, 17-71.

Etkind, A. 1996. *Eros des Unmöglichen. Die Geschichte der Psychoanalyse in Russland*. Leipzig: Kiepenheuer.

Fedorov, N. 1997. *Byla li tachka u ministra? Ocherki o stroiteliach kanala Moskva-Volga*. Dmitrov: Spas.

Fedorov, N. 2006a. "Dmitlag (Iz istorii stroitel'stva kanala Moskva-Volga)." *Khram novomuchenikov i ispovednikov Rossiiskikh v Butove*. <http://archive.martyr.ru/content/view/14/17/> (last accessed 10 October 2016).

Fedorov, N. 2006b. "Dvigatel' perekovki (nachal'nik Dmitlaga S.G. Firin)." *Khram novomuchenikov i ispovednikov Rossiiskikh v Butove*. <http://archive.martyr.ru/content/view/21/17/> (last accessed 10 October 2016).

Figes, O. [2]2008. *Die Flüsterer. Leben in Stalins Russland.* Berlin: Berlin Verlag.

Firin, S. 1934. *Itogi Belomorstroia: Doklad na Prezidiume Komakademii.* Moscow: Politizdat.

Firin, S. 1936. "Shtrikhi." *Literaturnaia gazeta*, no. 36, 26 June.

Fischer von Weikersthal, F. 2011. *Die „inhaftierte" Presse. Das Pressewesen sowjetischer Zwangsarbeitslager 1923-1937.* Wiesbaden: Harrassowitz.

Fitzpatrick, S. 1993. "Ascribing Class: The Construction of Social Identity in Soviet Russia." *Journal of Modern History* 65, no. 4, 745-770.

Frank, S. 2009. "Russische 'Reisetexte' um 1935." Kissel, W. St. (ed.), *Flüchtige Blicke. Relektüren russischer Reisetexte des 20. Jahrhunderts.* Bielefeld: Aisthesis, 223-260.

Geller, M. 1994. *Mashina i vintiki.* Moscow: Izdatel'stvo MIK.

Gestwa, K. 2009. "*Social* und *soul engineering* unter Stalin und Chruschtschow, 1928-1964." Etzemüller, Th. (ed.), *Die Ordnung der Moderne. Social Engineering im 20. Jahrhundert.* Bielefeld: Transcript, 241-277.

Gladysh, S. 2004. *Deti bol'shoi bedy.* Moscow: Zvonnitsa.

Goldt, R. 2005. "Einladung zur Enthauptung. Nikolaj Ustrjalovs Briefe und Tagebücher als psychologisches Stenogramm einer gescheiterten Heimkehr in die UdSSR." Göbler, F. (ed.), *Russische Emigration im 20. Jahrhundert. Literatur – Sprache – Kultur.* München: Otto Sagner, 33-60.

Gorcheva, A. Ju. 1996. *Pressa Gulaga. 1918-1955.* Moscow: Izdatel'stvo Moskovskogo Universiteta.

Gor'kii, M. 1953a. "O kochke i o tochke." *Sobranie sochinenii v tridtsati tomakh.* Vol. 27: *Stat'i, doklady, rechi, privetstviia.* Moscow: Gosudarstvennoe izdatel'stvo khudozhestvennoi literatury, 42-52.

Gor'kii, M. 1953b. "Ot 'vragov obshchestva' – k geroiam truda." *Sobranie sochinenii v tridtsati tomakh.* Vol. 27: *Stat'i, doklady, rechi, privetstviia.* Moscow: Gosudarstvennoe izdatel'stvo khudozhestvennoi literatury, 507-512.

Gor'kii, M. 1953c. "O vospitanii pravdoi." *Sobranie sochinenii v tridtsati tomakh.* Vol. 27: *Stat'i, doklady, rechi, privetstviia.* Moscow: Gosudarstvennoe izdatel'stvo khudozhestvennoi literatury, 58-66.

Gor'kii, M. 1953d. "Rech' na slete udarnikov belomorstroia." *Sobranie sochinenii v tridtsati tomakh.* Vol. 27: *Stat'i, doklady, rechi, privetstviia.*

Moscow: Gosudarstvennoe izdatel'stvo khudozhestvennoi literatury, 73-76.

Gor'kii, M. et al. (eds.) 1934. *Belomorsko-Baltiiskii Kanal imeni Stalina. Istoriia stroitel'stva.* Moscow: OGIZ; Reprint Moscow 1998.

Groys, B. and Hagemeister, M. (eds.) 2005. *Die Neue Menschheit. Biopolitische Utopien in Russland zu Beginn des 20. Jahrhunderts.* Frankfurt/M.: Suhrkamp.

Günther, H. 1996. "Der Bau des Weißmeerkanals als Laboratorium des neuen Menschen." Josting, P. and Wirrer, J. (eds.), *Bücher haben ihre Geschichte: Kinder- und Jugendliteratur, Literatur und Nationalsozialismus, Deutschdidaktik.* Hildesheim et al.: Georg Olms, 62-66.

Günther, H. 1993. *Der sozialistische Übermensch. Maksim Gor'kij und der sowjetische Heldenmythos.* Stuttgart and Weimar: Metzler.

Guski, A. 2009. "Der Präzeptor unterwegs: Gor'kijs Reiseskizzen 'Durch die Union der Sowjets'." Kissel, W. St. (ed.), *Flüchtige Blicke. Relektüren russischer Reisetexte des 20. Jahrhunderts.* Bielefeld: Aisthesis, 209-222.

Hartmann, A. 2012a. "Ordnungen des Zeigens und Sehens. Westliche Intellektuelle und ihre sowjetischen Guides Mitte der 1930er Jahre." Lampadius, St. and Schenkel, E. (eds.), *Under Western and Eastern Eyes. Ost und West in der Reiseliteratur des 20. Jahrhunderts.* Leipzig: Leipziger Universitätsverlag, 91-108.

Hartmann, A. 2012b. "'Perekovka'. Tschekisten und Schriftsteller als 'Ingenieure der menschlichen Seele'." *Jahrbuch für Historische Kommunismusforschung 2012.* Berlin: Aufbau, 11-26.

Hedeler, W. 2011. *Vom Schmieden neuer Menschen. Lagerkorrespondenten berichten. Artikel der Lagerzeitung des Karlag "Putjowka".* Leipzig: Leipziger Literaturverlag.

Heller, M. 1975. *Stacheldraht der Revolution. Die Welt der Konzentrationslager in der sowjetischen Literatur.* Stuttgart: Seewald.

Hillig, G. 2006. "Die Arbeitskommune der OGPU in Bolševo." *Jahrbuch für Forschungen zur Geschichte der Arbeiterbewegung* 5, no. 3, 42-58.

Ivanov, G. 1925. "Iz praktiki Saratovskogo gubernskogo kabineta." *Sovetskoe pravo* 1, 84-95.

Ivanova, G. M. 2001. *Der GULag im totalitären System der Sowjetunion.* Berlin: Schletzer.

Jakobson, M. and Smirnow, M. 2003. "Das System der Haftanstalten der RSFSR und UdSSR 1917-1930." Memorial International (ed.),

Das System der Besserungsarbeitslager in der UdSSR. 1923–1960. Ein Handbuch. Berlin: Schletzer, 3-17.

Klein, J. 1995/96. "Belomorkanal. Literatur und Propaganda in der Stalinzeit." *Zeitschrift für Slavische Philologie* 55, 53-98.

Koenen, G. [2]1992. *Die großen Gesänge. Lenin, Stalin, Mao Tse-tung. Führerkulte und Heldenmythen des 20. Jahrhunderts.* Frankfurt/M.: Eichborn.

Koenen, G. 2000. *Utopie der Säuberung. Was war der Kommunismus?* Frankfurt/M.: Fischer.

Krasnushkin, E. K. 1926. "Chto takoe prestupnik?" *Prestupnik i prestupnost'. Sbornik I.* Moscow: Moszdravotdel, 6-33.

Krasnushkin, E. K. 1925. "Kabinet po izucheniiu lichnosti prestupnika i prestupnosti." *Izuchenie lichnosti prestupnika v S.S.S.R. i za granitsei.* Moscow: Moszdravotedel, 21-35.

Krasnushkin, E. K. 1927. "Opyt psikhiatricheskogo postroeniia kharakterov u pravonarushitelei." Krasnushkin, E. K. et. al (eds.), *Prestupnik i prestupnost'. Sbornik II.* Moscow: Moszdravotdel, 7-33.

Lebina, N. 2015. *Sovetskaia povsednevnost': Normy i anomalii. Ot voennogo kommunizma k bolshomu stiliu.* Moscow: Novoe literaturnoe obozrenie.

Lichatschow, D. S. 1997. *Hunger und Terror. Mein Leben zwischen Oktoberrevolution und Perestroika.* Ostfildern: edition tertium.

Makarenko, A. 1958. *Ein Buch für Eltern. Vorträge über Kindererziehung. Reden und Aufsätze über Familienerziehung* (*Werke*, vol. 4). Berlin: Volk und Wissen.

Makepeace, R. W. 1980. *Marxist Ideology and Soviet Criminal Law.* London: Croom Helm.

Meditsinskaia inspektsiia Moskovskikh Mest Zakliucheniia 1925. "Predislovie." *Izuchenie lichnosti prestupnika v S.S.S.R. i za granitsei.* Moscow: Moszdravotedel, 3-6.

Mogil'ner, M. 2008. *Homo Imperii. Istoriia fizicheskoi antropologii v Rossii (konets XIX – nachalo XX v.).* Moscow: Novoe literaturnoe obozrenie.

N.N. 1928. "Voprosy izucheniia prestupnosti na Severnom Kavkaze" [Retsenziia]. *Revoliutsiia prava* 6, 161-163.

Podurets, A. M. 2013. "Kak Sarov ne stal Pogrebinskom." *Sarovskii kraeved.* <http://sarpust.ru/2013/03/kak-sarov-ne-stal-pogrebinskom/> (last accessed 10 October 2016).

Pogrebinskii, M. S. 1928. *Trudovaia kommuna OGPU.* Moscow: Gosudarstvennoe izdatel'stvo.

Prishvin, M. M. 2009. *Dnevniki 1932, 1933, 1934, 1935*. St. Petersburg: Rostok.

Rapoport, A. M. 1927. "Epileptoidy i ikh sotsial'nye reaktsii." Krasnushkin, E. K. et al (eds.), *Prestupnik i prestupnost'. Sbornik II*. Moscow: Moszdravotdel, 34-71.

"Razvitie kriminologii v 20-kh – 30-kh gg." Kudriavtsev, V. N. (ed.), *Ekonomiko-pravovaia biblioteka: Kriminologiia*. <http://www.vuzllib.su/beta3/html/1/13744/13785> (last accessed 10 October 2016).

Rolland, R. 1992. *Voyage à Moscou. Juin – Juillet 1935* (Cahiers Romain Rolland, no. 29). Ed. by B. Duchatelet. Paris: Albin Michel.

Rossi, Zh. 1994. "Real'nyi sotsializm." *Volia. Zhurnal uznikov totalitarnykh sistem* 2/3, 178-179.

Ruder, C. 1998. *Making History for Stalin. The Story of the Belomorkanal*. Gainesville et al.: University Press of Florida.

Rüting, T. 2002. *Pavlov und der Neue Mensch. Diskurse über Disziplinierung in Sowjetrussland*. München: R. Oldenbourg.

Sborniki Kabineta po izucheniiu lichnosti pravonarushitelia. 1927. Vyp. II. Rostov na Donu: Kraevoe upravlenie zdravookhraneniia.

Scherbakowa, I. "Gefängnisse und Lager im sowjetischen Herrschaftssystem." *Gulag. Memorial* <http://www.gulag.memorial.de/pdf/scherbakova_gefaengnisse.pdf> (last accessed 10 October 2016).

Shearer, D. 2009. *Policing Stalin's Socialism. Repression and Social Order in the Soviet Union, 1924-1953*. New Haven et al.: Yale University Press.

Shikhantsov, G. G. 2001. "Kriminologiia." *Ekonomiko-pravovaia biblioteka*. <http://www.vuzllib.su/books/1483> (last accessed 10 October 2016).

Shirvindt, E. 1925. *Nashe ispravitel'no-trudovoe zakonodatel'stvo*. Moscow: Iuridicheskoe izdatel'stvo NKIu RSFSR.

Shirvindt, E. G. and Utevskii, B. S. 1927. *Sovetskoe penitentsiarnoe pravo*. Moscow: Iuridicheskoe izdatel'stvo NKIu RSFSR.

Shirvindt, E. G. and Utevskii, B. S. 1931. *Sovetskoe ispravitel'no-trudovoe pravo*. Moscow: Izdatel'stvo Narodnogo komissariata vnutrennykh del RSFSR.

Shneider, S. M. 1927. "Rastratchiki." Krasnushkin, E. K. (ed.), *Prestupnik i prestupnost'. Sbornik II*. Moscow: Moszdravotdel, 72-105.

Shubinskii, V. 2006. "Perekovka (Obzor knig o perestroike russkikh pisatelei v 1920-1930-e gody)." *Novoe literaturnoe obozrenie* 79, 336-347.

Solomon, P. H. 1980. "Soviet Penal Policy, 1917-1934. A Reinterpretation." *Slavic Review* 39, 195-201.

Solonevich, I. L. [1938] 1999. *Rossiia v kontslagere*. Moscow: Prilozhenie k zhurnalu Moskva.

Solzhenitsyn, A. 1973a. *Archipelag GULag 1918-1956. Opyt khudozhestvennogo issledovaniia*. Vol. I-II. Paris: YMCA-Press.

Solzhenitsyn, A. 1973b. *The Gulag Archipelago 1918-1956. An Experiment in Literary Investigation*. NewYork: Harper & Row.

Solzhenitsyn, A. 1974. *Archipelag GULag 1918-1956. Opyt khudozhestvennogo issledovaniia*. Vol. III-IV. Paris: YMCA-Press.

Stettner, R. 1996. *"Archipel GULag": Stalins Zwangslager. Terrorinstrument und Wirtschaftsgigant. Entstehung, Organisation und Funktion des sowjetischen Lagersystems 1928-1956*. Paderborn et al.: Schöningh.

Ushakin, S. 2005. "Pole boia na lone prirody: ot kakogo nasledstva my otkazyvalis'." *Novoe literaturnoe obozrenie* 71, 263-298.

Vyshinskii, A. 1934. "Predislovie." Vyshinskii, A. (ed.), *Ot tiurem k vospitatel'nym uchrezhdeniiam*. Moscow: Gosudarstvennoe izdatel'stvo sovetskoe zakonodatel'stvo, 5-15.

Vyshinskii, A. 1936. "Predislovie." Averbakh, I. L. *Ot prestupleniia k trudu*. Moscow: OGIZ, V-IX.

[Zhdanov] 1990 [1934]. "Rech' sekretaria TsK VKP(b) A.A. Zhdanova." Luppol, I. K. (ed.), *Pervyi vsesoiuznyi s"ezd sovetskikh pisatelei 1934. Stenograficheskii otchet*. Moscow: Sovetskii Pisatel', 2-5.

Zhuravlev, S. V. 1997. *Fenomen "Istorii fabrik i zavodov"*. Moscow: Institut rossiiskoi istorii RAN.

III. Political and 'Other' Prisoners – Literature of the Gulag

Criminals in Gulag Accounts

Renate Lachmann

Criminality in Russia was studied in historical, sociological and psychological perspectives and a substantial body of literature exists on the subject. The special topic of criminals in the Gulag has also attracted interest in recent years. Here, however, reliable statistics and criminological investigations are scarce. Studies on criminals in the Gulag must primarily rely on eyewitness-accounts of the political prisoners (Applebaum 2003, 280-306; Petzer 2007). As far as I know there are no reports by the criminals themselves. All the accounts on which I draw are therefore those written by political prisoners who shared the camps with the criminals and became, as will be shown, their victims.

Even an expert may not have complete knowledge of all the reports published or preserved in other forms, e.g. in archives. In my contribution, I will select from the available corpus those accounts which seem to me most relevant in characterizing the criminals in jails and camps. All of them are victims' accounts, some written by frequently quoted authors, such as Aleksandr Solzhenitsyn, Evgeniia Ginzburg, Varlam Shalamov, others by less quoted ones, such as Dmitrii Likhachev, Karlo Štajner (Karl Steiner), Julius Margolin. For reasons that will be explained I will make one exception and draw on fictional texts by a writer belonging to a later generation, Danilo Kiš. Kiš is neither a victim nor a witness. He was inspired by Karlo Štajner's autobiography, *Seven Thousand Days in Siberia* (*7000 dana u Sibiru*, 1971) to write about the Gulag and the criminals imprisoned there (Lachmann 2017). His book *A Tomb for Boris Davidovich* (*Grobnica za Borisa Davidoviča*, 1976) became a bestseller in France at the end of the seventies. Almost two decades after Camus' death it supported the latter's position against Sartre who blindly maintained the communist party line which denied the existence of the Soviet concentration camps.

Introduction

Two very different types of prisoners were bound to meet in Soviet prisons as well as in forced labour camps. On the one hand, there were the political prisoners (*politicals*), whose number was at first rather small until the Second World War. On the other hand, there were criminals, ranging from those who broke minor laws, petty thieves up to those who, although lacking any political ambition, were sentenced for sabotage and laziness. The main body of the criminals were thieves and robbers, more or less successfully organized in camp gangs, and murderers. These two groups, by threats of violence, held power in prisons and camps. They developed their own regime and forced all the other prisoners in jails and in camps to submit to it. Violation of the rules of behaviour committed by their own were fiercely prosecuted; disobedience by lower ranking criminals and, more generally, disrespect shown by other inmates, especially the politicals, was punished by humiliation, beating and even killing.

This criminal power structure in prisons and camps shaped the lives and behaviour of inmates. It became a central topic in the autobiographies and memoirs written by the politicals, i.e. those who were sentenced according to article 58. All of them stress the fact that life was governed by the basic dichotomy between the criminals and the non-criminals and that the latter were dominated by hard core bandits. In her contribution to this volume, Leona Toker points out another important aspect: a peculiar coexistence, in fact co-operation, that was tolerated by the authorities, between the guards and the criminal regime.

The dichotomous structure insistently distinguishing between the criminals and the politicals was ideologically motivated. The former, whatever their crimes, were considered "socially near elements," closer to the Soviet society than the "socially distant, dangerous elements," the politicals. The criminals were somehow still part of the society, even of the working class, while the politicals stood outside the society, being members of a dying class – the bourgeoisie. Despite the basic aim of the Soviet ideology – a replacement of class society by a classless one, – the class struggle continued in jails and camps.

The re-forging of the socially near – *perekovka*

It is difficult to precisely define the period when the attribute "a socially near element" emerged and what its precise definition was. Was it a judicial term, which played a role in the structure of the penitentiary system, or rather a quasi-sociological term that distinguished the criminals from the politicals? The term, referred to in the Gulag reports, certainly has a 'moralistic' connotation as it clearly favours the socially near, who were considered guilty neither of treason nor of conspiracy against the party and its top members.

The expression "a socially near element" was already used in the 1920s and referred to thieves and robbers, who were then sent to work in the construction of the White Sea-Baltic Canal (the "Belomor Canal"). Subjecting these people to hard labour was meant as an experiment to test the new doctrine of re-education, re-forging (*perekovka*)[1] of the criminals. In the propaganda texts about the completion of the Belomor Canal "in less than two years" the association of the two concepts ("socially near elements" and *perekovka*) is taken for granted. The famous (infamous) memorial book *History of the Construction of the White Sea-Baltic Canal* (*Belomorsko-Baltiiskii kanal imeni Stalina. Istoriia stroitel'stva*, 1934), edited by Maksim Gor'kii, Leopol'd Averbakh and Semen Firin (accompanied by Aleksandr Rodchenko's photographs) praises the success of the *perekovka* even more effusively than the effort of building the canal. One passage celebrates the triumph of re-forging:

> [...] it was an extraordinary victory which people won over themselves, people who had been anarchisized (*anarchizirovannye*) by the recent, beastly power of the autocratic petit bourgeoisie.[2]

---

1 | The *perekovka* concept has to be seen in the context of the ideology of the new communist individual (Günther 1993). On *perekovka* see Anne Hartmann's contribution to this volume.

2 | "[...] но еще более изумительна победа, которую одержали над собой люди, анархизированные недавней, звериной властью самодержавного мещанства" (Gor'kii et al. [eds.] 1934, 12). Unless otherwise noted, here and elsewhere translation into English is mine – RL.

"Anarchization" was a euphemism for criminality. According to the prevailing official doctrine it suggested that the criminals were victims of the former decadent society.

Well-known authors – Aleksei Tolstoi, Mikhail Zoshchenko, Viktor Shklovskii, Boris Pil'niak and others – visited the canal in 1933 shortly after its ceremonious opening. They were to help in establishing the myth of both the fantastic completion of the canal building, and the rebirth of the former negative elements – thieves, robbers, murderers. The canal was not completed at the time and the *perekovka* was a failure. This must have been obvious to the editors and contributors to the volume. They all played a part in constructing another Potemkin village. Even the workers the visitors saw and talked to were fakes (well-dressed members of the Komsomol replaced the working prisoners with their ragged clothes who were shut away). The reports about and photographs of well fed, well clothed, happy workers in the official publication were received enthusiastically. The documentary photographs, which were most likely taken in the same period and which now can be seen in the Karelian State Regional Museum in Petrozavodsk, would have exploded the official myth. Newspapers such as *Pravda* and *Izvestiia* eulogized the first successful *perekovka* with portraits of "re-forged workers;" they proudly reported that the *perekovka* included not only criminal recidivists but even political enemies (Klein 1995/96).

Aleksandr Sidorov (the pseudonym of Fima Zhiganets),[3] an expert on the role of criminals in the history of the Belomor Canal, studied the so called criminal folklore – the bandits' songs and poems as well as their jargon (*fenia*). He claims that the texts can be taken as an authentic expression of their "work ethics." In the songs and poems which he quotes the bandits heap ridicule on official notions such as the duty to work, labour service, work efficiency, not sparing the main propaganda slogan "Work is an honour, a duty, a matter of pride [...]." These people scorned those from their own group who dared to break the chief rule of the criminal regime: avoidance of work. And those who broke this rule were to be punished. That is what the poems and songs propagated.

Contrary to the official view, already in the 1920s the implementation of the *perekovka* doctrine was obstructed, and the re-education program

3 | See his site: Zona Fimy Zhigantsa. Lichnyi sait Aleksandra Sidorova. <http://zhiganets.tyurem.net/> (last accessed 10 October 2016).

by means of work turned out to be a complete miscalculation. One of the song-poems Sidorov quotes presents an ironic version of self-accusation: the criminal confesses his former sins (robbery, theft, embezzlement, larceny, pilfering) and enthusiastically praises the virtue of work to which he converted, which saved him and granted him a better life. Other songs quoted by Sidorov are unconcealed hymns to the boundless enjoyment of theft and robbery, to the temptation of coming in possession of other people's property and the pleasures of doing nothing. The texts exhibit a preference for hyperbole, use *fenia* without any inhibition, their rhyming scheme and style follow the pattern of traditional folk verses.

Nikolai Pogodin's propaganda play *Aristocrats* (*Aristokraty*, 1935) takes these songs straight. In the song of the main hero, a gang leader (*pakhan*), self-conquest and reformation are praised as the victory of *perekovka*.[4] The play was performed 1935/36 in the Vakhtangov theatre[5] at a time when the official ideology of re-forging through work was already on the brink of being abandoned. The characters of the play (quoted by many historians of the Gulag) respect neither state nor the party nor the camp administration. These are prostitutes, petty thieves, hooligans (*zhuliki*) and "thieves in law" (*vory v zakone*).[6] It also features two politicals – engineers. The opening scene presents a characteristic entertainment of the bandits: a card game. They gamble for women and this at first seems to be the very plot of the play. It turns out, however, that the overarching intention is to glorify the success of *perekovka*. The thieves steal from each other for fun, only in order to then return the stolen items. The comic effect is accentuated by their boasts that they had never worked in their whole lives. These characters are made to appear as simple, harmless and even sympathetic fellows. At this point the main

4 | The play is thoroughly analyzed in Klein 1995/96.

5 | In the "Realistic Theatre", Moscow, the play was performed as well (since 1935) and at the end of 1936 the film *Zakliuchennye*, based on Pogodin's play, was shown in cinemas.

6 | The phenomenon of the *vor v zakone*, its history and present state in Russia as well as its role in the criminal world is the subject of the study by Gurov (1990). Gurov gives an account of the functioning of the criminal subculture - governed by a law system of its own - in which the *vor v zakone* enjoys an elite position which includes several privileges and means the authority over the lower status members. The newly chosen thief in law is honoured by a "coronation."

agent in the ideological theory of re-education, the "educator" (*vospitatel'*), appeals to the bandits to abandon their policy of abstaining from labour and to embrace the joys of work. The political commissar, not surprisingly a *chekist*, adds his own exhortations praising the rewards of work. Pogodin skilfully juxtaposes the commissar's elevated rhetoric with the jargon (*fenia*) of the bandits. The prostitutes for their part use a vulgar language, while the engineers, not without irony calling themselves "parasites" (*vrediteli*), discuss construction plans for the Belomor Canal in technical terms. These *vrediteli* become the central figures in the gigantic project and are finally awarded with an order. Thus the audience learns that not only the professional criminals but also "parasites," counterrevolutionary elements, can become useful members of the communist society.

The bandits' boss, the *pakhan* Kostia-Kapitan, is the first to convert. He is portrayed as a witty character with great authority who, justifying his own conversion to the right cause, tries to convince the members of his gang that it is both profitable and an honour to have a part in the Belomor Canal enterprise. He addresses his gang with a speech:

> I can tell from your heartbeat that you don't understand anything. What the chekists say is not empty talk. They hold out a ladder to you and urge you to climb it. From the first rung with better clothes you step up to better food. And then there is the rung which entitles you to engage in the "shock work" system with its own rewards. And you will forget that you are in a camp. They will allow you to have your wives with you. On the highest rung your ten years are crossed out and vanish like a nightmare after a bad hangover (Pogodin 1935).[7]

The boldest and naughtiest of the prostitutes, Sonia, all of a sudden appears with the wheelbarrow (*tachka*), one of indispensable tools of the Belomor Canal workers. In order to justify the fact that she too had been re-forged, she uses the clichés of the *perekovka* ideology. Pogodin allows

7 | "Я вижу по вашему сердцебиению, что вы ничего не понимаете. Чекисты – не фокусники, они перед каждым человеком ставят лестницу и предлагают: 'Поднимайтесь'. Чем выше, тем красивее жизнь. На одной ступеньке вы получаете лучшее обмундирование, потом питание, потом бывает ступень ударности, и вы забываете, что вы сидите в лагере, вам разрешают выписать жену. Но бывает такая высокая ступень, когда все ваши десять лет зачеркиваются и исчезают, как кошмарный сон с похмелья."

only one person to resist re-education – a woman, referred to in the play as "the Tattooed" (*tatuirovannaia*): "The devil take the *perekovka*. Me, I don't give a hoot [...]" (*ibid.*).[8]

Pogodin does not hesitate to use hyperbole to characterize the friendly relationship between the criminals and the politicals, as well as between the criminals and the chekists in having his main figure, Kostia-Kapitan, say to the mother of one of the engineers:

Mum, [...]. Did you ever expect that the life of your extraordinary son would be destined one day to become intertwined with the life of a renowned tramp? I never expected that my destiny would bring me to cross paths with this extraordinary man, the chekist comrade Gromov (*ibid.*).[9]

In the closing statement the theme of crossing paths in life is taken up by Gromov, who addresses the successfully re-forged individuals:

Yes, comrades, our destinies did become intertwined and this gave rise to many touching, sublime and genuinely human moments. Why is the Belomor Canal so famous? Here, with an unheard-of hardiness, with Bolshevist persistence, outcasts and people who went astray and real enemies join forces in Stalin's all-embracing geniality and commitment to the socialist goal. This is recognized throughout the country. Nobody is better equipped to understand this than we, those who took part in the construction of the famous Belomor Canal. My greetings and my heart-felt handshake to all those whom I encouraged to work and who fought with me to gain such a glorious victory. That's it! (Curtain) (*ibid.*).[10]

---

8 | "Ни черта я не перековалась – и плюю на все через плечо [...]."

9 | "Мамаша, ...Вы не ожидали, что судьба вашего замечательного сына переплетется с судьбой знаменитого жулика? А я не ожидал, что моя судьба переплетется с жизнью замечательного чекиста, товарища Громова."

10 | "Да, товарищи, наши судьбы переплелись, и в этом сплетении тысяч жизней много трогательного, высокого, истинно человеческого. Почему будет славен Беломорский канал? Здесь с невиданной смелостью, с большевистской суровостью, со сталинской широтой действуют силы приобщения к социалистическому труду таких людей, как Дорохов или Садовский. Отщепенцы, отверженные, потерявшие себя и даже прямые враги – сегодня они признанные люди на своей родине. Никто, может быть, не поймет этого с таким волнением, как мы, прошедшие славный путь Беломорстроя. Всем, с кем я дрался, кого я

The propaganda effect of the play must have been tremendous. In his *Gulag Archipelago* (*Arkhipelag GULag*, 1973) Solzhenitsyn sharply criticizes Pogodin's *Aristocrats*. In his view the romantization of criminals, which has roots in the Russian literature of the 19th century (and parallels in the German and English literatures) and is perpetuated by authors like Il'f and Petrov, Leonid Leonov, Isaak Babel' and others in the Soviet era, is overshadowed by the crimes the bandits commit in the camps intimidating, pestering, robbing, assaulting, murdering their noncriminal inmates. Shalamov, too, in his study *Sketches of the Criminal World* (*Ocherki prestupnogo mira*, 1959) condemns the heroization of crime by those authors.

Ideological change

The attitude towards criminals changed dramatically with the beginning of the Great Terror in the late 1930s. The Stalinist purges were meant to extinguish "dirty elements" which threatened the "hygiene" of the Soviet Union in the process of building communism. Yet, now these did not include as before only class enemies, enemies of the people, foreigners (especially communists from foreign countries), internal enemies in the leading ranks of the party, treacherous members of the politburo, members of the communist party, and counterrevolutionary activists. The country had to be cleansed of bandits, especially robbers, thieves and murderers, as well as of prostitutes, hooligans, beggars, drunkards, juvenile delinquents. As a result of this change the criminals who had been considered socially near now became socially dangerous. In his contribution to this volume, David Shearer defines this change as the "politization of the criminals," who were now seen as belonging to the same species as the so called counterrevolutionaries, the "enemies of the people" (*vragi naroda*). Shearer shows that it was Stalin who was directly responsible for this radical change, assisted by Genrikh Iagoda in whose view repeated offenders were incorrigible. As a consequence of this change and as a result of Stalin's condemnation of the criminals, the politicals and the criminals shared the same destiny. The shift from socially near to "de-classed" (*deklassirovannye*) elements determined the way they were now

брал в работу, как мог, с кем побеждал и соединен глубокой дружбой, – привет и крепкое рукопожатие. Все! ЗАНАВЕС."

treated. Because state property, i.e "socialist property" and social order were at stake, Stalin demanded a planned extermination of these groups in all regions of the Soviet Union.[11]

Stalin was particularly alert to the possibility that bandits with their own hierarchy and customs, a state within the state as it were, might rival his own power structure. It should be noted that some of the literature on the camps pointed to parallels between the official and the criminal regimes. Thus Stalin whose career began as a robber was likened to the boss (*pakhan*) of one of two rivalling gangs. As a matter of fact any organization not under direct party control, be it legal or not, was feared as a potential threat and fiercely persecuted. Many thousand criminals, including juveniles, were relentlessly killed in order to protect the social (socialist) order. Besides, the threat of a wide-spread criminal activity existed not only in Stalin's and Iagoda's mind but had a foundation in fact. On Stalin's initiative the *perekovka* and its key concept of criminals being socially near and capable of re-education were officially given up in 1937. Accordingly the camp journal *Perekovka* was closed in the same year.

Class system in the camps

After the Great Terror mass executions were stopped. The criminals, "socially harmful elements" (*social'no vrednye elementy* – as the term went), as well as politicals were imprisoned, sentenced and sent to forced labour camps. Still, the criminals remained a privileged group. The notes of those politicals who had a chance to write down their experiences while in camps during the Great Terror show that they had no exact knowledge of the mass trials of repeated offenders and their executions. What they did know was that criminals were treated as a privileged group. Although the

11 | See Binner et al. (eds.) 2010, 40-45. The authors, referring to statistics and archive materials maintain that already in the beginning of the 1930s, the criminals lost their privileged status. They point out that the attribute "counterrevolutionary" could be addressed not only to the politicals but also to the professional criminals. In the end of the 1920s sentences (punishment) varied according to the groups who had been arrested: the kulaks, the criminals, the politicals. To the criminals three categories were applied: 1. Organized criminals, 2. Recidivist thieves, 3. Minor delinquents. The authors stress the fact that criminals had to be persecuted in jail and camp and insist on their being the "forgotten victims."

distinction between the socially near and the socially distant was banned from official discourse it must have seemed to the politicals as if it had never been abandoned. Solzhenitsyn and other memoirists continued to use the term "socially near" to describe the status of the criminals. In fact, things got even worse. With the toleration of camp authorities, or even with their active encouragement, the criminals were allowed to establish their own cruel rule within the camps. Guards (the blue caps) and the criminals, regarded as fellow proletarians, became allies. They performed a variety of roles, such as managers of labour brigades, instructors and were absurdly entrusted with guard duties.

The distinction between the socially near and socially distant, whether officially sanctioned or not, may have been the source for the establishment of a two class system in the camps. The politicals stigmatized as parasites and enemies of the people were enslaved. In the complicated camp system they were the only ones to work. The former class system stood on its head. If in the old system it was the proletariat that was exploited, now it was the politicals, regarded as members of the bourgeoisie, whose labour was exploited.

Many accounts express the astonishment of newcomers not yet familiar with the facts of life in these camps at a regime run by a top layer of serious criminals, with the help of their underlings and other minor criminals. The power exercised by the underlings against the politicals was delegated power; they themselves remained at the mercy of the criminal elite.

A peculiar hierarchy evolved in the camps. In the background there was the unlimited power of the guards. In the daily life of the inmates the power of the top rank criminals also seemed unlimited. They could punish with utmost brutality, even murder another inmate (not only politicals but even their underlings), without being called to account. Štajner in his autobiography *Seven Thousand Days in Siberia* gives a picture of it:

A rather motley crew lived in that cell. Ivanov, the *pakhan* (boss) of the criminals, lounged on his bunk all day long, feeling like a *tsar'*, while the *kusochniki* danced around him like courtiers. Even the other *urkas* respected him. He was constantly issuing curt little commands: "Belyi, bring me some water!" – "Korsubyi, hand me the towel!" – "Belaia ruchka, give me a light." None of Ivanov's "subordinates" dared contradict him, for the other *blatnye* would have beat him to a pulp (Štajner 1988, 105).[12]

There were instances where the line dividing the two classes could be and was crossed. A political, for example, could win respect from a leading *urka* by proving his physical strength. Štajner mentions the case of a Hungarian lawyer, Kerosi-Molnár, who was assaulted by a criminal. The ensuing fist fight was decisively won by the Hungarian who then calmly returned to his bunk and continued with his translation of Pushkin's poetry into Hungarian. Marlen Korallov, who later became a co-founder of Memorial, was highly respected after he defeated an opponent; the ring-leader granted him special favours (for instance a better sleeping place) and everybody in the gang was aware of his having become the chief's protégé. He recounts:

The camp understood: if I become part of the troika around Nikola [the chief – R.L.], then I become part of the camp elite [...]. All attitudes to me changed instantly (quoted from Applebaum 2003, 285).

As a rule, however, the world of the camp was split into two spheres. Some reports present a picture one could best describe as showing a world upside down. The boss of the gang (a thief, robber or murderer) with his entourage appears as the carnival king claiming the position at the top, with non-criminals playing the role of those at the bottom. The political inmates perceived this as a breakdown of all moral standards.

Accused of belonging to conspiratorial circles, of treason, espionage and Trotskyist deviations, the politicals were sentenced according to article 58 and had to learn that they were deprived of all rights and left at the mercy of the ruling class, the gangsters. The power structure the latter established in jail and in the camps allowed them to humiliate, to beat, to

12 | "Bilo je to šareno društvo. Najstariji među kriminalcima tzv. 'pahan', bio je neki Ivanov, izležavao se posebno i uvijek izabirao položaj da leži s rukom naslonjen na pričnu, a da gornji dio tijela malo istakne, a oko njega plesali bi 'kusočniki' i slušali sva njegova naređenja. Pa i ostali kriminalci gledali su ga sa strahopoštovanjem i izvršavali svako njegovo naređenje. 'Bijeli, daj mi vode, Karsubi, ručnik, Bijeli podloži peć' – čulo se kako Ivanov podanicima zapovijeda. Teško onome koji ne bi poslušao, taj bi bio nasmrt isprebijan" (Štajner 1986, 114).

rob, to kill those at the bottom. The guards did not intervene. Solzhenitsyn reports:

> The most inveterate and hardened thieves were given unbridled power on the islands of the Archipelago, in camp districts, and in camps - power over the population of their own country, over peasants, petty bourgeoisie, and the intelligentsia, power they had never before had in history, power they had never in any state in all the world, power which they couldn't even dream of out in freedom. And now they were given all other people as slaves. What bandit would ever decline such power? (Solzhenitsyn 1978, II, 450).[13]

The two class system was accentuated by yet another factor. The politicals were predominantly members of the educated class, many belonging to the intelligentsiia. This put them in sharp contrast to the people without education. To show intellectual superiority was risky. The criminals responded to every sign of it with disdain, obscene mockery and occasionally even abuse. The generic name for intellectuals, Ivan Ivanovich, had a strong negative connotation. Compensating for the extreme hardships and inequities of the external world, the politicals in camps re-established an order in which they were the cultured, educated and morally superior class, while the others were the scum of the earth to be looked at with contempt.

The politicals recognized one another by the way they talked, walked and by the way they looked at each other. They could read and write, they were familiar to a greater or smaller extent with Russian literature and art. The criminals were generally illiterate (*negramotnye*). When they needed or wanted to write something they had to turn to a literate (*gramotnyi*) member of the other class.

There were also some other points of contact between the two groups where the criminals found themselves dependent on the more educated inmates. The criminals wished to be entertained and demanded from the

13 | "[...] самым заядлым матёрым блатнякам передавалась безотчетная власть на островах Архипелага, на лагучастках и лагпунктах – власть над населением своей страны, над крестьянами, мещанами и интеллигенцией, власть, которой они не имели никогда в истории, никогда в одном государстве, о которой на воле они и помыслить не могли - и теперь отдавали им всех прочих людей как рабов. Какой же бандит откажется от такой власти?" (Solzhenitsyn 1974, 424).

intelligentsiia to tell them stories, preferably adventure stories, which they called *romany* ("romances"). Shalamov in *The Snake Charmer* (*Zaklinatel' zmei*, 1954) tells the story of a newcomer whom the bandits intimidate, humiliate, punch in the face, drive away from a bunk, order to sleep near the fecal container. He is forced to empty the container and perform oth-er unpleasant tasks. Shalamov describes the abrupt improvement of the status of the newcomer when it turned out that he was a good story teller. Whereas Shalamov himself refused to tell stories to the criminals, the newcomer in his tale was only too glad to provide the criminals with 'literary' entertainment in return for a bowl of soup or a better sleeping place.

The politicals had many things in common. They shared a similar background and a common fate; they were "enemies of the people," the lowest of the lowest. But they were individuals who remained individuals. Regrettably for them, they were incapable of joint action. Whatever solidarity they might have felt, they could not organize a cohesive group. That, however, might have been their only possibility to resist the brutalities of the criminals. The latter, as was shown, managed to form a well-organized group that was based on a strict hierarchy of power. As it was, the political criminals were the weaker part in confrontations with the relentless brutality of the bandits, mainly because they were physically weaker but also because they could not count on the solidarity of their co-prisoners. Solzhenitsyn writes about the passivity of the other inmates when one of the politicals was attacked:

> But all your comrades, all your fellow Article 58's, who have been plundered one by one even before you got there, sit there submissively, hunched over, and they stare right past you, and it's even worse when they look at you the way they always do look at you, as though no violence were going on at all, no plundering, as though it were a natural phenomenon, as though it were the grass growing and the rain falling (Solzhenitsyn 1978, I, 503).[14]

14 | "Ты смотришь на соседей, на товарищей – давайте же или сопротивляться или заявим протест! – но все твои товарищи, твоя Пятьдесят Восьмая, ограбленные по одиночке еще до твоего прихода, сидят покорно, сгорбленно, и смотрят хорошо еще если мимо тебя, а то и на тебя, так обычно смотрят, как будто это не насилие, не грабеж, а явление природы: трава растет, дождик идет" (Solzhenitsyn 1973, 500-501).

The criminals viewed by their victims

As noted above, the coexistence with criminals is a central topic in the autobiographical texts written by ex-convicts who were sentenced according to article 58. All testimonies convey a strong sense of moral outrage; in some instances the writers also express a complete bewilderment.

Some of the politicals tried to comprehend what to a newcomer to the camp seemed to be incomprehensible. They observed the criminals in action, tried to describe and classify their behaviour, the foundation of the power structure which they developed. Although the accounts written by these observers vary in detail, what all of them have in common is a combination of two perspectives in how they narrate the events. One is primarily descriptive, as it were, "ethnographic," or, if some attempts were made at an analysis of the social mechanisms at play, "sociological." The other perspective could be defined as moral, or perhaps that of philosophical anthropology.

The ethnographic perspective

The non-criminal prisoners were victims of the bandits but at the same time some of them were observers curious to understand or to find out how this strange 'society' functioned. An example of how the non-criminal inmates perceived the structure of the criminal collective is quoted by Applebaum. It is a passage from the report of Karol Colonna-Czosnowski, a Polish prisoner, who was confronted with the bandits as the only political prisoner in a "northern logging camp." He describes the hierarchical structure of their community putting stress on the class aspect:

> The Russian criminal was extremely class-conscious in those days. In fact, class to them was everything. In their hierarchy, big-time criminals, such as bank or train robbers, were members of the upper class. Grisha Tchorny, the head of the camp Mafia, was one of them. At the opposite end of the social scale were the petty crooks, like pickpockets. The big boys would use them as their valets and messengers and they received very little consideration. All other crimes formed the bulk of the middle class, but even there, there were distinctions (quoted from Applebaum 2003, 281).

As a rule, the politicals were not expert social scientists. They observed the behaviour of the criminals, witnessed acts of violence and tried to make sense of it. This resulted in a more or less perceptive analysis of the power structure and rank order, of the code of honour, and the variety of punishments applied to those who broke the rules. Some accounts provide a certain degree of insight, others show that the writer finds the criminals so strange as to be beyond any rational interpretation. A comprehensive account of the criminal world in the camps was presented by Shalamov. He was a writer, not a social scientist. Yet, his description of the criminal rank order, for example, is an outstanding example of ethnography, and his analysis of the social relations within the criminal hierarchy and between the criminals and the politicals could have been written by a gifted sociologist. His account *Sketches of the Criminal World* – thoroughly analyzed by Leona Toker in her contribution to this volume – is quoted as a source in encyclopedic articles on the subject.[15]

---

15 | Shalamov's treatise is mentioned as a source concerning the criminal hierarchy (*ugolovnaia ierarkhiia*) in the internet article *Tiuremnye kasty v stranakh byvshego SSSR* (<http://dic.academic.ru/dic.nsf/ruwiki/1504289>; last accessed 10 October 2016) which draws on the investigation of Aleksandrov 2002 (Chapter: *Tabel' o rangakh v prestupnom soobshchestve [delenie na masti]*), which presents some data in Pre-Soviet and Soviet time: The term 'caste' (*kasta* or *mast'*) is applied to the social order of gangster communities in jails and camps. The application of the term is partly metaphorical because the system is not based on heredity, but the rank order from the representatives of the highest rank, the *blatnye*, to the untouchables, the *neprikasaemye*, has a certain resemblance to the Indian caste system. The politicals witnessed degradations, discriminations, even the killings of members of the higher ranks who trespassed laws, ignored the code of honour or violated secrecy rules. The cooperation with the official organs was strongly forbidden, trespassers harshly punished. Criminals who joined the Red Army in the Second World War and were sent back to the camps after the war, experienced degradation and discrimination as 'bitches' (*suki*) which resulted in the so called *such'ia voina*, the bitch war, a deadly fight between the thieves in law and the deviants. (Shalamov, too, gives an account of this event.) The members of the second rank, the *muzhiki*, do not cooperate with the administration, but are willing to work and intend to return to normal life after their release. The *kozly*, forming the third rank, cooperate overtly with the administration, they accept posts as *zavkhoz*, *komendant*, *brigadir*. The *neprikasaemye*, *izgoi*, the untouchables or

Another camp inmate, Julius Margolin,[16] who gave an excellent description and analysis of camp life paying special attention to the criminals, was not a social scientist either, but a philosopher who had studied in Berlin in the 1920s. In his autobiography *Journey into the Land of the Z/K* (*Puteshestvie v stranu ze-ka*, 1952)[17] he writes about a camp on Lake Onega to which political prisoners, mainly Polish Jews (he himself being one of them), were sent. He describes their shock when, after making themselves at home as best they could, they were suddenly assaulted by raiding groups of criminals. "The urki arrived" – he writes laconically (Margolin 2013, 178). As part of his account of life in the camp Margolin attempts to describe the criminal as a social type, characterized by a combination of features: readiness to engage in physical violence, in theft and robbery, and the use of obscene language. Because greed is a dominant feature of this type, Margolin calls them "beasts of prey" (*ibid.*, 179). It appears, however, that he had little knowledge of the criminal hierarchy and the group's rules of behaviour. His observations apply only to the ordinary members of the criminal community, none the less he calls them *urki* – a term in the non-criminals' accounts which seems to cover all ranks of the criminals.

Margolin stresses the fact that the administration treated the *urki* mildly because they were considered to be politically harmless and always willing to cooperate with the camp administration as spies. The *urki* aroused his anger, especially when they called the "westerners" (non-Russian inmates) "fascists" and addressed the Jews as "Yids." This reminded him of the pogroms before the revolution. Margolin observed that young men, even among the westerners, ran wild and soon became *urki* despite their origin and education. He describes with some empathy

outlaws, represent the fourth rank which has subdivisions. They are either *chushki*, that is those who neglect themselves, *opushchennye*, *shkvarnye*, *obizhennye*, or *petukhi* and *musora*, former collaborators with the police, and the *shesterki* – weak, submissive men.

16 | See Leona Toker's comprehensive characterization of Margolin as a writer (Toker 2000, 80-96).

17 | I am referring to the German edition (Margolin 2013). This is the first complete German edition, based on the unabridged, yet unpublished Russian original; a shorter Russian version *Puteshestvie v stranu ze-ka* was published in 1952. There is no English translation.

the inevitable transformation of a normal nice young boy into a criminal, step by step.

It may be noted that Solzhenitsyn describes the same process not only without empathy but with utter revulsion, stressing the aspect of moral decay:

And it was then that the twelve-year-olds crossed the thresholds of the adult prison cells, were equated with adults as citizens possessing full rights, equated by virtue of the most savage prison terms, equated, in their whole unconscious life, by bread rations, bowls of gruel, their places on the sleeping shelves - that is when that old term of Communist re-education, "minors", somehow lost its significance, when the outlines of its meaning faded, became unclear - and Gulag itself gave birth to the ringing and impudent word "kids". [...] But the young people, by the laws of their young life, were not about to be flattened by this life style but, instead, grew into it and adapted to it. Just as new languages and new customs are learned without difficulty in childhood, so the juveniles adopted on the run both the language of the Archipelago - which was that of the thieves - and the philosophy of the Archipelago - and whose philosophy was that? From this life they took for themselves all its most inhuman essence, all its poisonous rotten juice - and as readily as if it had been this liquid, and not milk, that they had sucked from their mothers' breasts in infancy. They grew into camp life so swiftly - not in weeks even, but in days! [...] And in a few *days* children became beasts there! And the worst kind of beasts, with no ethical concepts whatever (Solzhenitsyn 1978, II).[18]

---

18 | "И вот когда двенадцатилетние преступали пороги тюремных взрослых камер, уравненные со взрослыми как полноправные граждане, уравненные в дичайших сроках, почти равных их несознательной жизни, уравненные в хлебной пайке, в миске баланды, в месте на нарах, – вот тогда старый термин коммунистического перевоспитания несовершеннолетние как-то обесценился, оплыл в контурах, стал неясен – и сам ГУЛаг родил звонкое нахальное слово малолетка! [...] Но молодые по законам молодой жизни не должны были этим укладом расплющится, а – врасти и приспособиться. Как в раннем возрасте без затруднения усваиваются новые языки, новые обычаи – так малолетки *с ходу* переняли и язык Архипелага – а это язык блатных, и философию Архипелага – а чья это философия? Они взяли для себя из этой жизни всю самую бесчеловечную суть, весь ядовитый гниющий сок – и так привычно, будто жидкость эту, эту, а не молоко, сосали они еще младенцами. Они так быстро врастали в лагерную жизнь - не за недели даже, а за дни! [...] И в несколько *дней* дети становятся

Generally, the criminals are experienced by their victims as beings from another reality. Among the features that make them alien is not only their criminal behaviour as such but also their language, and their peculiar entertainments, in particular card games.

The most comprehensive analysis of both can be found in Likhachev's accounts. Likhachev spent four years on the Solovki Islands. During his stay there he listened to the way the criminals spoke, sang, played and was able to take notes. After his return to his family and academic life, the scholar published a notable book on the criminals' language, their jargon (*fenia*), in the expressivity of which he was particularly interested (*obraznyi iazyk*).

Solzhenitsyn is not interested in studying the vocabulary of the criminal language. What he is concerned about is the criminals' distinct pronunciation and the distortion of the Russian language:

> They hiss when they speak, enjoying that hissing more than the vowel and consonant sounds of speech - and the only thing about their speech that resembles the Russian language is the endings of verbs and nouns. It is gibberish (Solzhenitsyn 1978, I, 502).[19]

What perplexes him most is the impossibility of communication with the criminals:

> In one moment, all the customs and habits of human intercourse you have lived with all your life have broken down. In your entire previous life [...] you spoke words to other people and they answered you in words. And those words produced actions. One might persuade, or refuse, or come to an agreement. You recall various human relationships - a request, an order, an expression of gratitude.

тут зверьми! – да зверьми худшими, не имеющих этических представлений [...]" (Solzhenitsyn 1974, 438-439).

19 | "Они кривят рты, будто собираются куснуть тебя избоку, они при разговоре шипят, наслаждаясь этим шипением больше, чем гласными и согласными звуками речи – и сама речь их только окончаниями глаголов и существительных напоминает русскую, она – тарабарщина" (Solzhenitsyn 1973, 499).

But what has overtaken you here is beyond all these words and beyond all these relationships (*ibid.*).[20]

Even prisoners without academic training were struck by the peculiarities of the criminals' language. For example, when Štajner, uninterested in linguistic analysis, reports about the life in the barracks (see the quotation above), he matter-of-factly employs words from the criminals' own vocabulary, such as: *pakhan, fraer, urki, blatnye, kusochniki.*

There is a basic opposition between the two key terms corresponding to the elementary two class system within the camps: the inmates of the camps are either *urki* or *fraery* (non-criminals). The terms are used in most camp accounts. Dictionaries of the criminal jargon offer some etymological explanations and trace the idiom to the gangster world of Odessa which was Yiddish. *Fraer,* for instance, derives from Middle High German "Freier" and means "a free man," but also "a bridegroom," the latter being a reference to a prostitute's customer. "Freier" then travelled via the Odessa Yiddish into the language of Russian speaking bandits with a slight shift of meaning: a "*fraer*" in a camp was a dumb and naïve inmate, someone to be exploited. Semantically, the English terms "sucker" and "mark" come close to this latter sense. From the criminals' point of view everybody but themselves was a sucker. Solzhenitsyn comments:

And what did their word "frayersky" - "of the suckers" - mean? It meant what was universally human, what pertained to all normal people. And it was precisely this universally human world, *our* world, with its morals, customs, and mutual relationships, which was most hateful to the thieves, most subject to their ridicule, juxtaposed most sharply to their own antisocial, anti-public *kubla* - or clan (Solzhenitsyn 1978, II, 450).[21]

---

20 | "В один миг трещат и ломаются все привычки людского общения, с которыми ты прожил жизнь. Во всей твоей прошлой жизни – особенно до ареста, но даже и после ареста, но даже отчасти и на следствии – ты говорил другим людям *слова*, и они отвечали тебе *словами*, и эти слова производили действие, можно было или убедить, или отклонить, или согласиться. Ты помнишь разные людские отношения – просьбу, приказ, благодарность, – но то, что застигло тебя здесь – вне этих слов и вне этих отношений" (*ibid.*, 500).

21 | "И что значит само их слово 'фраерский'? *фраерский* значит – общечеловеческий, такой, как у всех нормальных людей. Именно этот

Another insight in the completely foreign world of the bandits was provided by a study of their central occupation: card games. The criminals' card games are mentioned in many accounts. The most precise description is given in Likhachev's article *Card Games of Criminals* (*Kartezhnye igry ugolovnikov*, 1930). Likhachev came into close contact with the criminals (after one of them happened to save his life), which allowed him an opportunity to study their behaviour at close quarters. The paper published in the journal *Solovetskie ostrova* is the product of a close observation of the peculiar piece of theatre unfolding before his eyes (Likhachev 1930). Winning in a game of cards was an important step in one's criminal career, even more important for gaining a status in a gang, among the *shpana*, than achievements in robbery or theft. A successful gamester became a big shot (*dukhovyi zhygan*) in the gang. Whoever was not able or willing to risk money, clothes (*triapki*) or even – on occasion – his own life, was considered a low character committing a breach of the criminal code. A true *zhulik*[22] (as the criminals liked to call themselves) was never without his cards, always ready to play, no matter when and where, even when engaged in "business."

In the conditions of a prison or a camp playing cards provided the excitements otherwise associated with criminal life: taking risks, counting on luck, enjoying the promise of a suspense. Likhachev speaks of a thief's physiological need to experience risk which the cards seemed to satisfy. Likhachev quotes a thief saying that to win in a card game is like feeling how a wallet slips from beneath the lining of a *fraer*'s jacket into one's hand. Likhachev refrains from moralizing comments (only in the end of the piece does he mention that as far as thieves were concerned, the labour camp failed in its intended corrective function).

Within the rigid criminal hierarchy there evolved internal fractions on the basis of one's place of origin, so that those who came from a certain street or neighbourhood in Moscow or Leningrad associated with others

---

общечеловеческий мир, *наш* мир, с его моралью, привычками жизни и взаимным обращением, наиболее ненавистен блатным, наиболее высмеивается ими, наиболее противопоставляется своему антисоциальному *кублу*" (Solzhenitsyn 1974, 433).

22 | *Zhulik* has the connotation of hooligan. In other instances the criminals call themselves *brodiagi*, *bosiaki*, *putevye* etc. giving their criminal profession a completely different connotation.

coming from there. Such affiliations also played a role when it came to playing cards. Likhachev notes the most minute details of the process of the production of cards: the search for paper (an easy task if the particular camp had a prison library), the skilful manufacture of a glue necessary to ensure that paper sheets stuck together. Then there was also the paint (water colours), without which the cards' suits could not be differentiated, as well as the carefully made paper cut-outs with representations of the figures and values of the cards.

In the Solovki camps card games were played in the barracks on the bunks and on the floor, as well as under the bunks that were shared by criminals with non-criminals. When a game began, onlookers gathered. In case a guard approached, the gamblers immediately stopped. Likhachev provides a comprehensive list of different games, analyzing their varying complexity.[23] The inmates played either for money or for various kinds of goods, often for clothes. Only underwear (the *otvetnoe*) was exempt. Likhachev not only gives an overview of the different games, but also reconstructs the concrete process of an entire game, the players' moves, the reactions of losers and winners. Once again, the importance of the code of honour is noted. The loser had to honour his debts under any circumstances, even when the demands of the winner were excessive. Likhachev writes about an inmate who, after having lost all his belongings, cut one of his fingers in lieu of money and clothes.

Cheating was an essential and accepted ingredient of the game when played by criminals among themselves, and even more so when *fraery* were asked to join the game. Having been robbed of most of their possessions by the criminals upon entering the camp, the non-criminals now had the dubious pleasure of being cheated out of the rest of them.

There were two categories of games with two different sets of rules, with the main difference being that the rules regarding cheating and trickery were much relaxed when it was just the criminals playing (*shpanskaia igra*), and a bit more strict when the game was played with "the suckers" (*fraerskaia igra*). When *fraery* were invited to join the game and consented to it, it was as if an invisible line was crossed. (It appears that *fraery* could decline such invitations without immediate sanctions). Interestingly enough, Likhachev observed a certain evolution of rules in

23 | Key terms of the criminals' jargon concerning names of different card games and tricks are listed at the end of Likhachev's article.

the game played among the criminals, so that trickery and cheating were becoming even more tolerated.

His observations convey the impression that the criminals' days were filled, quite literally, with card playing rather than hard labour, and the outcomes of games generally determined the social relations within a gang. Both the criminals' life in the camps and their card playing were based on the same organizational structure which, in turn, emerged from their passion for risk-taking and games of chance. This was the framework that enabled the criminals to live according to their own rules and to avoid to a considerable extent the official camp regulations.

In this context, theft itself seems to be a kind of game. In the camps the criminals did not steal out of necessity, rather, it was a sport to assault the exhausted newcomers (frightening them at the same time), to strip them nearly naked, to take their 'fancy' clothes, jackets, trousers, pullovers etc. or to fetch their hidden precious bread portion from under their heads when sleeping. The card games with their tricks, ranking order, brutal demands, and murder commissions represented the very essence of the criminal world.

Incidentally, Štajner, who spent his first months of imprisonment in the Solovki camps and had the unasked-for opportunity to observe camp life from the inside elsewhere for another 18 years, also noted the crucial importance of card games for criminal inmates and reported many relevant details:

> The criminals spent all their time playing cards. These cards were made of little cut-out pieces of newspaper pasted together with a glue made of soft bread, and then marked with an indelible pencil they had hidden away (Štajner 1988, 105).[24]

The transformation of bread into a component of playing cards showed the criminals' disregard for non-criminal inmates who were always close to starvation. The criminals, on the other hand, were never hungry, one of their skills being to provide themselves with an adequate food supply.

In one chapter of his book Štajner gives an account of a card game which the criminal prisoners played in the camp. The winner would order

24 | "Kriminalci su stalno igrali karata. Izrezali bi novinski papir na komadiće, od mekog kruha napravili bi ljepilo, tada bi nekoliko slojeva papira zajedno slijepili, iz neke rupe izvadili bi tintenu olovku i obojili karte" (Štajner 1986, 114).

the loser to commit a crime, for instance, a murder. Štajner reports that the crime was in fact committed:

Once in a while, the object of the game would be a human life. A victim would be designated - either because no other stake was available or because a conflict had erupted among the criminals - and the loser had to carry out the murder. If the victim was present, the murderer would pick up a suitable instrument and take immediate action. But if the victim was in another cell or in another section of the camp, the killer had to find a way to reach him. Sometimes the victim would be warned in time; then a regular manhunt would ensue. In some cases, it was years before a killer caught up with his victim. But if the elected killer refused to carry out his assignment, he would be killed himself. Among criminals, treason was punishable by death (*ibid.*, 106).[25]

Danilo Kiš's version of the card game story is an extension of Štajner's rather short mention of this labour camp entertainment with its fatal consequences. In his story *The Magic Card Dealing* (*Magijsko kruženje karata*) from *A Tomb for Boris Davidovich*, Kiš develops this passage from Štajner's memoirs into a complex plot, featuring the winner, the loser and the victim (Kiš 1989, 53-72). What intrigues him in Štajner's account is the fact that the person who fell victim to the winner's verdict had no premonition of what was in store for him and could be killed by the loser even after years. Kiš introduces the victim as the surgeon Dr Taube, Jewish by descent, a political prisoner with a socialist past. He also mentions Štajner in his story as a fellow prisoner of Taube's. Kiš explains the rules of the game, its history and terminology in the chapter called *Treatise on Games of Chance*, informing the reader of the "code of honour" of the criminal players and retelling in detail the execution of the verdict.

25 | "Igralo se i za živote drugih ljudi. Kad su izbili sukobi među kriminalcima i kad je iz neke grupe trebalo nekog likvidirati, onda bi onaj koji je igru izgubio morao likvidirati osuđenog. Ako je osuđeni bio tu, na licu mjesta, ubojica bi to uradio vrlo brzo, kamenom ili kojim drugim predmetom. Ako je žrtva bila u drugom logorskom odjeljenju, onda je ubojica bio dužan da po svaku cijenu pronađe onoga kojeg je trebalo ubiti. Bilo je slučajeva da je žrtva bila unaprijed obaviještena, onda je nastala potjera. Nekada je trajalo godinama da se ubojica dočepa svoje žrtve. Onoga pak koji bi se usprotivio da izvrši ubojstvo, ili bi ga odgađao izgovorima, osudili bi na smrt zbog izdajstva" (*ibid.*, 115).

In order to restore his honour as a ruthless criminal, the loser, a Georgian, pursued his prey for years, finally killing Taube with an axe while the doctor was on duty in a hospital in Tiumen', thousands of miles away from the original scene.

The short story *On Tick* (*Na predstavku*) in Shalamov's *Kolyma tales* (*Kolymskie rasskazy*) tells of a card game with a deadly ending. The narrator presents in a matter of fact manner the course of a game in which the gambling bet includes anything in the room – or rather, the barracks. The loser, obliged to honour his debt by any means, feels free to demand the property of others in order to satisfy the winner's wish. With an extreme economy of words, one of Shalamov's masterly procedures, the narrator describes how the loser demands a pullover from a prisoner who at that moment happened to pursue some task in the room. The man, who cherishes the pullover as the only thing that was left as a memory of his wife, refuses and is immediately stabbed by the loser. The blood-stained pullover is drawn from the corpse. The narrator, who had entered the room together with the victim just shortly before the incident, leaves without, it seems, experiencing any emotion whatsoever, his only thought being that he would now need to look for another helpmate at his next shift at work.

Sasha stretched out the dead man's arms, tore off his undershirt, and pulled the sweater over his head. The sweater was red, and the blood on it was hardly noticeable. Seva folded the sweater into the plywood suitcase - carefully, so as not to get the blood on his fingers. The game was over. I went back to my barracks. Now I had to find a new partner to cut wood with (Shalamov 1994, 10).[26]

This is what Shalamov calls his version of factography. Štajner, the documentarist, confirms the related event:

The *urkas* didn't just gamble for their own clothes but for the clothes of the other men in the cell. It was an honor to steal from a political. A criminal would step up

26 | "Сашка растянул руки убитого, разорвал нательную рубашку и стянул свитер через голову. Свитер был красный, и кровь на нем была едва заметна. Севочка бережно, чтобы не запачкать пальцев, сложил свитер в фанерный чемодан. Игра была кончена, и я мог идти домой. Теперь надо было искать другого партнера для пилки дров" (Shalamov 2013, 53).

to his unsuspecting victim, point at the desired article of clothing, and say: "Take it off!" Only rarely did anyone refuse (Štajner 1988, 106).[27]

The moralistic perspective

The anthropological moralizing view of the criminals by their victims is marked by an initial shock and perplexity. All newcomers to prisons and forced labour camps describe their first contact with the criminals as a terrifying experience which left them absolutely helpless. The descriptions of theft and robbery, rapes, beatings and murders convey the impression that all these acts were executed as a matter of course. Those who fell victim to theft observed with astonishment that the stealing of their clothes or other belongings was performed routine-like, as a rightful transfer of ownership. The perpetrators demonstrating their superiority did not bother to conceal their deeds.

The first published report about the camp world which we owe to Evgeniia Ginzburg is explicitly moralistic. She describes the first contact with the criminals in her autobiography *Journey into the Whirlwind* (*Krutoi marshrut*, vol. I):

> They were the cream of the criminal world: murderers, sadists, adept at every kind of sexual perversion. [...] Without wasting any time they set about terrorizing and bullying the "ladies", delighted to find that "enemies of the people" were creatures even more despised and outcast than themselves [...]. They seized our bits of bread, snatched the last of our rags with our bundles, pushed us out of the places we had managed to find (Ginzburg 1967, 353-354).[28]

---

27 | "Ali kriminalci nisu igrali samo za svoju odjeću, nego i za odjeću drugih zatvornika. Osobito j bilo časno kad je trebalo oteti stvari nekom 'frajeru'. Žrtva je sjedila mirno na svome mjestu ne sluteći ništa. Prišao je kriminalac i rekao: 'Skini to!' i pokazao na komad odjeće koji je maloprije proigrao. Nitko se nije usudio usprotiviti" (Štajner 1986, 115).

28 | "Это были не обычные блатнячки, а самые сливки уголовного мира. Так называемые 'стервы' – рецидивистки, убийцы, садистки, мастерицы половых извращений. [...] Они сию же секунду принялись терроризировать 'фраеров', 'контриков'. Их приводило в восторг сознание, что есть на свете люди, еще более презренные, еще более отверженные, чем они, – враги народа! [...] Они отнимали

All memoirists describe the 'event' of being robbed; it is one of the topoi of their narratives. Margolin gives a similar account of his being robbed: completely perplexed, he was forced to witness how all his belongings (including mementos) fell victim to the greed of the criminals who approached him in joint action. Solzhenitsyn, too, describes his first contact with the criminals which was being assaulted by thieves: "From that moment, nothing that belongs to you is yours any longer. And all you yourself are is a rubber dummy around which superfluous things are wrapped which can easily be taken off." He states: "They are not people. This has become clear to you in one moment" (Solzhenitsyn 1978, I, 503).[29] Here Solzhenitsyn, in addition to being a kind of ethnographer looking at the alien tribe of the bandits, is a relentless moralist whose background in philosophical anthropology inclines him to doubt the humanity of that tribe.

Ginzburg served time in a penitentiary camp for female criminals under especially severe conditions, and experienced this time as the apex of her sufferings. She is nauseated by the abominable creatures to whose attacks she is exposed. To her these women are beyond comprehension. She makes no effort to understand why they are what they are, where they come from, what fate had shaped them (some of them had certainly been *besprizorniki*, children left alone after the death of their parents in a camp). What she sees in them is the very face of inhumanity. She does all she can to avoid physical contact with them, she neither listens nor talks to them. She does this even when she is screamed at, berated in the most obscene ways. Such scenes regularly occur when she, in the capacity of a medical aid, refuses to certify the physical inability for hard work of those who merely try to shirk labour. In *Within the Whirlwind* (*Krutoi marshrut*, vol. II) she describes her stupefaction (*izumlenie*) when she is facing a scene of unseen before debauches:

у нас хлеб, вытаскивали последние тряпки из наших узлов, выталкивали с занятых мест" (Ginzburg 1985, I, 363-364).

29 | "С этой минуты ничто твое – уже не твое, и сам ты - только гуттаперчевая болванка, на которую напялены лишние вещи, но вещи можно снять. [...] Они – не люди, это объяснилось тебе в одну минуту" (Solzhenitsyn 1973, 500).

The criminals are beyond the human. I am not willing to describe their orgies, though it happened that I had to endure it, becoming their forced eyewitness (Ginzburg 1981, 330).[30]

Ginzburg is not the only victim-observer who is struck by the total lack of inhibition, the giving in to every urge, the crude performance of sexual acts. Similar observations are made by Margarete Buber-Neumann, who spent two years as a political convict with the criminals in a Soviet camp in Kazakhstan before she became a prisoner in the Nazi concentration camp in Ravensbrück (Buber-Neumann 1949). Applebaum quotes the reaction of a Polish prisoner, Antoni Ekart, who writes about "the complete lack of inhibition on the part of the *urkas* who would openly carry out all natural functions, including onanism. This gave them a striking resemblance to monkeys, with whom they seemed to have much more in common than with men" (Applebaum 2003, 281). All these testimonies of what the witnesses considered beastly behaviour are filled with the most acute moral revulsion. The female criminals did not act as human beings any more than the male ones did.

An extreme case of inhumanity is experienced by Ginzburg when she witnesses cannibalism. The passage in her memoirs concerning this event is a narrative of its own. One day she unexpectedly receives a love letter written in Latin. Her future husband, a German by origin, sentenced to ten years and working in his profession as a surgeon, sends her the following message: "Meus amor ... mea vita ... mea spes ..." (Ginzburg 1981, 329). This pleasant incident ends with a poignant counterpoint: a man caught eating human flesh is brought to the hospital by the officials. Having advanced to the status of a nurse in the infirmary, Ginzburg is charged with the task of improving, by injections, the poor health of this man, who has to be made fit to stand trial. The cannibal was not originally a professional criminal: he became one. Did the camp conditions and starvation transform him into a cannibal or was it the beastly nature of this man that erupted in the camp? Ginzburg refrains from giving an answer.

---

30 | "Уголовные – за пределами человеческого. Их оргии не хочу я живописать, хоть и пришлось немало вынести, становясь их вынужденным свидетелем." (Ginzburg 1985, II, 16). See the impressive interpretation of these passages by Franziska Thun-Hohenstein (2007, 114 and *passim*).

Solzhenitsyn, often a keen observer and generally reliable historian of the Gulag, alternates between an ethnographic perspective and a relentlessly moralizing one. He points out the sharp contrast between the self-image of the thieves, rapists and murderers as being free, resistant to authority, obeying only their self-created code and their own law, and their contemptible and brutal behaviour, the exploitation of the helplessness and weakness of their victims. In his anthropology the criminals are the "others," the completely alien ones. He stresses the fact that they come from a world the intelligentsiia was not familiar with and that they successfully imported that world into jails and camps:

> You see three or four – oh, no, not faces! They aren't monkey muzzles either, because monkeys' muzzles are much, much decenter and more thoughtful! No, and they aren't simply hideous countenances, since there must be something human even in them. You see cruel, loathsome snouts up there, wearing expressions of greed and mockery. Each of them looks at you like a spider gloating over a fly. Their web is that grating which imprisons you – and you have been had! They squinch up their lips, as if they intend to bite you from one side (Solzhenitsyn 1978, I, 502).[31]

Solzhenitsyn points out the danger which any of their gestures may signal:

> [...] and he jabs two protruding fingers, spread into the "V" of a slingshot, right in your eyes – not even pausing to threaten you but starting to punch them out then and there. And this gesture of theirs, which says, "I'll gouge out your eyes, crowbait!" covers their entire philosophy and faith! (Solzhenitsyn 1978, I, 503).[32]

Still, Solzhenitsyn's anthropological moralizing does not entirely replace the interest of an ethnographer describing his experiences. His style remains thoroughly ironic, which is obvious, for example, in his

31 | "[...] и видишь там три-четыре – нет, не лица! нет, не обезьяньих морды, у обезьян хоть чем-то должна быть похожа на образ! – ты видишь жестокие гадкие хари с выражением жадности и насмешки. Каждый смотрит на тебя как паук, нависший над мухой. Их паутина – эта решетка, и ты попался! Они кривят рты, будто собираются куснуть тебя избоку [...]" (Solzhenitsyn 1973, 499).

32 | "[...] и сует два пальца тычком, рогатинкой, прямо тебе в глаза – не угрожая, а вот начиная сейчас выкалывать. В этом жесте 'глаза выколю, падло!' – вся философия их и вера!" (*ibid.*, 500).

descriptions of the criminals' clothing, and even more so – when he talks about their "skin decoration."

For the criminals marking their bodies with tattoo imagery was an essential tool to signal their distinct status. The skin-language created an exclusive mode of communication. The outsiders were not expected to decipher the images, the symbols which signified the rank position of a particular person in the gang, the length of his sentence, represented fantasies and conveyed cryptic information. The same person's body could feature tattoos with religious motifs, often masterly accomplished imitations of icons – the Mother of God with the child, saints or churches with bulbous spires – together with images of provocative obscenity. Solzhenitsyn, who is impressed neither by the symbolism of the signs and their sometimes hidden meaning, nor by the "art of tattooing," describes these bodily inscriptions referring to their colour, shape, and ironically pointing out their "message:"

> They surrendered their bronze skin to tattooing and in this way gradually satisfied their artistic, their erotic, even their moral needs: on one another's chests, stomachs, and backs they could admire powerful eagles perched on cliffs or flying through the sky. Or the big hammer, the sun, with its rays shooting out in every direction; or women and men copulating; or the individual organs of their sexual enjoyment; and, all of a sudden, next to their hearts were Lenin or Stalin or perhaps both (and this meant exactly the same as the crucifix around a thief's neck). Sometimes they would laugh at a droll stoker hurling coal into their rear orifice, or a monkey engaged in masturbation. And they would read slogans on each other which, even if they were already familiar, they nonetheless dearly loved to repeat! - "all the girls in the mouth!" And it sounded as triumphant as "I am King Assargodon!" Or else on a girl thief's stomach there might be: "I will die for a hot –!' And even the modest and tiny moral on an arm, an arm which had already buried a dozen knives in somebody's ribs: 'Remember your mother's words!' Or else: "I remember caresses. I remember my mother." (The thieves had a mother cult, a formality, however, which did not mean faithfulness to her teachings.) (Solzheni-tsyn 1978, II, 450).[33]

33 | "Бронзовую кожу свою они отдают под татуировку, и так постоянно удовлетворена их художественная, эротическая и даже нравственная потребность: на грудях, на животах, на спинах друг у друга они разглядывают могучих орлов, присевших на скалу или летящих в небе; балдоху (солнце) с

The sense of being confronted with inhumanity, which the quoted texts convey, arises from an experience of two forms of behaviour: the animal-like exercise of bodily functions, and the excessive brutality of the criminals' acts. Even Shalamov does not always remain a dispassionate observer, although perhaps his emotional responses are not quite as acute as those of Ginzburg and Solzhenitsyn. He, too, maintains that "the bandits are no human beings." When he describes and analyses the criminals in his *Kolyma Tales* and what they meant for the life of the others in the camp, he concludes that they were the source of moral deterioration that inexorably contaminated all the others. In the end, he believes it was the criminals who became the arbiters of camp morality (*The Red Cross, Krasnyi krest*):

> Hundreds of thousands of people who have been in the camps are permanently seduced by the ideology of these criminals and have ceased to be people. Something criminal has entered into their souls for ever. Thieves and their morality have left an indelible mark on the soul of each (Shalamov 1994, 411).[34]

The moral revulsion that infuses his description and supposedly detached analysis cannot be missed. Ginzburg's characterisation of the criminals as those who are "beyond mankind" (*za predelami chelovecheskogo*) is an anthropological statement. Her encounter with the criminals shatters her

лучами во все стороны; женщин и мужчин в слиянии; и отдельные органы их наслаждений; и вдруг около сердца – Ленина или Сталина, или даже обоих (но это стоит ровно столько, сколько и крестик на шее у блатного). Иногда посмеются забавному кочегару, закидывающему уголь в самую задницу или обезьяне, предавшейся онанизму. И прочтут друг на друге хотя и знакомые, но дорогие в своем повторении надписи: 'Всех дешевок в рот...!' (Звучит победно, как 'Я – царь Ассаргодон!') Или на животе у блатной девчонки: 'Умру за горячую...!' И даже скромную некрупную мораль на руке, всадившей уже десяток ножей под ребра: 'Помни слова матери!' Или: 'Я помню ласки, я помню мать.' (У блатных – культ матери, но формальный, бес выполнения ее заветов.)" (Solzhenitsyn 1974, 429).

34 | "Сотни тысяч людей, побывавших в заключении, растлены воровской идеологией и перестали быть людьми. Нечто блатное навсегда поселилось в их душах, воры, их мораль навсегда оставили в душе любого неизгладимый след" (Shalamov 2013, I, 185).

view of humanity. The familiar ideas of what is human and what is not hold no longer.

Final remarks

The accounts discussed in the forgoing passages deal with the hardships and horrors of camp life. Strikingly, it is not the camp guards and the official regime that is the focus of these accounts: it is the criminals. We, the readers, learn about their deeds: theft, rape, murder. We are informed that they are the dominant force in camp existence. We are made to under-stand the reactions of disgust, disdain, fear, horror and perplexity political prisoners (and the authors of the accounts) experience face to face with the criminals. Not all accounts, however, are limited to one's own experience of the criminal horror and one's moral judgment of them. Alien as it is to them, some victims take a closer curious glance at their torturers. In an ethnographic stance they describe their behaviour, their social organization, their relationships with the camp authorities and with themselves, the victims.

Some of the victims, members of the intelligentsiia, philosophers and scholars, make an effort to grasp what to them at first is not understandable at all and what to others remains incomprehensible. It is noteworthy that the attempts at understanding and analytical approaches to the phenomenon of the criminal do not make use or refer to academic theories either criminality (e.g. Lombroso) or criminology prevailing in the 1920s, hypothesizing about the causes of criminality in the social milieu in which the criminals grew up, about psychological factors, motivation etc.[35] In his contribution to this volume, Riccardo Nicolosi demonstrates to what extent theories concerning crime and criminality were differentiated. It is unlikely that these theories were entirely unknown to the intellectuals among the victims. However, it appears that their concrete experience and

35 | The criminals were of greater interest (than the politicals) to the authorities as well as to representatives of the police and of disciplines like sociology, anthropology, psychology and last not least of jurisdiction. Theories about the origin, nature, psychological or physiological distinctive features of the criminals emerged leading to controversial decisions concerning the methods of their treatment.

the attempts of some of them to understand what they faced in the camps did not favour the application of such theories.

The contribution of the authors of camp accounts to defining the "essence" of criminality consists in the precision of their reports, but also in their ethnographic or anthropological approach which is, as was shown, a mixture of detached description and a moral stance. In coping with the helplessness the non-criminals felt in front of the bandits, the only way to regain their dignity was to write about them. In writing autobiographies, memoirs, diaries, stories, the victims recovered their intellectual and moral superiority. What the authors say about their criminal oppressors is based on experience, physical and psychic alike. Experience, of course, is transformed the moment it is expressed. The question of whether the texts of the eyewitnesses and victims are fictional or documentary does not grasp their essence. Their authors follow genre rules and stylistic conventions. Finding an adequate form of expression allowed these people to write the texts. Fiction is a necessary part of transforming experience into an account of experience (*opyt*)[36], making for a calculated arrangement of events, a refined style of description – all those elements that arouse tension, compassion, rage, anger on the reader's side.

References

Aleksandrov, Ju. 2002. *Ocherki kriminal'noi subkul'tury*. Moscow: Prava cheloveka.

Applebaum, A. 2003. *Gulag. A History*. New York: Doubleday.

Binner, R. et al. (eds.) 2010. *Stalinismus in der sowjetischen Provinz 1937-38. Die Massenaktion aufgrund des operativen Befehls Nr. 00447*. Berlin: De Gruyter.

Buber-Neumann, M. 1949. *Under Two Dictators*. Transl. by E. Fitzgerald. London: Gollancz.

Ginzburg, E. 1967. *Journey into the Whirlwind*. Transl. by M. Hayward. New York: Harcourt, Brace & World.

Ginzburg, E. 1981. *Within the Whirlwind*. Transl. by J. Boland. New York and London: Harcourt Brace Jovanovich.

Ginzburg, E. 1985. *Krutoi marshrut*. Vol. I-II. New York: Posev.

36 | *Opyt* is a notion which plays a major role in Russian camp literature.

Gor'kii, M. et al. (eds.) 1998 [1934]. *Belomorsko-Baltiiski Kanal imeni Stalina. Istoriia stroitel'stva.* Moscow: OGIZ.

Günther, H. 1993. *Der sozialistische Übermensch. Maksim Gor'kij und der sowjetische Heldenmythos.* Stuttgart and Weimar: J. B. Metzler.

Gurov, A. 1990. *Professional'naia prestupnost'. Proshloe i sovremennost'.* Moscow: Iuridicheskaia literatura.

Kiš, D. 1976. *Grobnica za Borisa Davidoviča. Sedam poglavlja jedne zajedničke povesti.* Zagreb: Liber et al.

Kiš, D. 1980. *A Tomb for Boris Davidovich. A Novel.* Transl. by D. MikićMitchell, Introduction by J. Brodsky. Champaign (IL): Dalkey Archive Press.

Klein, J. 1995/96. "Belomorkanal. Literatur und Propaganda in der Stalinzeit." *Zeitschrift für Slavische Philologie* 55, 53-98.

Lachmann, R. 2017. "Affekttherapie durch die Form? (Zu Texten von Karl Steiner/Karlo Štajner und Danilo Kiš)." Nicolosi, R. and Zimmermann, T. (eds.), *Ethos und Pathos. Mediale Wirkungsästhetik im 20. Jahrhundert in Ost und West.* Wien et al.: Böhlau, 241-268.

Likhachev, D. 1930. "Kartezhnye igry ugolovnikov. (Iz rabot kriminologicheskogo kabineta)." *Solovetskie ostrova* 1, 32-35.

Margolin, Ju. 1952. *Puteshestvie v stranu ze-ka.* New York: Chekhov Publishing House.

Margolin, Ju. 2013. *Reise in das Land der Lager.* Transl. by O. Radetzkaja. Berlin: Suhrkamp.

Petzer, T. 2007. "Der Olymp der Diebe. Spurensicherung bei Varlam Šalamov und Danilo Kiš." *Osteuropa* 57, no. 6, 205-219.

Pogodin, N. 1935. *Aristokraty.* LibreBook (elektronnaia kniga).

Shalamov, V. 1994. *Kolyma Tales.* Transl. by J. Glad. Harmondsworth: Penguin.

Shalamov, V. 2013. *Sobranie sochinenii v shesti tomakh.* Ed. by I. P. Sirotinskaia. Moscow: Terra; Knizhnyi klub knigovek.

Solzhenitsyn, A. I. 1978. *The Gulag Archipelago 1918-1956. An Experiment in Literary Investigation.* Transl. by T. P. Whitney. New York et al.: Harper and Row.

Solzhenitsyn, A. I. 1973. *Arkhipelag GULag 1918-1956. Opyt khudozhestvennogo issledovaniia.* Vol. I-II. Paris: YMCA-Press.

Solzhenitsyn, A. I. 1974. *Arkhipelag GULag 1918-1956. Opyt khudozhestvennogo issledovaniia.* Vol. III-IV. Paris: YMCA-Press.

Štajner, K. 1986. *7000 dana u Sibiru.* Zagreb: Globus.

Štajner, K. 1988. *Seven Thousand Days in Siberia*. Transl. (from the German) by J. Agee, Introduction by D. Kiš. New York: Farrar, Straus and Giroux.

Thun-Hohenstein, F. 2007: *Gebrochene Linien. Autobiographisches Schreiben und Lagerzivilisation*. Berlin: Kadmos.

Toker, L. 2000: *Return from the Archipelago. Narratives of Gulag Survivors*. Bloomington: Indiana University Press.

Varlam Shalamov's *Sketches of the Criminal World*

Leona Toker

Though the protagonists of Gulag literature are, like their authors, usually political prisoners, criminal convicts also figure, sometimes more and sometimes less prominently, in narratives about Soviet prisons and concentration camps. In the memoirs and fictionalized accounts of Stalin-period concentration camps, they are most often represented as the other main scourge of the political prisoners, the first one being, of course, the authorities – such as camp commanders, NKVD operatives, corrupt team leaders, and callous guards. The criminals steal the property of the "suckers" (*fraery*), as they call those who do not belong to their world, in particular the intellectuals, or sometimes simply take away their things by force (the term for this is *kurochit'*), get the production output of the working teams recorded as their own, thus depriving the others of a large share of rations, and often use the others for their own amusement, sometimes sadistic. The political prisoners are thus trapped between the criminals and the bosses, who are sometimes in collusion with the criminals as sources of corrupt gain or as instruments. One of the choice ways of punishing political prisoners was to throw them into the criminal prisoners' camp. Among the reasons why, as Varlam Shalamov noted, the camp described in Solzhenitsyn's *One Day in the Life of Ivan Denisovich* (*Odin den' Ivana Denisovicha*, 1962) was actually a "light" one is that it is a strict-regime camp for political prisoners; the conditions in it may be harsh, but it is free from the sway of the *blatnye*, the so-called "criminal world" (Shalamov 1998, IV, 435-436).[1]

The constant threat of the criminals, in one's own camp or in transit, or in special punitive camps, is dealt with in Julius Margolin's *Journey into the Land of the Z/K* (*Puteshestvie v stranu ze-ka*, 1952),[2] Evgeniia Ginzburg's memoirs, *Alexander Dolgun's Story: An American in the Gulag* (1975), Solzhenitsyn's *The Gulag Archipelago* (*Arkhipelag GULAG*, 1973), Lev Konson's *Brief Tales* (*Kratkie povesti*, 1983), Jacques Rossi's *It Was Beautiful, That Utopia* (*Qu'elle était belle cette utopie!*, 2000), and many other works, including those dealing with post-Stalinist camps, such as Eduard Kuznetsov's *The Mordovian Marathon* (*Mordovskii marafon*, 1979). A systematic analysis of the criminal world as a sociological phenomenon is presented in Varlam Shalamov's *Sketches of the Criminal World* (*Ocherki prestupnogo mira*) written, according to I. P. Sirotinskaia's dating, in 1959, that is, while he was still also composing the *Kolyma Tales* (*Kolymskie rasskazy*) collection. The present paper interprets Shalamov's agenda in writing this essay cycle and attempts to solve some of its puzzles in terms of this agenda.

I

Shalamov notes that the term "criminal world" (*prestupnyi mir*) is the one used by the criminals themselves (Shalamov 1998, II, 31), whereas members of this world are usually referred to as "thieves." Gulag literature draws a clear distinction between these professional "thieves" and *bytoviki*, that is, people who committed embezzlement or minor theft (sometimes motivated by hunger), or some other transgression in the midst of regular non-criminal life and who do not belong to the criminal underworld. From Shalamov's analysis, that underworld emerges as a shadow or

1 | Quotations from Shalamov's works are given in my translation. Shalamov's remarks about the camp in *Ivan Denisovich* are made in his correspondence with Solzhenitsyn.

2 | See Margolin 2016. First published in a shorter form in 1952 (New York: Chekhov Publishing House); the French translation by Nina Berberova and Mina Journot, *La condition inhumaine*, came out in 1949; recent full French version: *Voyage au pays des Ze-Ka*, trans. and ed. Luba Jurgenson. Paris: Le Bruit du temps 2010.

a photonegative of what in 1899 Thorstein Veblen represented as the aristocratic leisure class, whose predatory ancestors arrogated power and capital by various kinds of prowess, force, or fraud and who continually reassert their membership in the élite through "invidious emulation" that consists of "conspicuous consumption" and "conspicuous leisure" (Veblen 1899, 35-102 and 212-245). The professional criminals (*urki, blatnye, vory v zakone*) reflect the customs of vassalage, with the word of the leader (*pakhan*) being law; some of their property is status symbols (while other items are just stakes in card games); they refuse to do any work in the camps; they amuse themselves by card duels in which it is legitimate to cheat but a matter of life and death to pay up when one loses; they hold their own strategy meetings and their own courts of honor (*pravilki*) which frequently pass death sentences and appoint executioners. Special respect among these people is accorded to second- and third-generation thieves (*potomstvennye vory*; Shalamov 1998, II, 12), the aristocrats, whose status can never be matched by that of any of the up-starts or recruits.

The main theme of Shalamov's representation of this counter-society is its corrupting influence on others, especially the young. The accidental victims of Stalin's draconian laws and purges, young people of peasant and worker origins, orphans, and just easily swayed youngsters resentful of the regime that victimized them, are easily attracted by the thieves' sense of their might, their conspicuous exertions of power, their skills, their boastful or real bravado. Even intellectuals sometimes tend to romanticize the thieves (as in Shalamov's story *Pain* [*Bol'*]). This tendency, as Shalamov writes in the first of his sketches, *On One Error of the Belles Lettres* (*Ob odnoi oshibke khudozhestvennoi literatury*), is encouraged by a long tradition of literary romantization of the criminal world, from Hugo to Il'f and Petrov. Recruits are also attracted by crumbs of the criminals' food trophies (what Veblen [1899, 77ff.] would call "vicarious consumption"), and hence all the more ready to endow the criminals with an almost parental function. Once entrapped in the criminal world, the converts have almost no way of breaking free. Shalamov does not mention the possibility of exit, for which the term *zaviazat'* is sometimes used, but hints that the long arm of the criminal world (like, one might add, the long arm of the KGB) can reach the defector wherever he may be. This, indeed, is staged in Vasilii Shukshin's famous tale *Snowball Berry Red* (*Kalina krasnaia*): the protagonist is a criminal convict who decides to break with the criminal world upon being released from prison and goes to live with the woman who had corresponded with him when he was inside (the so-called *zaochnitsa*). He turns out to have been exactly one of the peasant children, the son of a family that fell victim of the de-kulakization; he had gravitated towards the criminal underworld, and his former criminal associates will not forgive him for wishing to endorse normal life.

Shalamov devotes a special sketch to the position of women in the criminal world. The women fall into two groups: thieves, whose status in their environment is rather high and similar to that of men, and so too are the demands on their "honor," and prostitutes, who are treated like dispensable property that passes from hand to hand and are not punished for rendering services to guards and camp bosses.[3] The entrapment of women by the criminal world illustrates Shalamov's principle, conveyed, for instance, through the words of Isai Rabinovich in the story *The Love of Captain Tolly* (*Liubov' kapitana Tolli*; Shalamov 1998, I, 432), that the moral fiber of a man emerges from the way he talks about or deals with women. In that respect too the criminal underworld is irredeemable.

II

Though Shalamov frequently mentions that the thieves are capable of totally inhuman acts (*v blatare i net nichego chelovecheskogo*; Shalamov 1998, II, 21) and sometimes specifically refers to their sadism, whether punitive or undertaken for amusement or out of cold curiosity, there are two phenomena that Shalamov seems to avoid, as if these were for him a kind of Orwellian ultimate torture chamber 101 ("Room One-Oh-One" in *1984*), where he fears to tread. These phenomena are dealt with by other witnesses.

One of these is the issue of the specific system of relationships around homosexuality. Shalamov mentions that all the thieves are homosexuals: leisure and ability to obtain food keep their libido alive (by contrast to that of the mass of depleted political prisoners), and they satisfy it by turning some of their younger dependents into passive homosexuals. Shalamov mentions the presence of the effeminate young men around the seasoned criminals. He has little sympathy for these youngsters, referred to by feminine names such as "Mashka" or "Zoika," and seems to believe that

3 | This distinction is partly blurred in Georgii Demidov's story *Amok* (Demidov 2008, 45-100).

their roles were more or less of their own choosing. What he does not mention is that young boys, adolescents, and youths are often raped by the criminals and by guards recruited from among the criminals – this is explicitly stated in Konson's *Brief Tales* (Konson 1983, 131). What Kuznetsov demonstrates in *Mordovian Marathon* is that while the rapists enhance their status as strongmen heroes, the male victims of rape are immediately and irrevocably degraded. In Kuznetsov's time their status becomes that of the *petukhi*, subject to every humiliation including having to sleep next to the slop bucket. The rape is sometimes undertaken not so much to satisfy the rapist's desire but as an instrument in the power game; its aim being to destroy the status of the victim (*opustit'*). The only way out of this life-sentence to degradation is for the victim to kill his rapist. This is the subject of one of Kuznetzov's stories, *On the 'Strange People,' Albert, and in General* (*O 'strannom narode', Al'berte i voobshche*; Kuznetsov 1979, 53-105), where the protagonist also kills a chance witness to the retaliatory murder, and explains his action to the narrator by a reference to Dostoevsky's *Crime and Punishment* – "Lizaveta and the ax."

The other issue that Shalamov does not develop is cannibalism among the criminals during escape attempts, an issue mentioned with horror also by Ginzburg.[4] This phenomenon is referred to in *The Green Procurator* (*Zelenyi prokuror*), Shalamov's long sketch about escapes in the cycle *The Artist of the Spade* (*Artist lopaty*) of *Kolyma Tales*, yet Shalamov does not explore it: for him cannibalism remains a marginal issue, whether because beyond the pale of his own in-camp environment or because it is unthinkable, locked up in "Room One-Oh-One." The writer who makes it thinkable and conjures it up for us is Konson, whose story *Misha Kriuchko* represents such an escape of a small group of friends: at a certain point, having run out of provision, they begin to suspect each other of wishing to kill one another for food. They fear going to sleep, make each other tearful promises not to commit murder, and break promises under the pressure of starvation (Konson 1983, 43-53).[5] A starker representation of cannibalism during escapes is to be found in the slightly fictionalized memoir of Jacques Rossi, author of the famous *Gulag Handbook* (*Spravochnik po*

4 | For interesting remarks on Ginzburg's account of her learning about cannibalism see Zholkovsky 1988.

5 | See Toker 2014 for an analysis of a Joseph Conrad story that likewise attempts to imagine, and make the reader imagine, starvation cannibalism.

Gulagu, 1987), an invaluable resource for anyone who studies this field. Rossi's second book, *Qu'elle était belle cette utopie!*, part of the corpus of the "literature of disillusionment" by former communists (Toker 2000, 63-65, 219-220, and *passim*), contains a chapter called *The Cow* (*La vache*; Rossi 2000, 89-91).[6] The corpse of a healthy young man is found on the trajectory of one of the escapes; on examination, a wound is discovered in the lower part of his body. The conclusion is that this was a person whom the criminal jargon referred to as "a cow," a piece of cattle to be well fed and lured to join the escape attempt, only to be butchered for food, when the provisions end. The organ extracted and consumed in haste is, according to Rossi, the kidneys.

III

One of the reasons why Shalamov does not dramatize such events for the reader is that he must have been spared witnessing their traces first-hand. It may also be that dwelling on them might have constituted a kind of pornography for him. Indeed, Shalamov's treatment of the main subject of the *Sketches of the Criminal World* is suffused with literary concerns. Shalamov's story cycles always start with self-reflexive narratives, dealing with some aspects of literature as testimony.[7] The cycle *Sketches of the Criminal World* is no exception. The first sketch is a critique of the literary topos of the thief as a romantic rebel; it also discusses the characters of Dostoevskii's *Notes from the House of the Dead* (*Zapiski iz mertvogo doma*) and of Tolstoi's *Resurrection* (*Voskresenie*) as accidental rather than professional criminals. It suggests that Chekhov was traumatized for life by what he saw of the professional criminal world in Sakhalin and never had the courage to tackle it. Shalamov annotates and critiques Gor'kii's representation of the criminals, deplores the "fashion for raiders (*naletchiki*)" that invaded Russian literature in the 1920s under the guise of a "fresh stream" (*svezhaia struia*; Shalamov 1998, II, 10) – Babel's stories about Benia Krik in *Odessa Tales* (*Odesskie rasskazy*, 1931), Leonov's *The Thief* (*Vor*, 1927) as well as some of the works by Sel'vinskii, Vera Inber, Kaverin, and Il'f and Petrov, and represents the works of the *perekovka*

6 | The phenomenon is also explained in Rossi's *Gulag Handbook* under *korova* (Rossi 1987, 168).

7 | For a discussion of the sequence of stories see Toker 2000, 160-176.

period, epitomized by Pogodin's play *The Aristocrats* (*Aristokraty*, 1934) as a return, full circle though with a difference, to the old error of romanticizing the criminal world. Throughout the *Sketches* Shalamov will consistently critique this literary tendency as well as sundry urban legends glorifying the prowess of the thieves.

The second sketch *The Crook's Blood* (*Zhul'nicheskaia krov'*), whose title, taken from the criminal parlance, refers to the sometimes ineffable signs by which the criminals recognize their like, has nothing to do with genetical transmission of criminal tendencies. Shalamov is totally on the side of those who regard environment rather than heredity as the source of criminality, and for him a major constituent of the environment is precisely the wish-fulfilling legends about the criminal as a free agent and hero as well as the literature that sustains such legends. "It can be said," he writes, "that instead of condemning the sway of criminality literature did the opposite: it prepared the soil for the flowering of poisonous sprouts in the inexperienced and unversed soul of the youth" (Shalamov 1998, II, 14).[8] In view of the thrill that the peak experience of risk-fraught robbery gives the thief, Shalamov refers to it in terms of the thief's wish to experience again and again "the lofty illness" of the theft, thus alluding to Pasternak's poem about poetry, *Lofty Malady* (*Vysokaia bolezn'*). In the sketch *The Prison Ration* (*Tiuremnaia paika*) he dismantles one of the myths about prison life, that of the sacredness of the prison rations, their immunity from theft. In the sketch *Apollo among Thieves* (*Apollon sredi blatnykh*), he deals with the cultural and would-be spiritual needs of the thieves, the kind of verse and folklore that they produce and consume. The subject is further developed in the next sketch, *Sergei Esenin and the Thieves' World* (*Sergei Esenin i vorovskoi mir*), where Shalamov registers the criminals' partiality for the poetry of Esenin, though they remain deaf to the "profound humanity and bright lyrical essence of Esenin's verse" (Shalamov 1998, II, 89),[9] attempts to reveal its cause – as associated with the kinship of some intonations in Esenin's verse, especially notes of the macabre reveling in *Moscow of the Taverns* (*Moskva kabatskaia*) (perhaps

8 | "Можно сказать, что художественная литература вместо того, чтобы заклеймить уголовщину, сделала обратное: подготовила почву для расцвета ядовитых ростков в неопытной, неискушенной душе молодежи."

9 | "[...] что им до глубокой человечности, до светлой лирики существа есенинских стихов."

also notes of maudlin self-dramatizing self-pity), and cites the cult of the mother as a common denominator of Esenin's poetry and the criminals' songs (alongside the criminals' abuse of other women). Finally, the last sketch, *How One Spins Novels* (*Kak tiskaiut romany*), deals with the criminal's love of listening to specific kinds of narratives, often based on detective novels or such classics as *The Count of Monte Cristo*, as well as with the way the ability to narrate such stories according to the thieves' tastes can save the lives of some of the intellectual prisoners. This sketch makes it clear why Shalamov himself refused to improve his condition in this way. This was not only a matter of dignity mentioned in his story *The Snake Charmer*, where spinning yarns for the criminals is likened to scratching their heels: having someone do it for them was another of the criminal leaders' favorite pastimes. Apparently, the yarns had to belong to a specific kind of banalized discourse, which Shalamov would not allow to contaminate the language of his own prose.

Thus, the collection of sketches that starts with an essay on a misguided literary topos in respect to the criminals ends with an account of the literary catering to the tastes of the criminals. Moreover, most of the material of the sketches provides, as it were, an external frame of reference that can shed light on a number of Shalamov's stories, in particular *On Tick* (*Na predstavku*), *A Day Off* (*Vykhodnoi den'*), *The Artist of the Spade*, *Pain*, and *The Snake Charmer*. It can also be mined for indirect commentary, whether reliable or controversial, on details of later works by other writers, such as Shukshin's *Snowball Berry Red*, Felix Roziner's *A Certain Finkelmeyer* (*Nekto Finkel'maier*, 1981) or Mikhail Jakobson's *Karzubyi: A Tale of the Camps* (*Karzubyi: Lagernaia povest'*, 1983). For Shalamov, however, the system of relationships around homosexual rape and cannibalism is clearly not a suitable subject for detailed literary treatment.

IV

There is, however, one subject, in the middle of *Sketches of the Criminal World*, where the concern is not literary but a matter of giving first-hand historical evidence from the standpoint of Shalamov the camp medic (a specially trained male nurse) rather than Shalamov the writer. This issue is the so-called "bitch war." To some extent the sketch bearing this title, *Such'ia voina*, is the closest to Shalamov's short stories: it opens with the dramatized scene of a wounded prisoner's arrival to the hospital and the bosses' need to determine his identity before he is assigned to a ward. Things fall into place when to the operative's question "What are you?" (*Ty kto?*), the wounded man answers, to everyone's satisfaction, "*Su-u-ka*" (Shalamov 1998, II, 57). He can now be assigned to the ward for the so-called "bitches."

"Bitches" were members of the criminal underworld who had broken the laws of this world by going over to the service of the authorities.[10] Unless delegated by the criminals themselves (for example, young thieves were often sent to work in the regular work teams, to ease the food problem among the thieves), such traitors were usually condemned to death and indeed killed when opportunity arose. However, their numbers considerably increased in the aftermath of World War II, for two reasons, which Shalamov carefully explains in this sketch.

His testimony unfolds the following picture. The first reason for the post-war leap in brutality among the criminals in the camps was that during the war many criminal convicts had been released and sent to the front.

> Rokossovskii's army gained notoriety and popularity precisely by its inclusion of the criminal element. The urkas made dashing scouts, courageous guerillas. Their natural leanings towards risk, decisiveness and effrontery turned them into valuable soldiers. Looting, striving to rob, was largely tolerated. True, the final siege of Berlin was not entrusted to these units. Rokossovskii's army was sent to other locations, whereas it was the more solid personnel of Marshal Konev's units, regiments of the purest proletarian blood, that was directed toward Tiergarten (Shalamov 1998, II, 58).[11]

---

10 | In his survey of the Russian camp culture of the present day, Igor' Sutiagin likewise explains that "the bitch wars" of the post-war period were "sparked by a disagreement over the limits of this specific taboo" (Sutiagin 2014, 29). Sutiagin's article is important for the understanding of the changes and continuities between the Soviet and post-Soviet prison camps.

11 | "Армия Рокоссовского приобрела известность и популярность именно наличием в ней уголовного элемента. Из уркаганов выходили лихие разведчики, смелые партизаны. Природная склонность к риску, решительность и наглость делали из них ценных солдат. На мародерство, на стремление пограбить смотрели сквозь пальцы. Правда, окончательный штурм Берлина не был доверен этим частям. Армия Рокоссовского была нацелена в другое место, а в

After the war, however, many of the demobilized former criminals returned to their erstwhile pursuits (their wartime looting was also a natural continuation of those pursuits) and were eventually brought back to the camps, especially to Kolyma and Vorkuta. They expected to be welcomed by their former associates with open arms, but were disappointed. The old timers, *vory v zakone* ("criminals in law"), rejected them as collaborators, that is, as "bitches": "You were at war? You held a rifle? This means you are a bitch, a most real bitch, and subject to punishment by 'the law'" (*ibid.*, 62).[12] Thus the former soldiers found themselves in the position of outlaws, not only in terms of the law of the land but also in terms of the "law" of their own criminal world, the "law" to which they had themselves adhered. Since their numbers were significant, they adopted not only defensive but also offensive strategies, entering an armed confrontation with their former associates.

The other reason for "the bitch war" that emerges from Shalamov's narrative was the 1947 law that introduced 20-year sentences for even minor criminal offenses. This meant that the former conspicuous leisure of the *vory v zakone*, which it was possible to maintain over relatively short periods of incarceration, became unfeasible under new conditions of long prison terms. This state of affairs, in combination with the hostility of criminal camp veterans, led, according to Shalamov, to the codification of a new criminal "law" by the former soldiers, under the leadership of a semi-legendary criminal known as *Korol'*, the "King": a law proclaimed in the transit camp in the port of Vanino in 1948 (*ibid.*, 63). *Korol'* entered an agreement with camp bosses that, placed in a command position, he would "introduce order" in the camps, provided the authorities did not raise difficulties about some bloodshed. Having received the appropriate assurances, *Korol'* initiated a massacre of *vory v zakone*, forcing those unwilling to die to undergo the ceremony of kissing the knife (other sources give more gruesome details) as a sign of passing over to the side of the "bitches." As a result, an uncompromising war ensued between the old-fashioned thieves and the "bitches": woe to a member of one faction if

Тиргартен двинулись кадровые части маршала Конева – полки наиболее чистой пролетарской крови."

12 | "– Ты был на войне? Ты взял в руки винтовку? Значит, ты – сука, самая настоящая сука и подлежишь наказанию 'по закону'."

he fell into a camp, or a hospital ward, belonging to the other faction. The killing was in many cases particularly sadistic.

This, incidentally, is the background for Shalamov's short story *A Piece of Meat* (*Kusok miasa*). It features a professional criminal whose principle of conspicuous leisure does not allow him to work in the camps; therefore, under the new circumstances, he chooses to avoid the camps by periodical murders which keep him in prisons and under investigations rather than in the camps. The protagonist-narrator of the story, which is set in a camp hospital, realizes that he is the prospective next victim of that monster, but he is saved when the criminal receives a letter from his associates in the camps, summoning him to the battle against "the bitches": since he cannot disobey the order, the criminal loses his motivation for murdering the protagonist.

As a result of "the bitch war," the criminal population of the camps is considerably reduced. *Korol'* himself is blown up by an explosive put under his place in the barracks in a remote camp (*ibid.*, 68). But then, according to Shalamov's testimony, a new development takes place.

Since the old-fashioned criminals do not distinguish between the old "bitches" and those newly converted by kissing the knife, when the latter wish to return to their old allegiances, they are not accepted back. In resentment, the recent converts work out a still new form of "law," the third one, devoid of any would-be ideological platform and dictated by nothing but bitterness and the wish to wreak gory revenge on both the old-fashioned criminals and the old-time "bitches." Members of this group came to be known as *bespredel* or *bespredel'shchina*, meaning the absence of any restraining principles. Their numbers became so great that, Shalamov says, the authorities had to assign them a separate mining camp. Various groupings of *bespredel* started proliferating, yet in Shalamov's times their members remained the most vulnerable and the least protected in the criminal world, since most of the facilities were divided among the two groups of their sworn enemies. It seems, however, quite likely that it is some combination of the collaborating "bitches" and the unpredictable *bespredel* that forms the legacy of the criminal world to the post-Soviet Russian society, with its racket, its "raiders," and its corruption.

V

Whereas Shalamov's story cycles, which, as noted above, tend to start with a self-reflexive narrative, usually end on a note of hope, the coda of *Sketches of the Criminal World* runs as follows: "Carthago must be brought to ruin! / The world of the *blatnye* must be destroyed!" (*ibid.*, 100).[13] Destroyed how? Shalamov is no advocate of initiating another outbreak of "the bitch war." He makes a point of surveying the types of brutalization that "the bitch war" caused in the camps, when murder became thinkable as a response to anyone's denial of anyone's request. Nor does he ever make a call for the death penalty. Moreover, in several of his stories, such as *The First Tooth* (*Pervyi zub*) and *Lida*, he shows that thieves are sometimes particularly proficient in camp semiotics, and a political prisoner can learn from them how to protect himself from inhuman conditions or assaults. Nor does he make a definite call for longer prison sentences, though he does deplore the authorities' favoring the thieves as "socially close" to the working class, or as sources of bribery at the expense of the political prisoners, and though he implicitly blames the authorities for the social conditions that have led to the spread of criminality.

What is Shalamov after? I think it is the meta-literary slant of *Sketches of the Criminal World* that may suggest an answer: one of the ways of destroying the criminal world is by disempowering the cultural tendencies that have enhanced its corrosive attractiveness, by telling the truth about it, by dispelling myths. As usual, every ideological position that Shalamov takes is riddled with self-contradictions. Though the inner agenda of his *Sketches* is part of the fight against the power of the criminal world, he plays no Solzhenitsyn-like games with censorship to gain an audience for these sketches. Just as he did not compromise his profession as a writer by telling stories to the criminals, so he does not cater to the cultural politics of the capricious "Thaw" in order to get his singularly urgent socio-political statement published in his country. Moreover, though he talks about the pernicious cultural effect of the literary misprision concerning the criminal world, he does not express an equally firm belief in the ability of literary works to counteract the deadly lure of criminal culture. The allusion to the speech of Cato the Elder in the Roman Senate in the coda of *The Sketches* suggests that, after all, the task of de-stalinization, initiated

13 | "Карфаген должен быть разрушен! / Блатной мир должен быть уничтожен!"

in Khrushchev's speech at the Twentieth Communist Party Congress in 1956, ought to be continued, by interventions from above, as a conscious concerted effort of the government and society. How such an effort is to be orchestrated, what place a literary intervention might hold in it, and how society must change in order for such a literary intervention to be possible or effective – these issues are beyond the meta-literary reflections of Shalamov's corpus.

References

Demidov, G. 2008. *Chudnaia planeta*. Moscow: Vozvrashchenie.

Konson, L. 1983. *Kratkie povesti*. Paris: La Presse Libre.

Kuznetsov, E. 1979. *Mordovskii marafon*. Jerusalem: Knigotovarishchestvo Moscow-Jerusalem.

Margolin, Iu. 2016. *Puteshestvie v stranu ze-ka i Doroga na zapad*. Ed. by M. Shauli. Jerusalem: Studio Click.

Rossi, J. 1987. *Spravochnik po Gulagu: Istoricheskii slovar' sovetskikh penitentsiarnykh institutsii i terminov, sviazannykh s prinuditel'nym trudom*. London: Overseas Publications Interchange.

Rossi, J. and Benech, S. 2000. *Qu'elle était belle cette utopie! Chroniques du Goulag*. Paris: Le Cherche Midi.

Shalamov, V. 1998. *Sobranie sochinenii v chetyrekh tomakh*. Ed. by I. P. Sirotinskaia. Moscow: Khudozhestvennaia literatura/Vagrius.

Sutiagin, I. 2014. "Russian Prison Culture Today: A Participant-Observer's View." Hansen, J. and Rogachevskii, A. (eds.), *Punishment as a Crime? Perspectives on Prison Experience in Russian Culture*. Uppsala: Uppsala University, 19-41.

Toker, L. 2000. *Return from the Archipelago: Narratives of Gulag Survivors*. Bloomington: Indiana University Press.

Toker, L. 2014. "Narrative and Talk-Back: Joseph Conrad's 'Falk'." Sell, R. (ed.), *Literature as Dialogue: Invitations Offered and Negotiated*. Amsterdam: John Benjamins, 115-134.

Veblen, T. 1899. *The Theory of the Leisure Class: An Economic Study in the Evolution of Institutions*. New York: Macmillan.

Zholkovsky, A. 1988. "Three on Courtship, Corpses, and Culture: Tolstoj, 'Posle bala' – Zoshchenko, 'Dama s cvetami' – E. Ginzburg, 'Raj pod mikroskopom.'" *Wiener Slawistischer Almanach* 22, 7-24.

On the Contributors

Anne Hartmann, Assistant researcher und lecturer in the Slavic Department at the University of Bochum. In her research she concentrates on the Soviet impact on GDR culture and literature, Western intellectuals visiting the Stalinist USSR and Gulag literature. Most recent publication: "Ich kam, ich sah, ich werde schreiben." Lion Feuchtwanger in Moskau 1937 (Göttingen, 2017).

Marc Junge, Privatdozent and lecturer at the University of Bochum. His research focuses on the history of Stalinism, notably the victims and perpetrators of the mass repressions during the 1930s. Recent publications: *Stalins Täter. Allmacht und Ohnmacht. Das "Kleine Berija-Tauwetter" im Gebiet Nikolaev in der Ukraine* (forthcoming), *Ekho Bolshogo terrora. Chekisty na skam'e podsudimykh* (co-editors Lynne Viola and Jeffrey Rossman, Moscow, 2017), *Stalin's Mass Repression and the Cold War Paradigm* (New York, 2016), *Bolschewistische Ordnung in Georgien. Der Große Terror in einer kleinen kaukasischen Republik* (co-editor Bernd Bonwetsch, Berlin, 2015).

Renate Lachmann, Professor em. of Slavic Literatures at the University of Konstanz. Her main topics of research are memory, intertextuality and dialogism, rhetoric, literatures of the fantastic, camp-literature. Recent publications: *Affekttherapie durch die Form? Zu Texten von Karl Steiner und Danilo Kiš (Ethos und Pathos. Mediale Wirkungsästhetik im 20. Jahrhundert in Ost und West,* eds. Riccardo Nicolosi, Tanja Zimmermann, 2017), *Zwei Brücken in Bosnien-Herzegowina und ihre kulturelle Symbolik (Le Pont des Arts,* eds. Julia Lichtenthal et al., 2016), *Poetics and Hermeneutics*

(*Theoretical Schools and Circles in Twentieth-Century Humanities*, eds. Maria Grishakova, Silvi Salupere, 2015).

Louise McReynolds, Cary C. Boshamer Distinguished Professor at the University of North Carolina at Chapel Hill. Her research interests include Imperial Russia, with a particular focus on "middlebrow" culture. Most recent publication: *Murder Most Russian. True Crime and Punishment in Late Imperial Russia* (Cornell, 2013).

Marina Mogilner, Associate Professor of History at the University of Illinois at Chicago, co-founder and co-editor of the international quarterly *Ab Imperio*. Her research focuses on a New Imperial History of Russia and the USSR. Recent publications: *Homo Imperii: A History of Physical Anthropology in Russia* (Lincoln and London, 2013), *Hybridity: Marrism and the Problems of Language of the Imperial Situation* (with Ilya Gerasimov and Sergey Glebov, *Ab Imperio* 17, 2016), *Human Sacrifice in the Name of a Nation: The Religion of Common Blood* (*Ritual Murder in Russia, Eastern Europe, and Beyond*, eds. Eugene Avrutin, Robert Weinberg, 2017).

Riccardo Nicolosi, Professor of Slavic Literatures at the Ludwig-Maximilians-University Munich. His research interests include the interfaces between science and literature, rhetoric, counterfactual fiction. Most recent publications: *Degeneration erzählen. Literatur und Psychiatrie im Russland der 1880er und 1890er Jahre* (Paderborn, 2017), *Ethos und Pathos. Mediale Wirkungsästhetik im 20. Jahrhundert in Ost und West* (co-editor Tanja Zimmermann, Cologne, 2017), *Blokadnye narrativy* (co-editor Polina Barskova, Moscow, 2017).

David Shearer, Thomas Muncy Keith Professor of History at the University of Delaware. His research interests are comparative 19th/20th-century Soviet and European political, economic, and social history and the history of modernity. Recent publications: *Stalin and the Lubianka: A Documentary History of the Political Police and Security Organs in the Soviet Union, 1922-1953* (with Vladimir Khaustov, New Haven, 2015), *Stalinskii Voennyi sotsializm: Repressia i sotsial'nyi poriadok pri Staline, 1924-1953* (Moscow, 2014), *Policing Stalin's Socialism: Social Order and Mass Repression in the Soviet Union, 1924-1953* (New Haven, 2009).

Leona Toker, Professor of English Literature at the Hebrew University of Jerusalem. Her research interests are 18th and 19th-century British novel, Joyce, and Nabokov, as well as documentary prose, especially narratives of concentration-camp survivors. Her recent publications include *Towards the Ethics of Form in Fiction: Narratives of Cultural Remission* (Columbus, 2010) and *Return from the Archipelago: Narratives of Gulag Survivors* (Bloomington et al., 2000). She is Editor of *Partial Answers: Journal of Literature and the History of Ideas.*